NEVER A SHOT IN ANGER

Major Gerald Mortimer MBE Royal Engineers, aged 26, drawn by a German prisoner-of-war, Diesex, in mid-December 1944 at 2nd Army Headquarters, Neerpelt, North Belgium, where the author was in charge of engineer stores supply

NEVER A SHOT
IN
ANGER

Gerald Mortimer CBE, DL, F.Eng.

A Square One Publication

First published in 1993 by
Square One Publications
Saga House, Sansome Place, Worcester, WR1 1UA

© Gerald Mortimer 1993

British Library Cataloguing in Publication Data.
Mortimer, Gerald
Never a Shot in Anger
I. Title
940.54

ISBN 1 87201 7 71 1

Typeset in Times 11 on 13 by Avon Dataset, Bidford on Avon,
Warwickshire B50 4JH
Printed by Biddles Ltd, Guildford, England

To my grandchildren —

Joanna and Jane Mortimer
Michael and Helen Osborne
Andrew and Matthew Bargh

I hope they get the point.

CONTENTS

Page

LIST OF MAPS

FOREWORD

Many readers of war books may have wondered what the staff officers at Brigade, Divisional, corps and Army headquarters did for a living, how they were organised and worked and how they got the necessary experience. A First World War joke asked, "If bread is the staff of life, what is the life of the Staff?" The answer was, "A long loaf". In those days, when Staff Officers all wore smart riding breeches and red arm bands, the jibe may have been true, though I doubt it. Few Staff Officers then or more recently have recorded their experiences and there may still be a story worth telling. I hope so.

This story has been written largely from memory. Keeping a personal diary in a war zone was not allowed. While my memory is very clear about the general trend of events and many of the places, there are a lot of gaps in those memories. I have no record of my own, made at the time, to which I can refer. However, for 48 years I have owned a copy of the excellent book "Normandy to the Baltic" written by Field Marshal The Viscount Montgomery of Alamein, indirectly under whose command I had the honour to serve and to whom I have paid tribute in a number of places. I have re-read parts of that book on numerous occasions and have taken it into my memory with my own recollections, but I still needed to refer to it again for confirmation of the dates and names of formations serving at particular times and places in the course of the campaign.

Maps are essential to any understanding of the complex series of massive battles and major troop movements but I have found it difficult to be original. My maps are necessarily free-hand copies, of some of those used by the Field Marshal in his book. I am grateful to his literary executors for permission to draw on them and to Mary Wilkinson for help in doing so.

The photographs are in two groups — the first batch all relate to the first eight chapters of the text and my service in the U.K. , when I was able to have my own camera with me. Except for the two groups, the other pictures are my own. On the Continent cameras were forbidden and, for the second batch, I copied photographs held by the Royal Engineers Library at Chatham, apart from the group taken by a German firm at Luneburg. The picture of myself, as a Staff Major, was drawn by a prisoner of war.

I have been assisted by my wife and my brother who have read large parts of my text and given me useful advice. My secretaries, Anne

Austin and Judith Harley have been indefatigable in their share of the work, particularly on the word processor, and in keeping my other business going in the meantime.

In conclusion, as a "hostilities only" officer, I would pay tribute to the leadership and professional skills of the senior Royal Engineers regular officers Brigadier Genet, Brigadier Godfrey, Brigadier Stone and Brigadier Campbell — under whom I served. They had to make Staff Officers out of very raw material.

Gerald Mortimer   June, 1993.

PRELUDE
Hitler's rise to power
(1924 To 1933)

Hitler was released from the Landsberg Fortress on 20th December 1924, after serving little more than ten months of a five year sentence for being one of the two leaders, with General Ludendorff, of the Munich "putsch", an armed attempt to take over the government of the state of Bavaria. His release on parole would have been possible as early as 1st October, but there were disagreements about its advisability. The Director of the State Police recommended that it "should not be considered" but the Governor of the prison, who had come greatly under Hitler's influence, with most of his staff, recommended strongly that he be released and said that "he proposes not to run counter to the authorities".

At the time, Hitler's National Socialist German Workers' Party ("Nazis") was only one of many different, extreme right-wing parties and some of the authorities were afraid that if he was released too soon he would work to combine these parties all under his wing, making him too powerful to handle. His supporters, however, including the prison governor, stressed his amenability, his moderate habits, his reluctance to enter into political discussion with his many visitors and his true patriotism. Eventually the latter group won the day.

During his time in the Landsberg Fortress, Hitler wrote his political testament, "Mein Kampf", a volume of turgid prose in which he paraded his hatred of the French, the negroes, the Jews, and the German statesmen who negotiated the Armistice. He saw the latter as having let down the German nation at the end of the First World War, when he and others like him believed the German army could still have won. It is bombastic and repetitive in style and it is difficult for a foreign reader to see in a translation any of the power and mesmerism which so animated his spoken word.

During the next eight years his followers and, particularly, his "storm sections" (the "sturmabteilung" or "SA", better known as the "brown shirts") fought constant street battles with the communists and trade unionists and even with other right wing parties. They gradually established a dominance and, indeed, a standing with the whole nation which led to his Party gaining a parliamentary position. This, in turn, led to Hitler being appointed Chancellor, or "prime minister" of the whole of Germany, on 30th of January, 1933 by the aged and senile President, Paul von Hindenburg.

1

CHAPTER 1 School and University in the 1930s (January 1930 — June 1939)

The late stage of Hitler's rise to power is a convenient stage at which to start my own story and to try to set the political background against which I was called into the army in 1939.

In January 1930 my parents had brought me down from Dunstable in Bedfordshire, where we were then living and my father was Minister at the Congregational Church, to Caterham School, in Surrey, where I was to be a boarder and spend most of the next seven years. I was eleven and took to the school and the life like a duck to water. At first the affairs of the great big world outside concerned me little. I doubt if I read the newspapers much. The serious news was mostly about the gradual recovery from the great depression and associated economic developments, together with home affairs. Foreign affairs featured very little. Unemployment was a major problem but, as in recent years, it was largely confined to Special Areas. The General Election in 1931 was marked by a mock election and parliamentary debate for the school debating society in which I took an early interest. The London Naval Treaty came and went without much comment, but disarmament was a big issue. I remember that I vaguely distrusted it and I think most of us at Caterham profoundly disapproved of the Oxford Union resolution in 1933 that "this house will not fight for King and Country". In the summer of 1933 I took my General School Certificate exams and matriculated. I passed into the sixth form that September, just after my 15th birthday, and settled down to a mathematics and science course which, almost inevitably, destined me for an engineering career. I was now a junior prefect and a member of various societies where we took an increasing interest in world affairs. Germany and Italy were very much at the centre of our thoughts. There was little doubt in our minds that the dictators were increasing dangers to the peace of the world, the residual "Pax Britannica" in which we had all been brought up.

We read fairly seriously: "Journeys End", "All Quiet on the Western Front", "English Journey", "Love on the Dole", "The Shape of Things to Come" and "The Seven Pillars of Wisdom" for example. We were interested in, but sceptical about The League of Nations which, faced with the defection of Japan, Germany and Italy, the non-involvement of the United States and the problems of Manchuria and Abyssinia, was experiencing increasing difficulties in being taken seriously.

3

Then there was the Peace Ballot in 1934/35. The staff at the school were mostly in favour and our church in the village was extremely so. We prefects were under some pressure for us all to sign; but had decided that appeasement and disarmament were not going to solve the world's problems at that stage. In this, we disagreed with ten million of the nation's households. In spite of all this, on average we worked hard enough — though I did not — and played harder still at a variety of sports, while watching with great interest the progress of Larwood and the "body-line" bowling controversy.

Then, in the Spring of 1935, the school received an invitation to send a hockey team to Germany to play in a festival at Jena in the state of Thuringia. I was in the second XI but was chosen to go and my parents scraped the money together. It was a chance not to be missed. Hitler was now in his third year as Chancellor of Germany and had set up the country as a full-scale dictatorship. Our mentors were not at all keen on that aspect but, with two of them to supervise us and a fairly responsible crowd of players, now all aged 16 or more, we ought to be alright. In any event, it was an honour for the school at a time when such overseas sports trips were most unusual for any school, and it recognised our fairly considerable status in the hockey world. We were the only foreign team taking part but there were a dozen or more German teams from towns all over the country. We won our first three games in a straight row and our fixture list was amended to give us a really tough assignment for our last game at Jena, which we won by a narrow margin. Next we moved to Goslar, a town in the Harz Mountains, where we played a club side and drew. Finally, at Hanover, we found ourselves up against a University side, which was much too mature for us and beat us heavily. It seemed that German honour had to be, and was, satisfied.

The real experience for us was that of seeing, at first hand, a nation under dictatorship. We had to admit to ourselves that Hitler's regime was extremely popular with just about everyone we met or, if it was not, they certainly were not saying so. The brown shirted uniforms of the SA were everywhere to be seen. My host — for we were billeted out on team members and adherents — was a hauptmann (captain) and proudly showed me his dirk with "Deutschland uber Alles" etched on the blade. Whether that meant "Germany over everything" or "everyone" I am still not sure. He wore the uniform all the week I was there, but quite what his job within the local unit was I did not find out.

What impressed me most was the vast range of languages in which he was wholly or partly proficient. They included Yiddish. He himself was dark in colouring where most Thuringians were blond, and I was far from certain that he and his parents did not have Jewish blood. Hitler's birthday occurred while we were in Jena and there were parades and

4

festivities to celebrate this, but we were under orders, from the two masters who were leading our party, to stay away.

The second experience was more marked at Goslar, which was a garrison town, and gave us many opportunities of judging the state of rearmament in Germany. Military despatch motor cyclists were constantly riding up and down the main street. In the railway marshalling yards there were long lines of railway trucks loaded with military equipment. For the most part this looked like relatively small calibre anti-tank guns or anti-aircraft guns, but there were some small armoured cars and small tanks to be seen with a lot of motor bicycles and side cars, all camouflage painted and standing out a mile in consequence in an urban area.

In conversation at Goslar our hosts laid great stress on what Hitler had already done for Germany since taking power and what he could be relied on to do for the future. In what they said could be seen some of the causes of the war to come and some of the possible war aims of the country's leaders. The reduction in unemployment and the stabilisation of the currency were strong and unexceptionable features, but the stress laid on restoring Germany's prestige and status in the world seemed to hark back too much to revision of the Versailles Treaty and a reversing of the decisions of the World War. We found the whole atmosphere of the country oppressive and seemingly dangerous.

At about this time I was much influenced — as were many others of my generation — by the writings of Sir Robert Vansittart, permanent under-secretary of the Foreign Office. He was convinced that German rearmament was moving much faster than we were allowing for and that it would certainly create a very dangerous situation for Britain. He stressed that Germany should be resisted but I can see now that he did not suggest how it could be done without provoking major conflict for which this country was not ready. The whole period, 1933/39, was bedevilled by this problem.

As Caterham's contribution to the cause, I proposed that we should have a debate on the issue and put up a motion "that Nazi rule in Germany will inevitably lead to war". It was a good debate but the motion was lost on the argument that nothing in life was inevitable. This seemed to me to be unrealistic and a dangerous attitude in itself but then, I was already convinced of the case.

During the holidays from school I had taken up membership of the scout group at my father's church in Stoke Newington, which we had moved to in the spring of 1930. Although, by 1935, we no longer lived near the church there was no problem in travelling to it or from it to our new home at Hendon. About this time, in mid 1935, the whole Scout movement was exercised by the problem of some boys becoming

5

members of the British Union of Fascists, who wore black shirts and had taken to marching provocatively through Jewish areas of the East End. There were then many Jews in the Stoke Newington area also and, not only might the BUF attract away our older boys, but the risk of trouble was almost on our own doorstep. Two of our senior boys, in fact, joined the fascists as drummers and were liable to be in the forefront of the marching. The scout movement ruled against joint membership and said that those who joined the BUF must leave the scouts. Accordingly our two were expelled but were no serious loss. The Government's decisions to ban the wearing of political uniforms and to give the police powers to forbid marches in certain areas soon took the steam right out of the BUF and it faded away.

In March 1935 Hitler took advantage of a British White Paper, which pointed out the threat of German rearmament, to justify his re-introduction of conscription in Germany. At the same time Britain's National Government did a private naval deal with Germany permitting Germany to have a navy roughly a third of the size of the Royal Navy. In the same month Ramsay Macdonald retired as Prime Minister and Stanley Baldwin took over. In October, with Britain leading, the League of Nations applied sanctions, but not oil sanctions, to Italy because of its invasion of Abyssinia. The German persecution of the Jews was growing in intensity and many refugees were beginning to arrive in Britain. One of these, a boy named Sondhelm, turned up at Caterham and was sympathetically received into the school. In November 1935 there was a General Election and, although rearmament and foreign policy should have been the main issues, they were pushed into the background by housing, unemployment and the Special Areas. The Conservative-led National Government retained its comfortable majority but Labour increased its vote substantially at the expense of the Liberals. Once again the school debating society held a mock election and a mock parliamentary debate, but they proved to be confused and inconclusive.

Nevertheless, things were moving behind the scenes and November 1935 can be seen as the real date from which British rearmament began. In what was more or less a Whitehall revolution, armament plans were re-cast for a possible major war, not merely for filling in gaps. It was a slow start but, previously, there had been no action at all. The results were slow to show themselves but the foundations were laid at a time when the Government was most discredited on this issue. Technically, an immense change in our air defence took place; radar had just been invented and the Spitfire developed. Nevertheless, disputes between the proponents of fighter defence and those supporting bomber retaliation commenced, came into the open and continued throughout the war and beyond.

Although general sanctions had had some effect on Italy's war effort in Abyssinia, they had not brought it to a halt and oil sanctions were being called for. Confusion reigned at the League of Nations. A plan to buy off Italy was revealed prematurely and a huge row ensued. The plan was abandoned but oil sanctions were not imposed and Italy went on to victory. The League of Nations was dead and Anthony Eden became Foreign Secretary. He was the white hope of young people like myself but in the end he proved largely ineffective. In March 1936 Germany re-militarised the Rhineland with the tacit support of the French and the reluctant acquiesence of the British, because action against Germany would have depended on the French and they were thought not to be capable of taking action at the time.

At Easter 1936 we had a return visit to Caterham from the Jena hockey club and a whole crowd of their female adherents came with them. My host of the previous year did not and there was no information available about him. I wondered whether he had been affected or involved in the purge of the SA (brown shirts) which had been carried out by Hitler during the winter. In part this may have arisen due to personal rivalry at the top, even to the extent of involving the leader. There was almost certainly a degree of corruption, vice and indiscipline in the higher ranks of the storm troopers but "the night of the long knives" was drastic and led almost to the dissolution of the SA as well as to the elimination of many of their leaders.

Another factor in the business did appear to be rivalry between the SA and the SS. The latter had come into being by somewhat obscure routes and may have derived from Hitler's own personal bodyguard, the "Stosstrupp Adolf Hitler" or, alternatively or in addition, from Goering's "Stabswache", or "staff guard". Both these units involved the concept of a smaller, harder, more brutal armed force than was to exist within the larger phalanx of Hitler's uniformed followers. In any event, no brown shirts came over with the Jena party in 1936 but one member of the SS arrived with them in full black uniform, with the ominous skull and crossbones badge of the concentration camp guards on his hat. He made himself very conspicuous on every possible public appearance and stalked around Caterham village giving everyone the Nazi salute. He did tend to cast a bit of a cloud over the occasion but, other than that, the visit passed off well, though guardedly.

The time had come for me to leave school. In June 1935 I had passed my Higher Schools (the equivalent of today's 'A' Levels) in Mathematics, Physics and Chemistry and had been accepted for entrance into the Royal School of Mines, part of the Imperial College of London University, to do the course in mining engineering. Unfortunately, it had been decided that 16/17 was too young to enter the second year of the course, even though I was otherwise qualified. It was cheaper for me to stay at Caterham than move up to Kensington, even though I would be living at home. Accordingly, I did a third year in the sixth form — largely wasting my time academically but enjoying myself immensely.

When I did go up to University in October 1936 the time was almost immediately enlivened by the constitutional crisis over the marital intentions of Edward VIII. I had become a King's Scout and was invited to be one of the Guard of Honour for the King at the Cenotaph in Whitehall on 11th November. It was a very cold day but we scouts were not allowed to retain our leather jackets and had to expose our bare arms to the icy conditions while the Guards, the Navy and the Air Force rejoiced in their greatcoats. The King emerged from the Home Office looking drawn and haggard but also wearing a heavy greatcoat.

The actual news of his complicated position did not break until 2nd December or no doubt the crowds would have been even larger, but rumours began shortly after Armistice Day. Once the matter became public events moved rapidly to a conclusion and to the Abdication on 11th December when Edward VIII was succeeded by Albert, Duke of York, who took the title of George VI. By this time Churchill, who continually pressed for rapid rearmament, was gaining prestige in the country again and he had played tentatively with the idea of forming a ''King's Party'' to resist the abdication but events overtook him, the idea was stillborn and he lost face as a result.

As a further complication of the international situation, the Spanish Civil War commenced in the summer of 1936 and gradually became more violent. The Germans and Italians gave increasing support to the nationalist rebels and the Russians entered the conflict on the side of the Spanish communists and their Government.

The Coronation of George VI took place in the spring of 1937 and was a magnificent day. As a King's Scout I sold programmes in the stand immediately opposite the entrance to Buckingham Palace and had a first class view of the processions, both coming and going. In the summer, on St. George's Day, I attended the annual parade of 1,000 King's Scouts from all over the UK at Windsor, where we marched past the Royal couple and their two small daughters. On that day Robert Baden Powell himself attended for the last time and I had the privilege of meeting and talking with him for some minutes.

All my three years at the Royal School of Mines were inevitably overshadowed by the cloud of approaching war. Although the evidence was hard to see in London itself, rearmament was proceeding inexorably as though war was inevitable. At the same time Hitler was creating crisis after crisis and our National Government was struggling to keep pace with them and preserve the peace, almost at all costs. Some of us were

8

beginning to feel the price we were paying for peace was too high. I have become convinced since that the delay in starting the war favoured us more than the Germans, quite apart from the potential benefit of peace if we had been able to find some way of acceptably satisfying Hitler's less unreasonable demands. In the meantime he entered Vienna and took over Austria in March 1938 and I joined the college rifle club! At near enough the same time my friends among the senior scouts at Stoke Newington joined the Territorial Army. Three of them were killed in the war.

My course at the Royal School of Mines required me to undertake and report on 1,000 hours of mining work done during the holidays, of which not less than 750 hours had to be underground work. The Professor and his staff found me a succession of interesting jobs. In the Easter holidays of 1937 I did a fortnight of geological fieldwork in Derbyshire. In the summer holidays of that year I worked for five weeks at a newish colliery at Bilsthorpe in Nottinghamshire and five weeks at an iron mine at Egremont in Cumberland. The following Easter I was at the Halkyn lead mine at Mold in North Wales and in the summer holidays of 1938 was for thirteen weeks at the Trepca lead/zinc/copper mine in Serbia. These were all first class experience and enjoyable into the bargain. I could have had no better preparation for my life as a mining engineer (and, indeed, for my immediate future as a military engineer).

Towards the end of my time at Trepca, the international situation became extremely grave, due to a further crisis in relations with Hitler. He was now asking for a "solution" of the Sudentenland problem in Czechoslovakia and the statesmen were flying to and fro all over the place. The mine authorities decided that their priority job was to get the students sent home. There were only two of us by then but we were packed off home slightly earlier than we had really intended to go. The other student was travelling via Austria but I was taking the classic Orient Express route through Italy.

Eventually the train arrived at Trieste and I was told that I would have a four hour wait there before the train resumed the journey to Venice, Milan, Geneva and Paris. I decided to get some lunch but first walked around the town. On the way into Trieste the train had gradually filled up with Italian Black Shirts, fully equipped and armed, and apparently accompanied by their entire families. It seemed to be a great day out and I gathered that they were going to a grand parade to hear Mussolini speak about the international situation. The large square to be used opened onto the waterfront where no less than four massive destroyers were parked, bows on to the quay, so that their guns would be facing the speaker when he mounted the rostrum. Stands had been erected for the spectators and the whole centre of the square was filling up with row upon row of Black Shirts.

I secured a good looking seat, but decided I had better eat first and then calculated that I would have very little time to spare to hear the speech. I went off to find a restaurant and was lucky to get an excellent one whose prices seemed reasonable. This was good as I was just about down on my beam ends for cash.

It was an excellent meal but towards the end there was a lot of movement in the street and I realised that the great man was about to pass by, so got up to go to the open window onto the pavement to see him. He came by standing in the back of a large open car but appeared to be adding to his height by standing on a box, with his black chin and his saluting arm both extended in front of him. There was only a small crowd and minor excitement in the street and as this died away I returned to my table. I asked the waiter why so little interest had been taken in Mussolini's passing. He told me that no one took any interest in him but I wondered if this would be a national reaction or merely one confined to this formerly Austrian area and town.

When I got home to England I found that the authorities were feverishly issuing gas masks to all concerned and volunteered for duty, taking them around to disabled and bed-ridden. The next week I returned to college, just at the time when Chamberlain returned from Munich with his famous "peace in our time" message. I read the news as I joined my underground train at Golders Green and wept with frustration. In January 1939, Parliament debated conscription and a proposal to call up the first batch of peacetime conscripts in July. The Bill went through quickly and preliminary notices were sent out calling on all twenty year olds to register forthwith. I did so and received a small registration certificate with which I attended for medical examination at Mill Hill Barracks. The examination was not exactly cursory, as the music hall jokes implied that it would be, but it was not exactly intensive either. As I recall, the doctor looked at my throat and listened to my chest, he checked my sight, merely by getting me to read from a wall chart, and I believe he examined my private parts for any sign of venereal disease. Apparently all were in order and in a relatively brief time I was passed A1 — as was everyone else in the room at the same time.

I recall that this medical exam must have taken place before mid February as it was then that we started the last half year of our course at the Royal School of Mines. This was to be devoted almost entirely to mine surveying. In the previous year we had done a course in land surveying in Kensington Gardens but now we were to do the real thing underground in an old Cornish copper mine, Tywarnhaile, near St

10

Agnes. We spent eight weeks over the Easter period doing the fieldwork in Cornwall and about the same amount of time subsequently in London doing the calculations and drawing our final plans.

My actual calling-up papers arrived one morning while we were preparing to go underground. I was required to present myself "for military training on Tuesday 18th July, 1939 at 10.00 a.m., or as early as possible thereafter on that day, to: 21st Searchlight Regiment RA at Pimperne, Blandford." A travel warrant was enclosed, as was a postal order for 4 shillings "being an advance which will be recovered from your pay".

There were about a dozen of us in all on the survey course. Seven were doing mining engineering and five were doing mining geology. Apart from myself only David Lloyd had received his calling-up papers. Of the others, two were South Africans and later joined the army there, one was a Canadian but was killed in an accident shortly after starting work, one was a German who spent the war working in the Barnsley coalmines and the other six were all either in the University Air Squadron or in the University Officer Training Corps. Lloyd had been called to a Royal Artillery Survey Regiment.

Two of the airmen were killed in the Battle of Britain but the rest, except the Canadian, all survived and I met them all again at one time or another after the war. It was a great joke to the rest that Lloyd and I were having to go for military training for six months but, as indicated, most of them were committed anyway. Even so, we could expect to be out on the mines and in employment — in my case in South Africa, in Lloyd's case in the coalmines in England — a fairly short time after our colleagues had started work.

On our return to London from Cornwall we were working, for the most part, in the Survey Drawing Office overlooking the Royal College of Music so our labours were lightened by snatches of magnificent harmony. The only trouble was that the performers never did more than a couple of bars at a time, which was extremely frustrating for us. Anyway, I finished the course with a first class honours degree and a row of most of the available prizes. I had to collect these from the office rather than wait for them to be awarded and, in fact, there was no degree ceremony that year for anyone in Imperial College, as so many of those eligible had been called-up or were already abroad before the due date.

CHAPTER 2

21st Searchlight Regiment,
Royal Artillery
(July, 1939 — September, 1939)

I suppose we actually joined the army at the moment when we received the King's four shilling postal order but, be that so or not, the arrangements at Waterloo Station on the 18th July and at Blandford Station on arrival were impeccable. At Blandford, as promised, there was a non-commissioned officer on duty to receive us and direct us onward. As I recall, he had two stripes and was no doubt a Bombardier. We were loaded into a three ton truck and conveyed three miles north-east of the town onto the Downs where a large bell-tented camp had been erected.

We pulled up near a flagpole and an embryo parade ground where the bombardier handed us over to an imposing looking regimental policeman wearing an armlet, with the letters RP, on his rolled-up shirt sleeve. He took over the dozen or so of us on board the truck and commanded us to follow him to a tent full of large cotton sacks which, he informed us, were palliasses which we had to fill with straw from a bale at the back of the tent to make them into mattresses. We were also given three blankets and a rather coarse pillow. Thus equipped we staggered down a row of tents until we reached one which he said was to be home for ten of us. The others moved on.

Next we followed him to a marquee, which was obviously where we ate, at the head of the lines, near to the regimental police tent. We went in and took our seats at wooden trestle tables where we were supplied with an enamel mug, two aluminium plates and a knife, fork and spoon each. There was bread, margarine and jam available on the table and, wonder of wonders, considerable wads of cake! The policeman instructed us to set to and said that a cook would bring us some tea very shortly. Accordingly, we set to and made a good meal. Afterwards we washed up in a small zinc bath of tepid water and took our wet utensils back to our tents.

The policeman re-appeared and took us to a marquee at the bottom of the lines. We gathered that this was the abode of the quartermaster sergeant, an all-powerful gentleman whom we would be well advised to obey promptly and keep sweet. He was indeed organised to cope quickly with large contingents of men. Odd bits of information were thrown at us from one side or another. We gathered that we were part of "D

12

Battery'', there being four batteries to a regiment, each battery being about 200 men and there being two regiments in the camp.

Each battery had three lines of eight bell tents and there were three marquees at the top of the lines — one was the mess (dining) marquee and the second was for the cooks. The third, we found out later, was our lecture hall. There were two other marquees at the bottom of the lines, one for the QM's store and the other for the Battery Office. The latrines and ablutions were slightly lower down the hill.

In the QM's store we were rapidly supplied with most of the rest of our clothing and equipment. Like the quartermaster sergeant himself, his helpers were regular army men drafted in to provide the permanent staff of such camps, as were the cooks, the regimental police, and the officers, of whom we only seemed to have two for the battery.

Selecting the right size of uniform for each of us took a little longer than issuing the other equipment and one or two mis-shapen types had difficulty getting anything suitable. One or two were instructed to report to the tailor at the back of the QM's store and had to wait until the next morning to get their modified tunics. Greatcoats were equally difficult for fitting.

Like me, most of our people were horrified to find that the Royal Artillery was not yet using the battle dress we had seen in the newspapers. Accordingly, we were being issued with brass-button-up-to-the-neck tunics and with riding breeches and puttees. I hated the lot on sight. The puttees were long lengths of khaki serge cloth about 4" wide and they had to be wound, starting at the top of the boot, round the lower leg up to just below the knee, where they were finished off with a tape tucked in. Wound too loosely they collapsed; wound too tightly you were almost in danger of gangrene. These ghastly appendages originated, like their name, in India where they were no doubt very useful for keeping stones and insects out of one's boots.

Then there was a suit of overalls, of stiff cotton cloth, called "denims", worn for most duty parades, there was a strange looking bag or wrapper known as a "holdall" and a brass plate with a slot cut in one end of it and called a "buttonstick". More welcome was the exchange of our civilian gas masks in their cardboard boxes for the military model.

We were also issued with our rifles and were warned on pain of death not to forget the number of our own, which was stamped on the butt and also on the bolt (the loading mechanism) which was easily removable but not necessarily completely interchangeable. All these we bore away to our tents. Some eager beavers immediately started cleaning their buttons and boots. I was not that keen and preferred to see whether and when someone actually wanted us to take on these chores.

Somewhere along the line we were also issued with our personal numbers, which had eight figures for the new recruits whereas the regulars appeared to have six or seven numbers. Mine was 10056002 and, as can be judged, recruits were required virtually to remember them in their sleep as well as at every waking moment.

We had barely looked at the tent when we had seen it before, but we were now at liberty to observe that we would not be sleeping on the soft ground but on hard, but relatively dry, baseboards cut in segments to fit the circular shape of the tent. Our rifles had to be strapped to the tent pole and we arranged our palliasses spoke-wise around the tent. Bell tents were and are still made up in twenty four segments, two of these being the door. In theory each tent accommodated twenty four men but we had the luxury of providing for only ten.

Shortly after this we heard a bugle playing the tune we came to recognise as the "Last Post". This was the time when the flag was lowered at the top of the lines and we were all required to stand to attention until the bugle had finished. The bugler was still a boy, and normally a very scruffy looking one at that, who hung around the regimental police tent or the battery office, running messages and perhaps making himself useful and occasionally tidy throughout the day. To play his bugle he smartened himself up completely, did up all his buttons, put his hat on straight and adjusted his steel-rimmed glasses. Then, with his brightly polished bugle to his lips, he looked and sounded the very spirit of the British army and I still thrill to the sound of that tune whenever I hear it.

It was now time to go to the latrines and the ablutions; then back to the tent, to make our beds quickly and put on the sports gear I had been given, which served me as pyjamas for most of my army time before I became an officer. There was a short argument as to whether we had the door closed or not — won by the fresh air men — and so to bed. With the brief sounding of the "lights out" bugle call at 10 o'clock and despite my palliasse being a little over-stuffed I, like everyone else, dropped off to sleep very promptly.

Thereafter, the passage of each day was marked by a succession of bugle calls that we all came to know intimately. First was "Reveille" — the wake-up call. Then came "Rations" — for breakfast and then "Warning for Parade" — about quarter of an hour before the formal parade and roll call, which was normally held at the start of the day's work or training, in the presence of an officer. We were told to answer our names with the reply "Sir" unless there was no officer present, when we answered the non-commissioned officer with the reply "Sergeant" or "Bombardier" as the case was. "Rations" sounded again for dinner, "Warning for Parade" for the afternoon roll call and "Rations" again for high tea, the day ending with "Last Post" and "Lights Out" as already described.

The parades were held on the camp road as the parade ground was not completed for two or three weeks. On the first one our battery commander, a very smart captain in the uniform of the Royal Scots, took the parade and addressed us briefly to the effect that he was sure that we would all get on very well. The circumstances under which we might not were not enumerated.

We then broke up into squads, each under a sergeant, for drill without rifles, which we had been told to leave in our tents. After about an hour of that we were told to go and change into our sports gear for physical training (PT) when a brisk, energetic looking sergeant of the PT Corps arrived from nowhere to take over and pursue us relentlessly for the next half hour. Then there was a break for a mug of tea.

This was followed by a session in a lecture marquee when we were taken — at an appallingly slow pace — through the first of ten lessons on the rifle. Lesson one was naming the parts of the rifle and stripping it down. That sounds a lot but to the best of my memory there were only two parts that we were allowed to remove, namely the bolt and the magazine. Anything else, we were told, had to be done by an armourer who could be found, inevitably, in the QM's store. I reflected grimly — and I'm sure others did too — on the quality of regular recruits who apparently needed an hour to learn six names and how to undo and replace two parts. On reflection I am sure that these tedious weapon training lectures were the worst thing I had to put up with during my recruit training but, on second thoughts, the afternoon programmme, which included an hour standing around our single searchlight, was even more tedious.

I would not want to imply that the system was wrong. By the standards of the time it was good; the instructors made an honest effort to present the material as well as possible, but it was adapted to the pace of the slowest (as, indeed, was all industrial training at the time!). High-flyers just had to be patient — which I never was!

A much earlier introduction of "cadre classes" for the quicker and more adaptable groups might have been useful but the question is would it have suited everyone equally? Not all graduates make good officers — some are just too clumsy for example.

The reader may wonder why I, a graduate mining engineer, had been posted to a searchlight unit? When we had first been registered for training we were asked in which branch of the service we wished to be trained. Thinking that I was going to spend the rest of my life in mining I asked to be posted to the Signals Corps as I was well aware that I needed

15

further knowledge and practice with radio and telephony. Unfortunately, most branches were getting very few of the first batch of 6,000 militia men (conscripts) and I am sure the Royal Signals did not wish to fill their small quota with men who had no specialist knowledge in line with their requirements. The Royal Engineers presumably could fill their quota too without taking someone who had not asked to join them.

The vast majority of the first batch were all being trained to take the place of the territorial army units who had been called up on June 11th to serve with the searchlights and anti-aircraft guns in case the Germans made a surprise attack, even before the declaration of war.

In fact, at that time, the War Office was not expecting the Germans to wish to begin the war much before 1941/42 and they expected to have time to train at least one year's intake, if not two years'. Our first batch of 6,000 seems small in comparison with a one year intake of, say, 250,000 but, bearing in mind that the camps were not even ready for us, and that they were going to take in new batches every two months, they might reasonably be expected to have had a large reserve of half-trained (six months) men at the end of a year or more.

We were destined, therefore, to move out of the Blandford camp after two months to take the place of the territorials on the searchlight sites and let them go home. To keep them much longer would have required another Act of Parliament which the Government did not wish to seek at that stage.

After we had been there nearly a month the captain decided to take us out for a route march. We all paraded in full uniform with our gas masks, rifles and webbing equipment (the belt and braces to carry our ammunition pouches and a haversack) and set off on a circuit of the local lanes which I see now must have been three miles at most but I did not get that far. About a mile after the start a rather plump youth collapsed with the strain. The captain came striding back down the files, took a look around, and detailed me to remain with the youth and await a truck which would come to take us back to camp, so I got off lightly.

One night the clouds opened and rain bucketed down on the tented camp where we were all trying to sleep through the thunder and lightning as water streamed under the door, lapping the boards. Every little moth-hole in the twenty year old tents spouted a small jet of water and sleep was impossible. The sounds indicated that many of our comrades in other tents were evacuating and heading for the nearly complete hutted camp. We decided to join them after debating whether to wait for orders. We left our rifles, wrapped in ground sheets round the tent pole, but that did us no good. We got a mild rocket anyway from the captain next day, not for deserting our tent but for leaving our rifles behind us,

16

which he categorized as a very unsoldierly act! Still, we had had a relatively dry night and had been able to sleep and had learnt a good lesson into the bargain!

At the end of the first month, we were given a rail warrant and allowed to go home for a weekend's leave, carrying home the civilian clothes we had brought with us. Morning parade was held on Sundays, as on ordinary working days, and was in full uniform, even though it was a no-work day. I cannot remember that we ever had a church parade or saw a visiting padre.

Mostly, on Saturday and Sunday afternoons a couple of us would walk around the adjoining lanes or visit Pimperne, which was a pleasant village with a good pub and cider which was equally as cheap and rather better quality than was avaiable in our canteen tent.

After about another week they — the captain and the NCO's presumably — had decided who their first new NCO's were going to be and half a dozen of us in "D" Battery were listed in Orders as promotions to Acting Unpaid Lance Bombardiers and instructed to hand in our tunics to have our first stripes sewn on by the tailor. The next step might not be long delayed and would mean that our pay would increase from one shilling and sixpence per day to two shillings and sixpence per day, which were riches indeed. (The unfortunate married men drew only one third of these sums and their wives drew 17 shillings per week to keep them and their young families.)

The only snag with pay was the pay parade itself which was highly formal, with the paying officer (the most junior available presumably) only slightly less confused than the recipients. They marched up to the pay table, saluted with the right hand, shouted out their number, held out the left hand for the money, saluted again with the right hand, about turned and marched off — all hopefully without falling over or turning in the wrong direction and being shouted at by the attendant NCOs.

The parade ground had been brought into use and, in fact, we had been visited by one of the Royal Artillery bands which had performed the ceremony and music of "Beating Retreat" on the parade ground as a sort of celebratory concert. We had been drilling with rifles for some weeks now and were really beginning to feel and look like soldiers too. Work on the permanent hutted camp, just a bit nearer Blandford than we were, proceeded apace and that was nearing completion too.

Suddenly the pace of life stepped up, except for the lectures on the anti-tank rifle and the searchlight. Following the Bren light machine gun the anti-tank rifle was simplicity itself but the weapons training sergeant insisted on making it still simpler for us. I well remember him introducing the rifle by saying, "This 'ere rooifle foires a bullitt wot goes froo tanks loike butter. Insoide the tank it whizzes rahnd and rahnd at

17

ever increasing velocity thus demoralising the enemy." Well, I always imagined it might.

We were loaded into lorries one day and taken back eastwards towards Portsmouth where we were told we were to erect as many bell tents as we could in a new camp. Having been a boy scout, with experience in a troop which had bell tents, I was able to organise and drill my small squad and get moderately effective performance. I think I was alone in this and it took some of my colleagues nearly two hours per tent but, by the end of the day, we had at least provided enough for the equivalent of one of our batteries. Nevertheless, I think that the captain was not very impressed with our alignment or inclinations to the vertical. I was sorry we didn't get a second try though.

By this time we had a junior officer in the battery who had literally come straight from civilian life into an officer's uniform. Nevertheless, he was friendly and prepared to talk to a couple of acting unpaid lance-bombardiers provided the captain was not watching him. We discussed the probable onset of war with him and what difference it might make to our future and our promotion. He knew very little, if anything, more than we did.

Then, on September 1st the sergeant asked on parade whether any of us knew anything about electricity. I thought it was either that they were looking for somebody to switch the searchlight on — which we hadn't yet got to in our instruction — or there was a soft job going, putting in electric light bulbs somewhere around the camp. As we were faced with another lecture on the anti-tank rifle, I volunteered, thus breaking the first rule of the army — "never volunteer for anything!". I was sent down to the battery office and the Battery Sergeant Major marched me in to see the captain. "Left-right, left-right, 'alt".

"What do you know about electricity, Mortimer?," said the captain. "I did it at University, Sir," I said glibly, "it was one of my subjects", failing to mention that it was my worst. "Did you now!" said he, "Right, back to your squad again then." and the BSM loyally chanted, "Left-right, left-right", as I left the tent.

The next day, Saturday, was my 21st birthday and with a friend I went down to the pub in Pimperne to have a couple of ciders. On Sunday, as we sat in the canteen tent having yet another cider, we heard Neville Chamberlain telling us that the war had begun. On Tuesday I was posted away to the Ordnance Corps to be a Vehicle Electrician, which shows the un-wisdom of volunteering as I was quickly to find out that I knew nothing whatsoever about the inside of a car or truck bonnet.

CHAPTER 3
1st Ordnance Base Workshops,
Royal Army Ordnance Corps —
(September – December, 1939)

There were three or four of us going by truck to the Ordnance Corps from Blandford. One of them, Bernard Anstey, was a graduate engineer like myself. The other one or two men I cannot remember at all. They dropped off somewhere on the way to our ultimate destination. Our immediate destination that day was the Ordnance Corps barracks at Hilsea, a suburb of Portsmouth.

Hilsea seemed to be a gathering point for men being transferred to the Ordnance Corps from other Corps and Regiments. With my precious Acting Unpaid stripes I was the only NCO amongst us so I got the odd jobs like marching the others to meals and calling the roll. The only difference now was that I was referred to as Corporal rather than Bombardier. This possibly explains why the pay clerk later made a mistake and credited me with being a paid lance corporal electrician of the Ordnance Corps itself. This favoured me with a greatly increased rate of pay and I did not argue too strongly, making a mild protest only for conscience sake and being overruled by the pay clerk who clearly knew best, in the opinion of the paying officer. My rate was now something like five shillings per day rather than one shilling and sixpence, until a much smarter clerk at the Officer Cadet Training Unit found out the error and I was put under stoppages of pay for some considerable period into my commissioned service. Nevertheless, I enjoyed the higher rate while I had it for six months or more, and the pay back period soon passed.

We had no particular duties at Hilsea and it was mostly a period of relaxation. That was easy because we had iron bedsteads and some short mattresses called "biscuits", about 2 feet 3 inches square, three making a complete mattress for a standard bed. As we were also supplied with sheets, it was luxury indeed. I suppose that, if the Ordnance Corps could not get themselves sheets, no one could.

After two or three days I was given a rail warrant for Anstey and myself and for two other men to transfer to Chilwell, in Nottinghamshire, which we accomplished successfully. Our sleeping quarters there were in a huge store shed where rows of mattresses were laid out on the concrete floor — not very comfortable, but acceptable enough. When we arrived only a few of the beds were allocated but, over

19

the next few days, the spaces gradually filled up as parties of reservists and other transferees came in to fill them.

Although I did not realise it at the time, we were being formed up as the 1st Ordnance Base Workshops and we were due to go to France to join the British Expeditionary Force (BEF) as soon as sufficient men had been assembled and the last trade vacancies had been filled. I might not know what we were or where we were going but we were clearly going somewhere pretty quick so it behoved me to be pretty quick too in attending to a couple of priority matters. First things first, of course, and here was my chance to get rid of my hated tunic, breeches and puttees. I went at once to the QM's Store and represented to the quartermaster sergeant the terrible indignity of an Ordnance Corps lance corporal being sent to do electrical work for his country overseas dressed as a First World War horsed gunner. He saw my point and I got my coveted battle dress without any money changing hands on the deal.

Only delaying to put my new tunic in the hands of the tailor, with the customary "pour boire", of course, to get my stripes sewn on quickly, I moved on to the regimental offices to enquire about making a move to get my name down for a commission in the Royal Engineers. The time had come for Mortimer to face the fact that he was now in for the duration, to stop mucking about with the Royal Regiment of Artillery (searchlights), the Royal Corps of Signals and the Royal Army Ordnance Corps and to get stuck in somewhere where he might be found to have some training, experience and ability which might merit advancement beyond his present proud but still lowly rank.

The clerk who dealt with me neither showed any particular interest in my application nor any particular surprise at receiving it. On the whole it seemed that he was aware that candidates for commissions were required and that a number of us were applying. I told Anstey of my doings and was gratified to see him grab his uniform and start off on the same errands — with ultimate success.

When I told my parents about my intentions, in one of my letters, I got a very quick letter back trying to discourage me from attempting to move to the Royal Engineers, which my father saw as being a move much nearer to the front line than that occupied by the RAOC. He had always been impressed by the carnage of the First World War and visualised the same sort of thing in this war. I attempted to allay his fears by pointing out, not only that I might be knocked down in the street just as easily in either occupation, but also that I might just as easily run into military danger as well, depending on where I would actually be working. More importantly, I stressed that it was surely right for me to do the job that I did best and that, in a long war, I was likely to be happier doing so.

20

I expected the war to last six years — half as long again as the First War — a prediction which proved remarkably accurate. As it happened the unit I would have joined, had I stayed with the RAOC, was overrun by the Germans in their big advance through France and, to the best of my knowledge, a fair number of them spent the war in prisoner-of-war camps.

Fairly soon we started parading outside each morning and the gradually lengthening roll was called. After that we were slowly sorted out into various working parties and sent to various departments in the depot workshops themselves. Chilwell was a vehicle and spare parts depot and the leading vehicle workshops in the army — a position which I believe Didcot took over later. It was a fairly compact mass of huge, hangar-size store buildings and workshops. Anstey and I were detailed to go to the electrical workshops. This department had just about the smallest number of tradesmen and was, apparently, the one with still the greatest number of vacancies.

We were all farmed out to work with individual civilian electricians. Mine was a cheerful, sharp-looking character, who greeted me amiably and suggested that we might start the day with a stroll out to the toilets. After paying our visit he suggested that we went round the corner and read the newspaper for a bit, explaining that it didn't pay to overdo things. Then we went back and looked at our day's work which was a sand-coloured, burnt-out truck which had to be re-wired. Looking into the bonnet, I had not the faintest idea where we would start or finish the job or, in fact, what we needed to do to fix it. However, my mentor decided that a visit to the store was the next thing on the list so we worked our way towards this, hailing and chatting with many other of his colleagues on the way, to whom he introduced me as "Gerry" all round. Gradually we reached the stores, a wired off portion of the shop, where he engaged in amiable chit chat for a while with one of the storemen. The latter eventually fetched us a box of tools and coils of cable of various sizes and colours.

Returning to our vehicle my friend decided it was time to visit the toilet again for another smoke and another read. When we returned we found that break time had arrived and so with all the others we trooped out to the canteen for a cup of tea.

At last he started work on the vehicle by pulling out every piece of cable he could get his hands on. His hands were then so dirty that a visit to the washroom was called for which, like the other visits, took us at least half an hour. So the morning passed. By the end of it we were actually putting in some new cable but, with intermittent breaks for the toilets and further visits to the stores, progress was incredibly slow. The afternoon seemed even slower. After two or three days we were finished

21

with the vehicle and handed it over. Curious, to me, was the fact that neither we, nor anyone else as far as I can recall, applied any paint to the blackened interior of the bonnet while we were on the job. As an example of the progress of work in government workshops it did not impress me at all.

Then some seven or eight of us were told that we were to come off the daily workshop parade and be formed into a "cadre class". It turned out that we had all applied for commissions in a variety of regiments. The lectures were to be given by the somewhat over-weight second-in-command of the depot, who was a major from the Middlesex Regiment and apparently in charge of regimental administration. He expressed himself as glad to be dealing with real soldiers again and not with a bunch of workshop loafers and storemen! The commanding officer was a full colonel of the Ordnance Corps, whom I never met or saw in the time that I was there. Our man told us at our first session that he was going to divide his course into three parts initially. First he would deal with some elements of military law, then with matters of procedure and etiquette, as they affected young officers, and then he would deal with certain matters of military organisation. This all sounded fine to us.

We were introduced to the Army Act by way of the Manual of Military Law. There were forty main clauses of the Act itself, which laid down the various offences that a soldier might commit and the appropriate maximum punishment in each case. Nearly every crime seemed as if it would possibly incur the punishment of death but about half of them were mitigated by the words "or some such less punishment as the court may decide". The other half were not mitigated in any way and death appeared to be mandatory. As many of these were really serious crimes, including mutiny, desertion and the civil crime of murder, perhaps this mandatory sentence was not really surprising and the punishment had certainly been applied very regularly in the First World War.

It behoved us, as potential young officers, to be well aware of the serious implications of some of these crimes. Not only might we, under stress, be personally tempted into desertion (not all that different in war time from the lesser crime of absence without leave) but we might, at some stage be faced with mutiny or something rather like it or, alternatively, be required to serve on a court martial as one of the "judges".

It was all fascinating stuff, particularly the procedure for the court martial itself where, depending on the seriousness of the offence and the possible punishment, the court might be quite large with five or seven officers, for example, constituting the "judges" in the court. Then there was a representative of the Judge Advocate's Department (a legal gentleman whose duty was to advise the court on the points of law), the prosecuting officer and the prisoner's friend, who had to do his best to defend him. All very complicated. Most daunting of all was the fact that, when it came to passing sentence, the first to speak had to be the most junior officer on the court. I never quite gathered what happened when the court disagreed on verdict or sentence except that I did know that the junior officer might well be over-ruled if the others thought that the sentence was too harsh and no doubt he was looked at pityingly if his sentence was too weak. We gathered that the navy and the airforce had similar but different Acts.

The most fascinating clause of all was the last, which was a clean-up, catch-all clause because it was also a crime to commit any act which was "contrary to good order and military discipline". In my experience this one formed the basis of more than nine out of ten charges for minor defaulting. It was also one of the only three or four crimes which did not permit death as a possible punishment.

The lectures on procedure and etiquette were all accompanied by cyclostyled notes distributed by the major and presumably copied from his own stored aide-memoires. These too were fascinating, some having an Anglo-Indian context, presumably because so many peacetime officers served in the Indian army. We were given, for example, notes on the procedure for joining a military "station" in India. Apparently, the first thing to be done was to walk or ride up to Government House, the residence of the senior British military or civilian officer on the station. "Up" was literally true, as the residence was usually on the highest point available. Here one signed the visitors' book, and left one's card on the silver tray produced by the servant who answered the door. Thereafter, one was literally a member of the community, able to be invited out to dinner, cards and tennis, or other sports.

However, a young officer had also "to leave his card on his colonel's lady" and, presumably, civilian officers did the same for their principal's lady. What the word "lady" encompassed was not made clear but presumably it was the practice to sign a visitors' book at her residence as well. The procedure for toasting the King was also worth noting as it was clear one might easily get landed with it at a very early stage. When the port or madeira glasses had been filled and the coffee cups put around the table at dinner, the mess president, usually the most senior officer member of the mess, would rise to his feet and call "Mr Vice". Then the most junior officer present would stand up, raise his glass and call "Gentlemen, the King". Thereafter the port or madeira decanters circulated clockwise, "with the sun" round the table and each officer topped up his glass as the opportunity came to him. To smoke before the King's health had been drunk and the president had given

23

permission to do so was a serious social error. Hardly less serious, but only just, was to prevent the decanters from moving steadily on their course. We were informed that, at the mess table or in the mess generally, officers did not discuss work ("shop"), politics and religion and ladies' names were not mentioned. That must certainly have led to either the broadening or stultifying of conversation. I cannot say because this last rule was not really observed in war time, particularly in so far as "shop" was concerned.

Unfortunately, the major never took us as far as military organisation which, although the other matters were fascinating, was the subject that interested me most then and later in my career. Gradually the major's work seemed to increase and we seemed to be called on for other jobs so that our lectures tailed away to an end.

In the middle of them I was called to Northern Command Headquarters at York for interview regarding my application to be an officer cadet. I presented myself at, I think, Fulford Barracks and was marched into the Chief Engineer's office. I saluted and the officer there raised his head from the papers he had been studying. "Graduate?" he asked without waiting for any reply and then "What school did you go to?" "Caterham, Sir" I answered. He might have asked "Where's that?," but presumably did not, either to spare my blushes or to conceal his own ignorance, so I filled in, "In Surrey, Sir". "Right Mortimer," he said, "we'll let you know".

That completed my interview. Later in the war they became more prolonged and formal with the setting up of the "WOSBies" (War Office Selection Boards) which both my wife and my brother later had to face. Still, we must have saved some money in my case and probably not made a mistake either.

One day, the whole cadre class was detailed to turn up for a job of work at the tyre store, a medium sized building in a considerable state of disarray. Most of the stacks had been built too high and had fallen over, scattering a mix of tyres of all sizes in every direction. Our task was to sort them out and re-stack and count them. At first glance it was a formidable task. Nevertheless, it was a good unstructured team test. We sorted ourselves out excellently and set to work with a will. Within an hour the store clerk returned and was horrified to find that we had progressed a long way towards completing the task. In injured tones he told us that the job was meant to last a week and here we were about to finish it before lunch time on the first day. We laughed him off and completed it nevertheless and he dismissed us with muttered imprecations about "taking the working man's bread" and so on. My impressions of honest working men and their trade unions were suffering a rapid set-back.

Anstey and I found ourselves a good job sorting out "impressed" vehicles. The army had apparently decided to call up vehicles, as well as men, and had selected, as one of the types in which they were interested, a Bedford two or three ton truck, usually fitted with a drop-side body. Many of them had literally been accepted on their last legs with flat batteries, no spare wheel and other disabilities. Our job was to identify any non-runners and see if we could correct the situation. Short of cannibalising (which was beyond our scope because it would require the condemning and scrapping of another vehicle) there was little we could do about missing spare wheels; batteries were easy to replace and some vehicles only required petrol and oil. Anstey had a learner driver's licence but I had none, and we were both at an early stage of learning to drive, but we improved our standard considerably by practicing on the impressed vehicles. Whenever we went to collect re-charged batteries or petrol we took the longest route around the depot to get there and reversed into every dead end to try out our three-point turns. Some vehicles required minor jobs in the workshops such as dealing with faulty lights but we had to be careful not to cause a pile up of trucks there.

When we had finally established a vehicle as a "runner" we delivered it to a separate car park, until that was full, or into one of the spare store sheds. In this manner, we attained a reasonable standard of driving proficiency on these simple vehicles (I later found the gearbox of the standard army 15 cwt truck far more difficult to compete with). From our services the army gained a considerable fleet of "ready-to-go" vehicles at the expense of a certain amount of petrol, a number of damaged rainwater down pipes and a number of chipped brick corners.

Long before Christmas the 1st Ordnance Base Workshops had moved out (leaving the cadre class behind) and had presumably gone to France to set up there to serve the BEF.

New contingents of reservists and transferees continued to stream in at a fair pace. We were all now looked after by a large squad of women (ATS) cooks, clerks and general administrators. Meanwhile the cadre class continued with only occasional special duties. Indeed, one or two were leaking away as cadets to one arm of the service or the other but no word had yet arrived for Anstey and myself.

I grew friendly with an ATS girl named Mary but she turned out to be a Catholic, which horrified my parents, and caused me to think carefully. She was a pleasant girl and we got on well but the Holy Father's conditions for marriage seemed too restrictive on the Protestant side, particularly in relation to the upbringing of children. This was unacceptable to me and Mary too had doubts about a mixed marriage. We therefore agreed that we would not suit and we parted amicably. The war had now been going on for four months and I had been in the army for nearly six months. The BEF was now established, in France on the left of the French army on the Belgian border, but no real action was taking place. On the Polish side of Germany intense action had started at the very beginning of the war. The "blitzkrieg" tactics of the German armoured forces and the virtual extinction of the Polish airforce led to the rapidly complete defeat of the Polish forces by the German army, while the Russians overran the east of their country. Hundreds of Polish airmen escaped by a variety of routes to join the RAF in Britain. The collapse of Polish resistance meant that Germany was now in a position to build up in the west to discourage any Allied reaction in 1939.

RAF bombing activity over Germany was virtually non-existent, except in relation to naval targets. Indeed, the only things dropped over much of Germany were bundles of propaganda leaflets.

With Churchill now in the Government as First Lord of the Admiralty there was some activity on the naval front but the balance of sinkings mostly favoured the Germans until they had to scuttle the "Graf Spee" to avoid further battle with three British cruisers. That definitely made the Navy one-up on both the other services and on the enemy.

Meanwhile, the Russians had started a minor war with the Finns which went badly for the former in the winter conditions.

Almost immediately the New Year commenced Anstey and I received our orders to report to the 142 Officer Cadet Training Unit (OCTU), Royal Engineers at Aldershot and we packed our bags. Incidentally, "our bags", while we were in the ranks, consisted of a small haversack worn at the side and a large pack worn on the back and a black kit bag. These, together with an eight pound rifle, made a formidable and awkward load to be lugging around the railway stations of England, but fortunately we were usually delivered by truck to our departure station and collected by truck from our arrival station. So, although the main war appeared to have entered a static or "phoney war" stage (except for the poor Poles), it had at least begun moving for Anstey and myself. In the meantime, though unintentionally, I had missed out on my first chance of embarkation (for France) — and avoided spending possibly the whole war in a prisoner of war camp.

CHAPTER 4
142nd Officer Cadet Training Unit,
Royal Engineers
(January – June, 1940)

The 142nd Officer Cadet Training Unit RE was housed in Malta Barracks, Aldershot, a new hutted complex in a clearing in the woods on Watts Common, to the west of the Farnborough Road. The abandoned Basingstoke Canal was its southern boundary and to the west and north was the Royal Aircraft Establishment and its airfield. On the near side of that was the Aldershot golf course. When Anstey and I first saw the camp, in the first week of January, 1940, it was still incomplete and, in particular, the regimental offices were only just being built.

We reported at the temporary orderly room and were shown to our quarters in one hut of the two six-hut "spiders" which comprised the cadets' barracks. These spiders appeared to be the latest thing in hutted camp layouts and they certainly made relatively comfortable quarters. A central block, forming the spine of each spider, included the latrines, the ablutions, the bathrooms and the heating equipment. Six barrack huts branched off, three on each side of each centre block.

We were to be in Class No. 6 and, as each class of between 50 and 60 cadets or Young Officers needed two barrack huts, the two spiders were now full, although I believe a third spider was still to be built. The Young Officers were men who had been directly commissioned from civilian life and wore officers' uniform and held the rank of 2nd Lieutenant. Their initial training was exactly the same as that of the cadets. Two whole classes, Nos. 1 and 5, were entirely made up of Young Officers and each other class contained one or two, No. 6 Class having four. If I remember rightly, cadets and YOs were not mixed in the same barrack hut in order, no doubt, to preserve the YO's dignity.

We soon heard, from one source or another, that the whole training programme was divided into eight separate courses of three weeks each, although courses 1 to 3 were literally identical. As No. 7 Class was presumably due to enter the OCTU in three weeks time, extra accommodation would be needed by then. It did not look at all likely that it would be ready and I forget now whether, indeed, it was or whether the entry of the Class was deferred.

Working to capacity, as I am sure it eventually did, 142 OCTU could therefore produce about 800 new officers a year. There was a second OCTU, the 141st, at Folkestone with about the same capacity and there

27

was also a flow of directly commissioned officers for Works Units, who did not do OCTU training, and this flow continued for much of the rest of the war. All this, of course, was added to the original number of regulars, recalled reservists and territorials with whom the army started the war. It seems a large number of officers but it has to be remembered that about one third of the total army was made up of Royal Engineers.

In the barrack room conditions were fairly spartan but were not uncomfortable. Each man had his bed and a small bedside cupboard (without a lock). The rifle racks and a full-length mirror occupied one corner near the door and in the other corner was a small room which, in a normal barrack block, would be occupied by an NCO but in our case I believe it was occupied by one of our YOs.

Each class had a regular officer (a captain or full lieutenant) in charge as Class Officer. He was assisted by a regular sergeant. Ours was, I believe, a Sergeant Walker, but I do not recall our having a corporal as well. Outside the class structure was the rest of the training staff under a major as Chief Instructor. There were quite a number of captains and lieutenants and Quartermaster Sergeant Instructors (QMSIs), all regulars, making up the rest of the team. In addition, there were the physical training instructors who came from the Army Physical Training Corps under the command of Sergeant Alf Gover, the Surrey fast bowler. The regimental staff was small, the Commanding Officer, (Lt. Colonel Binney), the Adjutant, the Regimental Sergeant Major and the Regimental Quartermaster Sergeant plus the orderly room staff and all the RQMS's cooks and administrative staff.

Apart from the barrack blocks and the regimental offices there were, of course, the mess room and the kitchen block, the RQMS's store and a number of lecture rooms and stores for training equipment of various types. The Motor Transport Training School was outside the complex and was, in fact, situated in the old Horse Transport Training School within marching distance. The Wet Bridging School was several miles away and had its own stores building. When we first saw the main camp it was blanketed in a moderate covering of snow and the pines and Christmas trees gave it an almost romantic look.

There were no sports facilities within the barrack perimeter, but running tracks and games pitches were all readily available at other barracks close to us on the Aldershot side of the Farnborough Road.

I can now only remember the names of half a dozen or so of the twenty five men in my hut and none of the half class in the other hut. The most notable character was Jonah Maunsell, a veteran of the First War. He was carefully concealing the fact that he had been commissioned in 1917/1918. He had left the army then with a minor wound, had claimed disability and drawn a pension throughout the intervening peacetime. When he had applied for a commission again in September, 1939 this had been refused on the grounds that he was unfit, as demonstrated by the pension he had drawn. Accordingly, he had gone round the corner and enlisted again in the ranks without mentioning his previous service or wound. Now he was in a dilemma as to whether to put up his medal ribbons as this might give the game away. Eventually, the Colonel, who had guessed the position, told him to do so and there were no adverse results. Between the wars he had lived and worked in South Africa as a mining official on the Witwatersrand. As that was where I too hoped to work after the war and, as I had graduated in mining engineering, it can be appreciated that I had plenty that I wanted to talk to him about.

Another mining engineer in the hut was my own age, a young man named Paul Bennett, who had been at the Camborne School of Mines, a Cornish establishment with which my own college, the Royal School of Mines in London, had an intense rivalry. Naturally we teamed up together although this tended to reduce slightly my association with Anstey.

There were three other slightly more senior men who teamed up with Jonah Maunsell. I cannot remember the name of one of them but the other two were Bradbury and Ferguson. Both of them did extremely well later, becoming lieutenant colonels but I do not know what civilian jobs they held before the war.

Then there was Hathaway, who was also a little bit older than most of us, and his friends Affleck and Harvey. All three came from Chippenham and had joined as territorials together. There were only two regular soldiers among the cadets, as far as I can recall, and both were young sergeants. Williams had done quite a bit of boxing in the army and represented our class well when we had an inter-class boxing competition. The other one, Gentry, was a fresh faced, outgoing young man. Both had some difficulty with the more academic side of our work but shone on the practical side where they had considerable experience already.

I can see a few of the others in my mind's eye but I do not recall any other names except Blayney who went through the whole course terrified of being "RTU'd". This ignominious fate, of being "Returned to Unit", could, in theory, be meted out to any of us if we were lazy, awkward, disobedient or just slow to learn. In practice two or three in each class were usually found wanting at some stage and quietly disappeared but, in general, the selection system — meagre as it was at that stage — seemed to work fairly well. I think we lost two but I cannot be sure of that even and most of us went through the course without any serious worries. Nevertheless, the whole atmosphere was highly

29

competitive and none the worse for that. It was largely because we were all intensely interested in the whole thing.

The first three courses were all on general military affairs common to all arms of the service. A very large amount of time was taken up with drill and, although this did not go far in complexity beyond what I had already learned in my recruit training at Blandford, we were soon taking turns at drilling the squad and giving the commands. This slowed down the progress but was absolutely essential and contributed, I am sure, to our general development as officers. A much higher standard was demanded than had ruled at Blandford. The sergeant was required to address us as potential officers but, nevertheless, made his feelings felt. He pursued us around the square bellowing "'Orrible, 'Orrible, Gentlemen!" — "'Alt!'", — "Stan' still!" — "Nah do it again".

When we came to drill the squad ourselves, we were mostly petrified as we immediately realised it was far more difficult than it looked. By the time one had made up one's mind whether to turn the squad on the march and if so whether to left or right or whether to halt them and then turn them, they were already marching off the edge of the parade ground and the sergeant was shouting "For Gawd's sake say something, Sir, even if it's only goodbye!"

All commands had to be given as the left foot hit the ground and the penultimate word had to be prolonged for two steps in order to give the squad time to realise what it was expected to do. Then there was the tricky question of "advancing" or "retiring". When the squad was halted in three lines, one behind the other, it could be moved forward by the command:

"Squad will advance — qui--ick march". Or to move it to the right:

"Squad will move to the right in threes — ri--ight turn", and then: "Qui--ick march".

Then to turn them on the march would require:

"Squad will advance — le---ft — turn" — cramming the first three words in on the first left foot, the directional information on the second left and right foot and the final executive word, in a louder sharper voice, on the third left foot.

To synchronise them all was hell and took no end of practice, with colleagues in the squad not all necessarily as helpful as they might be.

We spent some time also learning to salute on the march and at the halt and the mystery of the stately slow marching. At the end we were attempting to learn how to right and left form. This involves the squad marching in line when they are in three ranks, one behind the other, as opposed to marching in threes, and then turning the whole squad through a right angle, either to the right or to the left. This maneouvre can be seen to perfection each year when the Guards march past the Queen on Horseguards Parade at the annual Trooping the Colour ceremony. Unfortunately we did not quite reach that standard at the 142 OCTU.

Physical training is well known to everyone and needs no explanation. We had a period of this every day of the week.

Also among our "all arms" training was military organisation, starting with the detailed make-up of the infantry battalion. This was all fascinating stuff to me but some of my colleagues found it hard going. Nevertheless, it was essential to know that an infantry battalion consisted of four rifle companies, each of three platoons, each of three sections, each of eight men and a corporal and then there were separate small platoon and company headquarters sections. Each section was armed with rifles but one man carried the Bren light machine gun, the ammunition for which was spread around the rest of the section. Each platoon also had a 2 inch mortar.

In addition to the four rifle companies there was the rather bigger headquarter company, consisting of seven platoons, one of which was the headquarter platoon itself involving the clerks, cooks, storemen and the band who were organised as stretcher bearers. Then there was the carrier platoon with lightweight, open-topped armoured tracked vehicles to be used in battle to reinforce the rifle companies with extra Bren guns at points under pressure. They were also used to bring forward ammunition under fire to forward companies.

Next was the pioneer platoon — semi-engineers who could do odd jobs around the camp or barracks but were particularly equipped and trained to deal with field works, including wiring and trench works, booby traps and obstacles. The mortar platoon was equipped with two heavy 3 inch mortars with a section of men in support of each. The intelligence platoon was concerned with the gathering, transmission and use of all the information they could gather, or receive from above, about the organisation and activities of the enemy.

Then there was the signals platoon manned and equipped to provide a telephone system, if possible, and/or radio communications between battalion headquarters, the rifle companies, the headquarter platoons, higher headquarters and flanking units and formations. Finally there was the transport platoon, equipped with 3 ton lorries, largely under the direction of the RQMS for the distribution of rations, ammunition, other equipment and stores.

I give this summary of what formed two separate lectures, in order to indicate the sort of framework to which numbers of men were added and much other detail. Today the armament and equipment of the infantry battalion has been substantially changed and strengthened, in particular by the introduction of APVs, the armoured personnel vehicles now so familiar from Northern Ireland. These enable the rifle companies to advance or be switched across the battlefield under heavy fire in comparative safety and at speed. They replace the carriers which were much too light and limited in capacity.

In those days the infantry battalion was literally foot-borne, only battalions forming parts of armoured divisions had sufficient vehicles to lift the whole battalion at one go and without calling on the Service Corps (RASC) for help. However, though each battalion is now fully mobile at all times, with its own vehicles, the route-march is still not a thing of the past, as was demonstrated by the marines and airborne units in the Falklands battles in their famous "yomping" drive on Port Stanley.

Following the infantry battalion, we dealt with the divisional reconnaissance regiment (the successor to the former light cavalry screen), the machine gun battalion, the field artillery regiments and the anti- tank and anti-aircraft regiments, the divisional engineers (of three field companies and one field park company — with its own light bridging column) the divisional signals, motor transport companies, military police units, the medical corps and one or two other units all forming part of the standard infantry division's "Order of Battle".

Then we dealt with the higher formations and their organisation, such as the infantry brigade of three battalions (a "brigade group" is an ad-hoc grouping of the formal brigade with a selection of supporting arms to enable it to operate independently). Usually such a brigade group would include, beside the three infantry battalions, one artillery regiment, one engineer company, one signals section and possibly certain other companies or sections.

The infantry division, totalling some 15,000 men, usually had three infantry brigades under command, together with three artillery regiments, one engineer regiment and one of each of the other types of units. The organisation of an armoured division was also described but in practice it always seemed to me subsequently that every armoured division had a slightly different order of battle. Finally, we dealt with higher formations of corps, armies and army groups.

To back up this classroom, theoretical stuff, we spent some days and part days on TEWTs ("tactical exercises without troops") in which, armed with maps, sheets of plastic and chinagraph pencils we were taken through one or two situations in which an infantry section corporal, platoon lieutenant, company captain or major, and battalion lieutenant

32

colonel might find himself in the field. We decided where we would place our section and its individual men and machine gun on the ground and where we would start digging our weapon pits and joining them up into a trench system. Similarly we expanded that in theory into a battalion position for defence or a formation for attack but I must say that the defence was stressed more strongly than the attack at that time.

On another day, I remember we reconnoitred a railway line to see if its cuttings and embankments would form, or could be improved to form, an effective anti-tank obstacle and recognised the importance of being able to fire along the line of it to prevent infantry from advancing over it or to destroy the enemy tanks while they were slowed down in attempting to cross the obstacle.

I am bound to say that I sometimes felt that our instructors — not much older than ourselves — were somewhat lost in these exercises in imagination and that some of us were perhaps leading them rather than they leading us in trying to visualise the situations for another arm of the service and at another time and place. Nevertheless, I was sure the exercises were very worthwhile and I enjoyed them greatly.

The part I did not enjoy so much was weapon training, which I had found rather boring at Blandford and still tended to do so. The lecturers were rather better but the lesson layout was still far too slow for my liking. The final part of this section of the course was a visit to the range, but this was preceded by small-bore rifle firing on a range within the barracks and this was, of course, familiar to me from my time in the University Rifle Club.

The open range practice was rather different in that the full scale .303 ammunition had a substantially greater kick than the .22 ammunition. Firing at 100 yards distance was not demanding but by the time we got to 400 yards the targets seemed a long way away as, indeed, they were. On the whole I did well enough at this. At that time we were only allotted a very limited amount of ammunition for practice.

The military law lectures largely followed the same pattern as those we had from the second-in-command at Chilwell.

Finally, somewhere in the course we did "Appreciations". This odd term relates to a standardised form of mental approach to any military problem, to meet which a plan has to be made. I have always found it since to be a very useful process of thought. It starts with defining the object to be attained, for example, "to capture a given hill or village" or "to bridge a given river at a given place". The object had to be stated in a single sentence as briefly as possible. Then followed a listing of the factors affecting the attainment of the object, for example: —

the position of the enemy,

33

the position of friendly troops,

the weather and time of day,

the nature of the intervening country and the presence of
favourable or unfavourable features from the point of view
of ones own men,

the availability of equipment, weapons, etc., etc., etc.

Then might follow an assessment of these factors and any interim conclusions drawn from them, for example: –

the enemy has a good view of the intervening ground and a
night advance or smoke cover would be essential,

our own troops are or are not adequate in numbers and
equipment to give covering fire,

etc., etc.

Every problem had several possible answers. Even though some were clearly impossible they should perhaps be thought of also. In this section, therefore, it was appropriate to list the "courses open": –

Course "A"   a decoy attack with the real attack coming from another
direction,

Course "B"   a night advance with only a short exposure to fire,

Course "C"   an attack under cover of smoke, etc., etc.

Finally, having made a choice between these possibilities, it would be necessary to draw up a plan which would include not only the bare bones of the scheme but also such details as the individual men or units to be involved, the equipment required (including tools and materials), the ammunition to be carried or left behind and the route to be followed.

The officer making the plan would normally submit and discuss his plan with his senior and secure his appoval before issuing his own orders to his key subordinates.

This led on naturally to the discussion of such things as order groups and the format of sound military orders which give sufficient information to put subordinates in the general picture, as much as may be necessary, as well as their executive orders, in giving them some knowledge of what others may be expected to do at the same time. These lectures and the accompanying practice work were among the most valuable things we did, but they were also some of the most challenging, especialy when it came to acting out, for example, an order group.

It was with some relief that we reached the end of the first nine weeks and the three "all arms" courses, when we were given our assessments to date. These were guarded particularly at the upper end and left questions in one's mind as to who were the good and who were the very good. On the other hand they were all too clear to some at the lower end. Here at least one man left us for almost total incompetence on the parade ground as well as being weak in the classroom. A number of others were given warnings with mostly mild cautions in public but one or two having private sessions with the Chief Instructor. For the most part we were encouraged to believe we were doing well.

And so to the fourth course which was at the Motor Transport Training School. For the most part, instruction and practice was given with the army's then standard 15 cwt. truck, a ghastly machine to drive, with a primitive gear box, but no doubt a trustworthy and robust piece of equipment. To change gear in either direction demanded double de-clutching, a traumatic experience for most of us and especially for me. The corporal in charge of the vehicle which I shared with two other cadets always shuddered with horror when I took the seat and nearly tore his hair out when I crashed the gears seemingly almost to destruction.

We spent a lot of time driving around the roads south and west of Aldershot and did a fair amount of cross country work on the sandhills west of the Rushmoor Arena in the Long Valley. In the lecture room we were concerned with matters of maintenance procedures and general organisation of a military transport fleet. For our "passing out" event we did some night driving. We were warned to sit in the dark or semi-darkness of a March evening for our eyes to get accustomed to the very dim light.

However, when we paraded for duty we found that we were not to be allocated to our usual vehicles and a new list had been drawn up so that each vehicle had a cadet or Young Officer driver who had had considerable peacetime experience. The idea was that the rest of us would merely sit in the back of the trucks to observe. I, for one, did not think much of this idea. It seemed to me that those of us with the least experience needed to have a go and accordingly I protested on parade — possibly a rather unmilitary thing to do but I escaped a reprimand, though I did not get the practice anyway.

On the last Friday morning we did not parade at the MT school. Instead we went to the medical room for the dreaded inoculations. These were a formidable dose. One was anti-tetanus but the second was a three-in-one shot called the "TAB" injection — typhus, bubonic plague and enteric. They felt bad enough going in but the real effects were delayed. We were all allowed to disperse for weekend leave. I was not going home on this occasion but had accepted an invitation to join Hathaway, Affleck and Harvey in going off to Chippenham to stay at the Vicarage there. The Vicar was father-in-law to Hathaway's brother who was working in a reserved occupation at the local big industry — Westinghouse Brakes. We all piled into Harvey's little sports car, for which he fortunately had enough petrol coupons for the weekend, and off we went. At that stage of the war rationing was not yet too severe.

The vicarage was a delightful house with an exquisite garden sloping down to a clear slow stream. I fell in love immediately with it all and particularly with its hostess, a charming cool blonde, who was Hathaway's sister-in-law. She made us all feel completely welcome and clearly managed the big house with great efficiency. We had all brought a small supply of coupons with us to cover our rationing for the weekend so she was able to put on a very creditable dinner. Unfortunately, by then I was feeling sick as a dog with the after effects of the inoculations so I was sent to bed early. I woke during the night with an incredible headache and my moans and groans woke the household. Fortunately our hostess was equal to even that contingency and appeared in a delightful dressing gown and armed with aspirin and a hot drink. This put me into a healing sleep and let the household get back to bed without further trouble. Morning found me still weak but able to participate in the affairs of the day which included a short look around the town and then a round of golf — for those fit to swing a club — and a picnic at nearby Castle Coombe. It was all gorgeous country with daffodils everywhere. On the Sunday we went to church but after an early lunch we had to get back to Aldershot and to the second half of our training.

The fifth course was a mixture, but was essentially field engineering with quite a lot of lecture material, including the preparation of work tables (to indicate the men and time required for any particular job) and lists of equipment and materials required. The course also provided for one or two "EEWTs" — ("engineering exercises without troops") but these were not nearly as successful as the earlier "TEWTs".

Field works included trench digging using various types of revetment (to hold back the face of the sand in which the trench was being dug) using sandbags, corrugated iron and expanded metal sheets. The revetment itself was held in place by prefabricated "A" frames, the slatted trench boards being laid on the cross bar of the "A" in order to leave a good sized ditch underneath to drain the trench. Dug under ideal conditions with all the right materials available and with a good wire entanglement in front, the completed trench looked an ideal place to be when the enemy were attacking but I doubt if it would look as much like home after having been hastily dug, only partially revetted, and having been subjected to continuous bombardment with artillery. We spent one day at least on working with the various types of barbed wire, making a variety of fences and entanglements.

36

For the sixth course we were virtually "on detachment", leaving camp first thing in the morning and returning late in the afternoon. The wet bridging site was at Frensham Ponds some ten miles south of the barracks and close to the extreme south west corner of Surrey. With a period of early summer weather and delightful surroundings, the situation was almost idyllic but the sterner stuff of war intervened and it was only at lunch time that we could enjoy a swim in the lake or some mild sunbathing.

The Bailey Bridge development had not yet been completed and the army was still working with older types of equipment, namely, for wet bridging, the Folding Boat Equipment (FBE) and the old standard pontoon equipment with light decking. The folding boats did literally fold, the two sides collapsing inwards onto the bottom of the boat, which straightened out in the process. They were alright to handle as long as they were being transported on a standard light framework trailer, as the three boats carried were separated by the framework and slid in and out fairly easily. Once a single boat had been taken off and carried to the water's edge it was easy to open and secure before being launched. However, when three or more boats were loaded, one on top of the other with nothing to separate them, in the back of a 3 ton load lorry, they were bastards to move. The superstructure, i.e. the decking which carried the roadway, was in fairly light sections and was moderately easy to handle regardless of the actual transport being used.

This equipment provided a bridge which would carry 9 ton overall weights and could carry standard 3 ton load army lorries. I think that 5 ton load vehicles would have been just beyond the capacity of the equipment, but there were few of those about at that stage of the war. It would not carry tanks and very little in the way of a heavy armoured car but in general it would serve for most divisional loads, including guns. The Divisional Field Park Company had a set of this equipment permanently mounted on trucks and trailers so that it was readily available. I am not sure how long a single bridge could be made with the equipment available but it could handle two or more short bridges over, say, British sized canals, as bank seats and shore equipment were available for more than one bridge.

The standard pontoon equipment in those days would, I think, cope with 24 ton overall weight vehicles and that was sufficient then for any army load including tanks. There were special pontoon trailers, each of which carried two pontoon sections which joined together in the middle to form a complete pontoon.

In order to strengthen the pontoons they were all fully decked. With the correct trailers, again, the pontoons were easy enough to slide in and out so that an adequate sized squad could stand around the pontoon to

37

lift it down or up and carry it to the water's edge. On the other hand, when two were loaded on top of one another, on a ordinary 3 ton load truck, they were literally hell to get on and off. Fortunately, at Frensham Ponds, the equipment was all laid out on the shores of the lakes and the real problems of handling the equipment only arose later when I encountered them on maneouvres in Yorkshire with 2nd Division.

Equipment bridging, of either type, was rather like meccano, it all went together easily enough provided that you started in the right place. Therein lay the snag that faced every bridge commander. The first thing that he needed to know was the width of the river, and getting that was not as easy as it might seem. Second, he had to calculate how many sections of floating equipment (two complete pontoons plus the intervening decking) he would need to put in the water to ensure that the bank could just be reached with the end section of decking (ramp with no boats).

Third, he would now know, in theory anyway, how far from the water's edge to put the bank seat which would usually be made of sleepers dug into the mud of the bank. These had to be reasonably square with the centre line of the bridge. I seem to recall that the standard section of decking was 20 feet long and ideally, therefore, the bank seat would be 10 feet from the water's edge and the first pontoon would be nearly 10 feet out from the bank on the water. It never seemed to be, but somehow we managed. Unfortunately, once several lengths of the actual floating bridge were connected they seemed to take on a life of their own and only the best founded bank seats could resist the leverage of the flowing water, on the pontoons, even when the pontoons were held by ropes and anchors. Somehow the far bank never seemed to be as difficult as the near bank, which was just as well, as tempers were fairly short by the time it was reached.

We spent a short time on the Infantry Kapok Bridge. This was a light trackway for soldiers on foot only. The main elements were the floats which were — quite simply — a bundle of silky fibre from the hairs covering the seeds of a tropical tree wrapped in a piece of tarpaulin and fashioned into a rectangular pack about six feet long by two feet wide by six to eight inches deep. This pack had sufficient flotation to support a man comfortably. The packs had straps around them carrying the mountings for duckboards which made the trackway.

The idea was that such a trackway could be readily carried by infantry and launched into the water. Theoretically, when the ends were secured at the banks on either side, infantry could quickly walk across the track to cross canals, dykes or small, relatively slow rivers up to some fifty feet or so wide. In practice they were not so easy to guide across the obstacle or to walk across without spilling several men into the water. We also had some practice with the then available type of assault boat which was rather like a much smaller version of the standard folding boat.

I cannot recall any particular events on the wet bridging course; it was just a succession of beautiful days with many of the usual difficulties out of the way because we were working quite simply on the bank of the lake with the equipment immediately to hand.

The seventh course was back at Malta Barracks which had been provided with a large artificial "gap" for dry bridging. We had available to us at least three if not four types of obsolescent equipment, all eventually replaced by the Bailey bridge.

The one we were most likely to meet for some while was the Small Box Girder bridge. The standard section was, I believe, 10 feet long and about 2 feet deep by 18″ wide. This was fairly easily carried with lifting bars to which we became very accustomed. The box section itself was of welded strips of steel. The carrying rods therefore passed through the lattice work very readily and with three bars through the section six cadets could lift and carry it with ease. Two sections could be mounted on rollers and joined together to make the middle section of the total girder and then a tapering section was added at the front end. The sections were joined by toughened steel dogs. To launch the girder a special 15 foot long nose with a large wheel on the end was added. To counter-balance the forward weight, until it hit the bank on the far side, either one or two more standard sections could be added to the back as a false tail and, with the launching crew adding their weight to it, the girder could be pushed forward until the wheel contacted the bank. The false tail was then removed and a proper tapering tail section added instead, when the whole girder could be then be moved forward until both nose and tail were in position over the bank seats. These were heavy steel plates with lifting handles, which had been positioned beforehand on either side of the gap. Jacks were then used to remove the rollers and lower the girder onto the plates. Two girders side by side, and then decked over, provided the full bridge. The final work of levelling off the approaches on either side usually took far more time than building the bridge itself.

The small box girder was carried on ordinary 3 ton load lorries and I seem to recall that the Divisional Field Park Company had enough equipment and transport to provide two 40 foot bridges.

The carrying capacity depended on the length. A 20 foot bridge made up of the tapered sections only would, I think, carry 40 ton weight tanks comfortably with one centre section added on each side to give a 30 foot bridge. The safe load was reduced to perhaps 24 tons weight which would carry practically everything the infantry division had available to pass over. With two centre sections added, the 40 foot bridge was probably reduced to a safe load of 15 tons which would still be adequate for practically all divisional vehicles but a 50 foot bridge could carry restricted loads only.

The bigger brother of the small box girder was the Large Box Girder and I seem to recall that the sections were now 12 feet long by 3 feet high but still 18 inches wide. This was becoming a bit heavy for man-handling and I never saw another after leaving the OCTU.

Then there was the Inglis bridge — made up of equilateral triangles of 10 foot by 3 inch diameter pipes, with heavy connectors at the junctions of every two or more pipes.

Finally, we did a fully improvised bridge such as might be made in practice anywhere where a few rolled steel joists (RSJs) might be found — for example, from some demolished building — and provided suitable heavy timber was also available. For this type of bridge the span would normally be much shorter than an equipment bridge could provide. Heavy section RSJs were unlikely to be available in more than 12 to 20 foot lengths. To bridge a gap of say 50 feet it would be necessary to have two intermediate supports at least.

In our version one of these was provided from trestles made out of 9 inch by 9 inch square timber and fabricated on site. A complete trestle would consist of a "ledger" piece as a base, slightly longer than the overall width of the bridge, three verticals with a "raker" on either side leaning inwards to give some sideways stability to the structure and a "transom" (cap piece) on top, to match the width of the bridge.

A completed trestle would need to be handled by some form of lifting gear. We used a "gyn" made of a single strong pole, some 9″ or more in diameter, with four strong guy lines. A block and tackle was suspended from the top and the hauling rope led away to the side. With care, the gyn could be manoeuvred by the guy lines to lift the trestle from the bank onto prepared foundations at the required site.

Two trestles were erected side by side and braced in the upright position by cross pieces of lightish timber. The two caps were decked over and then the RSJs stretched from the bank seat to the first pier, again using the gyn to lift them. The bridge that we made had three spans only and our second pier was constructed of tubular scaffolding — easy and quick to build, if the material is available.

Beside the single pole gyn we also built one with three poles. This one did not swing, as did the single pole, but might be sited over a well or vertical shaft, as in a mining operation. Either during this course or the eighth we spent a short time on mining operations. We advanced slightly a tunnel being driven by successive classes of cadets under a sand cliff in one of the old sand pits, among which this part of Malta Barracks was situated. I suppose it was quite good for me professionally as my practical experience of mining had been largely confined to hard rock.

The tunnel was being completely lined with 9inch by 3inch timber and was suitable not only for sand, which might run, or clay, which might squeeze, and chalk, which might crumble, but also for such relatively hard rocks as the coal measures. The method being used would not be suitable for rock which would require blasting. The sand was dug out for a distance of about 1 foot ahead of the last completed section of lining then a "ledger" was laid on the floor, a cap piece was held in position, while two legs were hammered in from the centre to wedge the cap tightly at the top with the aid of some blocks and wedges to fill up the space to the roof. A variation of this could be used even when it was impossible to excavate fully one foot ahead before the face collapsed or the lining was inserted.

It was slow and tedious but it demonstrated the way in which the big mines had been dug on the Western Front in the First War right under the German lines at, for example, Messines Ridge. It was also the typical method employed by escapers tunnelling out of German prison camps or equally, but much less publicised, by Germans tunnelling out of prisoner of war camps in Britain.

So we came to the final course on RE Works type projects. We laid out and did portions of a water supply circuit suitable for a standing tented or hutted camp. We had a go at completing the erection of a Nissen hut. We made small quantities of concrete suitable for odd jobs and extended a light concrete road by a few feet. We also did various other forms of trackway, including timber trackways and Sommerfeld track — a sandwich of light reinforcing bars and chicken wire which was good as long as the ground did not become rutted by heavier than specified transport.

Pierced Steel Planking, later greatly used for making airfields and therefore able to carry moderately significant loads, had not, I believe, been developed at this stage or, if so, it was in extremely limited supply.

During this last course other matters began to intervene almost daily. Our quota of time for drill, which had been greatly reduced during courses 4, 5, 6 and 7, began to build up a little as we practiced for our passing out parade, due on the very last day of our training. Time was allocated to us to see a representative of the Cox's and King's branch of Lloyds Bank who were the army agents and from whom we would draw our pay. Those of us who did not have bank account, like myself, were advised to fix them up with this bank. This I did and stayed with the branch for 50 years afterwards.

Then two representatives of Austin Reed arrived to measure us for our officers' uniforms and take our orders for other items we would need on change of rank. Finally, we were given our gradings and invited to indicate our preferences for postings. The gradings were a simple A, B, C, anyone who might have got a D having been disposed of long since. Grade A might be said to be reserved more for those who had a clear maturity, rather than necessarily for those who might have done better than others on, say, the academic or theoretical side of the work. I am sure I came into the latter class rather more than into the former class and, indeed, had little experience of life at that stage outside school and university and my short period in the ranks. Nevertheless, I was discontented not to get an A and ought to have been contented with my B. Mind, I do think I had probably begun already to reveal my lack of respect for my seniors in addition to my lack of years. As before, in my experience, the army did not appear to take too much notice of any preferences we might have mentioned but certainly Jonah Maunsell, Paul Bennett and I had little reason to criticise our posting to the 1st Tunnelling Engineers whereas most of the others had been posted to Divisional Engineers — many of them to former Territorial Divisions.

During this last course the sad, incredible news began to come in of the British army's retreat to Dunkirk and the collapse of France. Apparently the YO's who had qualified and finished their training with Class No. 5 had all been rushed over to France as reinforcements for the harrassed army. I believe that few ever reached it and that they were mostly captured at St. Nazaire.

The possibility that Malta Barracks might be attacked by parachutists was obviously considered by our senior officers somewhere and we were issued with five rounds of ammunition each and paraded and marched out to line some of the ditches around the camp. It was an unlikely possibility, in the view of most of us, but it did serve to impress on us the gravity of the situation. I think that the five rounds were more significant in this respect than the lining the ditches.

Finally the great day arrived. We spent an inordinate time polishing our boots and cleaning our rifles and generally furbishing up our battledress and other equipment ready for the passing out parade. Almost before we realised where we were, we were marching past the saluting base with fixed bayonets and our most precise drill. The officer receiving the salute looked most inconspicuous but he undoubtedly was a hero of the Regiment, Captain Cloutman VC, MC and Bar, RE. no less.

I did not know then but I recollect now that the impression he made on me was that of a man who looked very much like Captain Mainwaring of "Dad's Army", the famous television show. I think he had the pince-nez and he bristled in a fiercely martial style, belied somewhat by his small stature. Our class officer led the way off the parade ground to one of the lecture huts where we settled down to receive the commissioning address. Colonel Binney introduced the guest by telling us briefly about a couple of his outstanding acts of valour. It seems that, in the face of the enemy and under intense fire, he had driven a cart load of explosives onto a bridge, which should have been demolished already, and blew it up just in time. On another occasion, with the retreating Germans still holding onto the far side, he advanced onto a bridge where the fuses were already smoking and cut them, saving the bridge from destruction and speeding the advance of our own troops.

His speech did make a great impression on me. He was clearly a man of great courage and considerable expertise but I fear that the parts of his address which I actually remember are not good illustrations of the whole. He did seem obsessed by the fear of our allowing our sappers to be used as infantry and to suffer casualties thereby which would deprive us of highly trained engineers and tradesmen. He portrayed for us the temptations which would be put in front of us to do so, the senior officers who would pressure us with offers of medals which they would dangle in front of us. Having warned us of these dangers he stressed again and again the importance of saving sappers for real engineer's work. He gradually warmed to his finale as he talked of the duties of officers.

"An officer's principal duty," he said, "is to set an example at all times. No example is more important than to shave every morning." With his voice rising to even higher levels he concluded, "Frenchmen, Spaniards, Italians and Russians may be able to fight looking like gooseberries but Englishmen never could!"

This stirring thought completed his message and, with a comprehensive glare at us all, he turned and left the room closely followed by Colonel Binney, leaving our Class Officer to murmur farewells and good wishes.

After that we put on our new uniforms, completed the packing of our bags and took off for a week's leave. I went home to my family in London for the week and, while there, I was invited to a tea dance at the Grosvenor House Hotel by the newly commissioned 2nd Lieutenant Blayney, who had survived the whole OCTU training without incurring the ultimate penalty of RTU. He was still looking surprised when I last saw him but he redeemed himself with me, at any rate, by having a charming sister who also produced a very presentable friend to give us a first class afternoon. Unfortunately, I never met them again. I am sure he would always be a survivor — but only just.

The six months for which I had been at the OCTU had seen a great change in the war situation. At first the pace of the "phoney war" had seemed to suit us in spite of being incredibly slow but it was soon being realised that the gift of time was not being used as well as it should have been. Defence had not been unified but remained in three parts. War policy did not exist. Rationing was badly organised and hardly effective at that stage. Prices and wages were largely out of control. Public relations were out of touch. The army high command was divided. The Government was living under the illusion that the war was going well where, in fact, it was turning its back on the whole situation.

It was the Chamberlain Government's own actions which finally precipitated the real war. They decided to interrupt the wintertime shipments of iron ore from the mines in the north of Sweden, which went by rail to Narvik and Trondheim, and then by sea to the north German ports. There was also popular, but ill-informed pressure to help the Finns in their increasingly difficult war with the Russians.

The plan was to send an expeditionary force to Narvik and to set up a blockade of the Norwegian coastline. It was hoped to develop from this by the capture of the Swedish mines and by a land link up with the Finns. The plan was ill-conceived in the extreme, and hopelessly executed into the bargain. The Germans got wind of it and moved in on 8th April to invade and take over both Denmark and Norway. The Finns made the best peace they could with Russia. With every Norwegian airfield in German hands the expeditionary force was scuppered and the Royal Navy was powerless to intervene. The Norwegian fiasco brought down the Chamberlain Government and on 10th May Winston Churchill became Prime Minister. Narvik was evacuated on 8th June thus ending an inglorious episode; yet there were some gains. The German Navy had been severely mauled and had lost two thirds of its surface fighting strength. The successful British evacuation from Dunkirk and the failure of the Germans to invade England may have been the real results.

On 10th May the Germans invaded Holland and Belgium and the French and British advanced to the aid of the Belgians. The great Belgian fort of Eben Emael fell to a paratroop attack on 11th May and the Germans broke through the French at Sedan on 14th May. On 20th May the British fighting retreat to Dunkirk began and the evacuation was complete by 3rd June. It was four years before we returned. There were 68,000 British casualties in the campaign, including prisoners of war, but 368,000 British were brought back, although most of their equipment was lost. The French position became hopeless and they concluded an Armistice on 22nd June. Italy entered the war on 11th June. An incredible period!

By being in Class 6 rather than 5, or perhaps because the Germans' timing was speeded up by the Norwegian episode, I had again missed my (second) chance of embarkation for overseas service but also a very likely chance of spending most of the war in a prisoner of war camp. I welcomed keeping my options open.

CHAPTER 5
1st Tunnelling Engineers and 172
Tunnelling Company, R. E.
(July, 1940 – March, 1941)

At that time the 1st Tunnelling Engineers were based in Chester so I met Paul Bennett, who was travelling up with me, at Euston Station. He had that morning come up from Cornwall where he had been spending his commissioning leave with his parents. We now travelled first class, though it was barely less packed than the third class we had been using for all our service so far. At Chester a truck met us at the station and took us to the headquarters, which was above a bootmaker's shop in the old part of the city, near the Grosvenor Bridge. This has since been completely changed by a new bridge and new roads giving better access to the centre of the city. There was then a little market place outside the shop and this was just across the road from the castle, which we came to know well later.

The accommodation was cramped, the colonel's and the adjutant's offices barely having room for their desks. If I remember rightly the two junior officers, of whom I was to be one, shared a desk in a small outer office but the clerks and NCOs did rather better in their general Orderly Room. Nevertheless, there always seemed to be something of a milling crowd in all the offices.

It seemed that there were currently three companies, the 170, 171 and 172 Tunnelling Companies, also at Chester and these were quartered, for the most part in tents, on the Roodee, which was the Chester racecourse. Their company offices were all situated in the grandstand. Their officers, like those of headquarters, were all billeted out in good accommodation around the city. The remaining 173 Tunnelling Company was at that time detached from headquarters, putting in anti-tank blocks and building pill boxes at Dolgelly.

Bennett and I were conducted by a corporal to what must have been the best accommodation of all, a beautiful house in a suburb, across the Grosvenor Bridge and overlooking the Roodee. It belonged to a Mrs Brown, who had just retired from being Lord Mayor of Chester. She lived with her son, Stephen, who was seemingly addicted to knitting socks because we never saw him do anything else and a mysterious Miss Brown who we thought for some time was the daughter of the house but was, in fact, billeted like ourselves, being a civil servant whose office had been evacuated from London. There were a number of servants and dinner was served in state, greatly assisted by the extra rations that we brought with us in the form of military ration books. At that stage of the war soldiers, when they were billeted out, enjoyed a much larger allocation of food coupons than the general public.

The officers of the regiment were in some disarray following the debacle which preceded the Dunkirk evacuation. When the Germans broke through the French lines in the Ardennes and did their swing to the right and to the sea at Calais they swept through the British lines of communication between their bases further west and their troops in the front line in Belgium. Among the troops in the area concerned were the 1st Tunnelling Engineers who were working on various underground headquarters and stores accommodation projects. They were taken completely by surprise, as were many other line of communication units, and half their number were rounded up and made prisoners of war. Some of the officers, indeed, were collected from socially embarrassing situations. Accordingly, the companies now on the Roodee had numerous vacancies for officers and I believe that one or two of the regiment were somewhat in disgrace or disfavour for what had happened.

Maunsell and Bennett were allocated to the 170 Company and I, as I have indicated, was posted to headquarters. During the following weeks reinforcements gradually trickled in. No more came from OCTUs but a number of experienced mining engineers — some with First War experience in the Tunnellers — arrived.

In the meantime the companies in camp were being kept busy on a tunnelling job at or underneath Western Command headquarters which was fairly near us and inside the city. The material in which they were mining was a fairly slabby and somewhat unconsolidated soft sandstone and it could be worked by small pneumatic picks with spade attachments. The equipment they had had in France had all been left behind. One of my first jobs was to get a decision made as to the type and make of picks required. I then had to make contact with suitable firms to supply this equipment and with the Ordnance Corps to be prepared to pay for it. The idea that anyone in the army, as a user of the equipment, should be in direct contact with the supplier and arranging prices to be paid was very strange to the military mind and ethical problems arose. Suppliers representatives moved into the best Chester hotels and plied tunnelling officers, especially myself as quartermaster, with invitations to lunch, drinks and so on. I realised quickly that I should have to watch my step or trouble would ensue. However, we soon got a sound drill worked out and matters went fairly smoothly.

Also in Chester there were one or two relatives of officers and other ranks who had been made prisoners of war. News of them appeared to be scarce at that stage, remembering that it was still only two weeks since the return from Dunkirk. These relatives presumably thought — and probably quite rightly — that some of the earliest news was likely to arrive in Chester. One of them was the sister of a Royal School of Mines man, Jim Rogers, who was three or four years senior to myself. She was a charming lady and I enjoyed her company while she still remained in Chester. We were to meet again later.

One evening Paul Bennett and I decided to sample the hospitality of the pub at Eccleston, a village some two miles south of Chester and also on the banks of the River Dee. We had by now established good relations with Miss Brown and persuaded her to come with us. Rumour had not lied about the quality of the pub and we enjoyed an excellent evening there but when we came to walk back up the straight Roman road to Handbridge, the suburb in which we were billeted, the air raid warnings began to sound and it appeared that the activity was taking place over the Wirral where there were many chemical works. Fires appeared to start some ten miles north of Chester though whether they were real ones or decoys it was hard to tell.

It was a beautiful night and gradually the beer began to take effect. Bennett and I began to drop back in turn while the other took advantage of the opportunity to kiss the very willing Miss Brown — or at least I did. As Bennett later married Miss Brown — Ursula — I assume he did also as she was a very pleasant armful. I am glad to say we all reached our temporary home safely and tiptoed up to our respective beds with many giggles.

My great professional problem at the time was how to get the companies on the Roodee reasonably re-equipped, particularly with clothing, including underwear and boots, without the troops selling them off to the second-hand shops in Chester faster than I could get the Ordnance Corps to supply them.

It seemed to me to be an easy enough job for the company officers to keep lists of what each man had or needed and then we could make a plan to replace missing items in a comprehensive manner. Unfortunately, there was too much change going on within the companies. Officers were coming and going, new men were being drafted in, some with fairly complete equipment, others with literally nothing, or so they said — and in any event, living in tents made it hard for any man to keep proper control of his own kit.

Anyway I decided to hold everything in store until we were in a position to make a complete issue to everyone, after which no excuses would be accepted. It certainly appeared that the German army must have been able to equip a couple of new divisions with the underwear the 1st Tunnelling Engineers had left behind.

47

To get this equipment together I had to go round scrounging from every Ordnance Depot for miles around. To do this brought me much into contact with Corporal Brady, the Regimental Motor Transport NCO. Corporal Brady was apparently a big man in motor cycling in those days — or so he said. He was certainly a good driver and rider and my own standards began to improve with some of his hints and observations. They needed to sadly following the scrappy way in which I had learnt to drive and my discouraging period on this subject at the OCTU.

I never really got to know my first commanding officer in the Tunnellers. He seemed a slightly morose individual which subsequent events may have explained. I suspect that he had received a substantial reprimand for something to do with events in France and he must have known that he was due to be replaced as soon as a suitable man could be found. One soon turned up, a Lieutenant Laurence Hill, a First World War tunneller with an MC and already a senior man in the Rio Tinto mining group in the City and Spain. He was a brisk, energetic, upstanding man who soon became our Lieutenant Colonel and made his mark. The only man who seemed to have emerged from France with much credit was the Adjutant, a regular Captain, N.S. (Sam) Cowan. In a crowd of amateurs he was the only professional soldier.

Another new arrival from civilian life was a Lieutenant Gilchrist who was rapidly promoted to be 2nd-in-Command of the 170 Company and fairly shortly thereafter became the officer commanding that company, with the rank of major. I think he also had First War experience. At about that time Deyman Eastmond, senior lieutenant in the 170 Company, was seriously injured in an accident underground at the Western Command Headquarters. It was said that he was "barring down", which meant that he was using a crowbar to remove loose pieces of rock from overhead before allowing men to work in one of the tunnels. Unfortunately, either the piece he was working on, or another, fell on his back and broke it. I found out later that he had experience in South Africa and, indeed, I met him there later but he never worked underground again. Still, he sold me my first car at a very fair price and he was always a very friendly fellow.

I never got to know the 171 Company or its officers because I believe they left Chester, in relatively good shape and short time, and moved down to the south of England to do tunnelling work of some sort there.

The 172 Company was well thought of. Its commander was a Canadian, Major Foss. I came to know him well when I served in his company in Dover later while awaiting a posting to 2nd Division. His principal support, 2nd Lieutenant Brandt, had graduated from Birmingham University as a Mining Engineer about two years before

48

and so was slightly more senior professionally than Bennett and myself. He was strongly tipped to become 2nd-in-Command of 172 Company.

As I have said, the 173 Company was at Dolgelly, but I had not previously met its Commander, Major Simpson. One of my duties as quartermaster was to handle the Regiment's petrol and oil returns. In Britain the regiment had to apply the peacetime army system whereby each driver's weekly work ticket had to show not only the hours worked and miles driven but also all petrol and oil drawn from stores. These work tickets then had to be balanced against the stores vouchers for petrol and oil received in bulk and issued in detail. It seemed a fairly simple operation and I quickly mastered it but the Companies found it very difficult indeed as they had become used, I judge, to rather more free and easy methods in France.

The 173 Company appeared to find it more difficult than all the others and, because they were detached, it was necessary to try to correct their reconcilliations by post. As an HQ staff officer I was entitled and expected to sign letters on my subjects on behalf of the Colonel. Theoretically, the letter came from him but in practice it was quite clear who had written it. On one occasion Major Simpson strongly resented, probably quite justifiably, the terms I used and came to my office and blasted me out of my chair. I knew him well much later when we were colleagues on the staff of the Head Office of Consolidated Gold Fields in London. I cannot recall that he ever reminded me of the choke-off he had given me but I am sure he always thought I was brash and lacking in respect for his age and seniority.

In due course, and all too quickly at that, the billeting officers got themselves organised and decided to find space for Bennett and I, and some of the other tunnelling officers, in the castle. This was the headquarters of the Cheshire Regiment who were in the course of moving out to a new hutted camp somewhere on the outskirts of the city. I never saw the whole of the barracks and only four buildings come to my mind.

The wide parade square stood behind substantial railings and gates close to the Grosvenor Bridge. On the right stood a massive building which was the Officers' Mess. Next to it was another building, closed at the time, which may have been the Regimental Headquarters, and to the east of the square was an even bigger building which I believe was the Law Courts. This was in constant use. To the north and slightly behind that was a much smaller building whose normal purpose we never found out but this had now been made available to the Tunnellers to house their officers. Bennett and I had a fairly spacious, though sparsely furnished, room on the ground floor. Cowan (the Adjutant) and Maunsell shared a similar room immediately above us. To the best of my

49

knowledge no trace of the original castle remained but I suspect that the parade square was its original outer bailey.

Feeding in the Cheshire's Mess was definitely a pre-war experience in style and content. On Sunday evening, particularly, we had a grand buffet supper which defies description but the centre piece was always a large Dee salmon fished from the river just below us. Beside the Tunnelling Officers there were several other mess members. One or two of them were officers of the Cheshire Regiment but not part of the battalion which had just left. There were also one or two officers who appeared to be part of the staff of Western Command. Conversation at the mess table was definitely limited by the peacetime rules of no religion, no politics, no ladies names. Nevertheless, it was merry enough as some of the non-tunnellers were fairly remarkable characters.

Compared with life with Mrs Brown, which was comfortable but stately, we seemed to have rather more time available to us in the evenings. On one of these Bennett and I decided to see if we could find out how many pubs there were in one of the City's main streets. We started out aiming to drink half a pint in each. Long before we had reached half way, closing time arrived but, unfortunately, just as we were about to leave the pub we had reached, the door behind the bar opened and revealed a considerable proportion of the Sergeant's Mess in session. We were invited in and by the time we managed to break off it was close on midnight and we had had a skinful. We staggered back to the castle and literally fell into bed.

It must have been about an hour later that we were wakened by Cowan and Maunsell coming into the room and telling us to get up. They told us that the threatened German invasion of Britain had begun and that we were to report to the Roodee immediately, giving the sentry the password "Cromwell, the flap's on". They repeated this, "Cromwell, the flap's on", and left the room. Bennett said, "O Lord, we'd better go!".

I said, "Hang on a minute, I'll bet they were pulling our legs, it would be just like those two. I'll go and see if they have gone to their rooms, I'm fairly sure they went upstairs". So saying I followed them, heard them moving about in their rooms and went downstairs again. "There you are," I said, "they are going to bed".

Bennett said that he felt we should still go down to the racecourse and began to pull on his trousers.

"Not likely", I said, "We'd look fools turning up in the middle of the night and telling the sentry, 'Cromwell, the flap's on.' That would take some laughing off. I'm going back to bed", and did so. Bennett followed me to his own. We woke about an hour later to find a fully armed and equipped sapper in the room with his gas mask on his chest, a gas cape on his shoulders and a steel helmet on his head, with his rifle and fixed bayonet in his hand. This familiar but disturbing figure convinced us at last, through the drunken haze, that something serious was happening. He had a note for Bennett in his hand. It was signed by his company commander, Major Gilchrist: —

"Mr Bennett, you will report to the Roodee immediately".

We both tumbled out of bed and were dressed like a shot. Fully arrayed with our gas equipment, belts and revolvers and carrying our steel helmets we went down to the racecourse at the double. I only gave the first word of the pass "Cromwell" and that seemed to do the trick, without the extra words "the flap's on" and the sentry did not seem to find that strange because he let us in with no difficulty. All was relatively ordered confusion and I decided that my duty was to open my store and issue all the stores I had at once. This took some time and by the time I had finished daylight had arrived and it was nearing breakfast time. I even issued thirty or forty rifles I had in stock although, even then, the 170 Company was still not fully armed. However, those that were armed had at least half-a-dozen rounds of ammunition each and my store was empty. I reported the situation to Major Gilchrist who expressed himself as satisfied.

It seemed to be a good time to show myself at headquarters. When I got there no questions were asked about my delay in turning out for the good reason that they seemed to know nothing about it. Sam Cowan had assumed that I was doing what I actually did, namely issuing the stores. Furthermore, the Colonel had not yet arrived. He was still using private billets and appeared to be sleeping out somewhere, — as opposed to the rest of us who were in the castle. Accordingly, everyone at headquarters was more concerned to get him to work than in checking up on their efficient quartermaster! I went to breakfast and found only two of the Cheshire officers in possession of the mess table. They were discussing the night's events. "Cromwell", said one, "a fellow came to my room talking about Cromwell and saying the invasion had begun. 'Cromwell', I said, 'who's he?'" They roared with laughter and then began to ask each other whether they had heard the bells which were supposed to announce the imminence of invasion. They decided they had not and that it was a bad thing. I had certainly not heard them either.

Nevertheless, there is no doubt that the authorities in London were convinced that Hitler had launched Operation "Sea-Lion" and later we heard stories about masses of troops embarking and being caught at sea by the Navy or, having landed, being caught in the fire of fougasses, devices which projected burning oil from buried barrels by means of explosives. The latter sounded unlikely but the first seemed highly probable. Even so, it seemed to be one of the turning points of the war because from that moment on invasion seemed less and less likely and without invasion we could not lose the war. However, neither rumour has ever been confirmed and officially no German attempt at invasion ever took place.

A strange reinforcement arrived for headquarters, straight from one of the training battalions for other ranks. He appeared to have some form of influence, possibly with the Colonel, because I was detailed to look after this young man and to see he got some training which might be helpful to him if he subsequently went to an OCTU. Remembering the kindly 2nd-in-Command of the Chilwell Depot I was quite willing to take this on. It appeared that he had spent very little time indeed at the TBRE because his knowledge of drill was practically nil.

Accordingly, I decided that the whole of our headquarters needed a refresher in drill and we had a number of pre-breakfast sessions for all the other ranks who sadly needed smartening up. I roared at them across the parade square much to the amusement of officers making their way to breakfast.

I was only slightly disconcerted when Bennett told me that Ursula Brown had reported to him that the young gentleman was persona grata with Mrs Brown. He had told her that Bennett and I were recruits to his own company, Consolidated Gold Fields, and that he would have personal charge of our postings to South Africa in due course — when the war permitted. After the war, when I did join Gold Fields — (but Bennett had been killed in action at Bremen) — I tried to find out who this young man was in the Gold Fields hierarchy and whether he had survived the war but I never found any trace of him. However, he stayed with us for three or four weeks and then disappeared as quietly as he had come.

About this time I had a certain amount of contact with 2nd Tunnelling Engineers but I cannot remember any names. While we in the 1st Tunnelling Engineers were being kept busy with conventional mining the 2nd were experimenting hard with a device called a pipe-pusher. This was already in use to some extent in civil engineering for laying pipes up to about 6″ in diameter without digging trenches. Obviously it only worked in soft ground and the difficulty was to keep the pipe moving in a straight line.

If it had worked properly — as well as it does now in civilian use — the device might have been very useful if anything like trench warfare had developed. What they were trying to do was push a pipe from one of our front line trenches to underneath one of the enemy's. The head of a 6 inch diameter pipe would be filled with explosives, jacked into position and fired causing a crater and a serious breach in the enemy line. I believe that a range of 100 yards was feasible without too much trouble but for 200 yards or so the pipe was apt to get badly off course and turn round on itself. As no one really knew where the head of the pipe was it was potentially quite exciting.

I did go down south for a visit to the 171 Company who were now attempting to tunnel at Aldershot to provide underground headquarters for that Command. They had run into real difficulties because the whole area lies on the London clay. In some spots there may be a thin covering of sand and gravel but once in the London clay the mining difficulties are immense as is well known to the makers of the London underground. The London clay is plastic and when any excavation is made in it it squeezes back with immense power and rapidly closes any space not protected by the heaviest of linings. The 171 were trying to work with light steel colliery arches and these were far from strong enough for the job. This work was eventually abandoned. A section of the Company, however, was working on a small portion of the Circle Line in London which had been damaged by a bomb and they were struggling to keep that clay ground open long enough to get the massive cast iron tubbing into place. It took them quite a while before they were successful.

As we were now reduced to only one Company, the 170, at Chester, (the 172 having moved to Dover a couple of weeks before the "Sea-Lion" incident) plans were made for HQ to move to Brighton.

There we were quartered in a small residential hotel on the sea front but this was no advantage with approaching winter and with the beaches choc-a-bloc with Dannert wire entanglements. Nevertheless, the morning walk from the hotel to our office, which was a few blocks along the front, was salubrious. The headquarters was comparatively well situated in Brighton to serve the group which was concentrating in the south. Before long the 170 Company moved from Chester to St. Margaret's-at-Cliffe, leaving a section behind to finish off the Western Command job. The 172 was now in Dover with jobs out to the west of the town along the coast. The 171 Company was still in the Aldershot area and the 173 had, I believe, also come south from Dolgelly.

My life was occupied in trying to help them with their stores problems, with timber being particularly difficult. I rapidly became acquainted with the forms for building materials controls and "standards" of timber. A "standard" of sawn timber is the unit in which such timber is measured and amounts to 165 cubic feet. Why 165 I do not know, but it does divide by 3, 5 and 11, though what that has to say to anything I cannot imagine.

Fortunately, the chalk in which two or three of the companies were then working was rather more suitable than clay for lining with colliery arches and corrugated iron backing and this was much more readily available than timber. I also remember being involved with ration supply as I seemed to spend quite a bit of time visiting ration depots but I am sure that was not really my job. There had been some changes in the headquarters. Sam Cowan had not come down to Brighton with us and we had a new Adjutant, a burly but pleasant gentleman named Fowke, and we also had a new workshops officer named Olver. With Colonel Hill and myself the four of us made up the officer establishment of headquarters.

The hotel was full of retired ladies who jealously guarded their small stores of marmalade, jam, honey, etc. which their rations allowed them and we, indeed, found it convenient to have our preserves clearly named. In other respects the hotel was passably comfortable but as much the youngest of our team I found myself reduced to haunting the basement games room where the other inmates were very close to being children. I say close but I am not really sure because the star was a very charming young Jewish girl. My guess is that she was 15 but she could have been up to three years younger or three years older. However, with the gramophone on she was a good dancing partner and we did once or twice go to the local dance hall. I went there rather more often. The usual stimulating conversation, inevitably began, "Do you come here often?" Still it improved my dancing a little which, like my driving, was badly in need of improving.

Before leaving Chester I had approached Colonel Hill with a request for a transfer from the Tunnellers. I told him that I realised that with little practical experience of mining I was obviously lower on the promotion list than many other of my colleagues. Furthermore, I hankered after a more stirring military life, more along the lines I had learned at the OCTU rather than those of my Univesity training. Accordingly I asked to be posted to a Divisional Engineers. Colonel Hill agreed and sent off an application to the War Office. I sat back to await events.

In spite of the apparent failure of "Sea-Lion" and the rumours that the Germans were reducing their strength on the Channel coast it never seemed impossible at Brighton that one morning we would see "ships in the bay" and landing craft pushing to the shore. It seemed to me to be a dreadful fate to be caught with a non-combatant unit (in spirit if not in theory) and put in the bag like Jim Rogers and others in northern France. The only effective way, though, of doing anything about it seemed to be with explosives so I secured a 50 pound case of dynamite and some fuses and detonators, determined to sell my freedom dearly if I could think of a way of using them.

More practically, I looked around for a chance to learn something about horse riding. My beautiful riding breeches, which were part of my originally prescribed uniform, had had little chance of exercise so far, but I yearned to provide it. Accordingly, I searched for and found a suitable riding school up on the Downs, somewhere near Patcham Place. The lady in charge looked very County and her horses looked good stuff too. Anyway, I felt a long distance from the ground when I mounted one of them. I will not pretend that I was God's gift to the equestrian art and my learning was slow but I made gradual progress through a trot to a canter and might even have graduated to a gallop had I stayed in Brighton long enough. I did not, at any rate, fall off.

While we were in Brighton we followed up our friendship with Jim Rogers' family, who lived in Worthing, and had a number of enjoyable evenings at their squash club. However, we were rather too conscious of the fact that we were indulging in unauthorised use of army transport and petrol to be entirely at ease.

Suddenly, news came that the headquarters was to embark for Malta and I think that both 171 and 173 Companies were to go with them. I was still awaiting news of my own posting and so, clearly, I was not to go. Instead, I was posted temporarily forthwith as an extra officer to the 172 Company at Dover. Company headquarters there was somewhere along the road leading out north west to Buckland and Lydden and my quarters were in a house on the other side of the road but further out still from the centre of the town.

The majority of the Company were working near the centre of town and were extending the old underground headquarters below the Castle. Another large contingent were on the west side of town and were working below the Victorian fortifications known as the Western Heights. The section allocated to me was already mining at Lydden Spout near the Abbott's Cliff about three miles from the centre of town.

Since the beginning of the war British coastal convoys working their way through the Straits of Dover in either direction and hugging the Kent coast fairly closely had been harassed from the French side by German big guns or by "E" boats. These were large, armed, fast motor boats and they could make a quick dash out of small French ports between Dunkirk and Boulogne and cause considerable damage. Firing at extreme range the big guns were not so dangerous but it was well known that the Germans were installing bigger ones which would be more accurate. To counter this firing, our own side were installing a number of batteries of medium and big guns along our coast, between Folkestone and Deal, which would also harass German convoys. The mining companies were in the process of supplying these batteries with safe sleeping accommodation for their crews. In general they were in the chalk about 50 feet below the surface and well up from sea level.

The railway line from Dover to Folkestone passed underneath Abbott's Cliff so the Lydden Spout "mine" had started in from a convenient recess at the top of the spout and was now well in under the

55

solid chalk. Small trucks on light track were being used to bring out the chalk and tip it into the sea down below. When I arrived they were actually cutting the sleeping (barracks) chambers, and the work in general was well advanced. The biggish barrack tunnels were being supported with colliery arches holding back corrugated iron lining between the arches and the chalk. The chalk was being dug out by pneumatic picks and shovelled up off a temporary board flooring into the waiting trucks. A sloping access tunnel was being driven upwards from the workings to break through to surface fairly near the actual guns.

Some twenty five years later I returned with my family one holiday time to locate the tunnels and did succeed in finding what was clearly the barricaded entrance to the access tunnel but I did not attempt to go down over the side of the cliff by the path we had used to reach the tipping point. Fifty years after we had mined there I saw the site again from a distance while visiting the Channel Tunnel workings. In between where we then stood and Lydden Spout there was quite a substantial bay which was being filled up by the spoil brought out of the tunnels on a much vaster scale than we had worked. It was interesting to see that their reclamation virtually reached our spoil tip but was subject to environmental controls which would have totally pre-empted our efforts had we to do the same.

I worked on that project for about two months. It was a three shift operation, as was all the mining work around the town. Every morning the day shift, including myself, paraded at the Company office, the men carrying their steel helmets, gas masks, gas capes and rifles but wearing their denim overalls, now very dirty and marked by the white chalk. It took two or even three 3 ton trucks to carry the shift and we proceeded in convoy down to the harbour where we dropped off the squad who were going to take over from the night shift at the navy headquarters under the Castle. The next squad was dropped off at Western Heights and my section finally went on to Lydden Spout. There we changed over with the night shift and the trucks returned by the way they had come, picking up the other night shift men. Sandwich rations and tea arrived at midday. For the men, about 25 of them, the work was not uninteresting and certainly not hard, but for the officer, myself, it was a dead bore, for nothing ever went wrong or needed attention except for a very small surveying job to establish where the access tunnel was likely to hit surface.

Life in Dover was occasionally enlivened by hostile shelling of the town from the French coast. The siren sounded, as for an air raid, and one was supposed to take cover and occasionally did, but I never saw a shell fall and the damage was minimal. One night, however, a couple of us had decided to go to the music hall. Because of the shelling many civilians had left Dover and so the audience was almost entirely male and military. Row after row of soldiers sat clasping their rifles between their knees while Salome gradually removed the seven veils. In the middle of the show the siren sounded and there was slight disquiet for a barely perceptible moment while the soldiers faced the possibility that the lady might stop disrobing, but the show carried on, while the men resumed sucking their rifle muzzles. Eventually, to a huge sigh and rapturous applause, she removed the last veil and disappeared from view very promptly, just as the authorities decided there was not going to be any serious shelling and sounded the "all clear".

In due course my posting arrived to the 2nd Divisional Engineers at Pocklington in east Yorkshire. Someone had considerately decided to send a truck almost the whole length of England to fetch me. I was interested in the fact that the posting was to so senior a division as the 2nd which was one of the few regular army divisions and it had featured well in the retreat to Dunkirk. The posting seemed to me an honour at least as great as any of my OCTU colleagues had received. If the powers that be at "Officer Postings" had decided that a young man wishing to transfer from a "safe" billet in his own chosen peacetime profession to a Divisional Engineers must be a regular fire eater, then one could see that this great thought, as to where to put such a man, might take them quite a little time — as indeed my posting had done.

The early autumn, while we were still in Chester saw Hitler trying to build up his forces and equipment in France ready for Operation "Sea Lion", the possible but always problematical invasion of Britain. At least he started right by attempting to establish air superiority over the likely invasion beaches by knocking out the fighter stations in the Home Counties. This was the Battle of Britain stage and it was won by the fighter pilots of the RAF with very great help from radar and from Beaverbrook, as minister of aircraft producton, who ensured that the RAF never ran out of fighter planes and, in fact finished the Battle with more planes than it had had at the start. The German Air Force nearly won the battle, but it could not maintain the pace and switched from the airfields to bombing by night. They could not then hit industrial targets significantly and could not defeat the civilian population. Without a navy and without air superiority Hitler had to abandon "Sea Lion" and turn his attention to the east and to Russia, but not until 1941. Fearing that Hitler would take over the French fleet, the Royal Navy eliminated it from the fight by shelling it in France's North African ports.

The night bombing "blitz" throughout the winter was borne manfully but it revealed weaknesses in defence; anti aircraft guns were few and largely inneffective without radar, as were night fighters, but techniques improved as winter went on. Fortunately German navigation was disrupted by technical devices and many bombs dropped in open country. The fire brigades were effectively reorganised and ARP services greatly improved. Even so, the raids were not as heavy as they might have been. 57 raids over the winter brought 13,500 tons of bombs. Three years later the British were delivering that quantity in a single week.

Churchill commenced negotiations with Roosevelt, but at first these brought only small returns as America was even less geared up to war production than Britain had been at the start of the war. We had to pay cash for everything and most of what we got on Lend-Lease was either obsolescent (the 50 destroyers) or surplus to American requirements (the 500,000 rifles) but that is not to deny their usefulness then and as preparation for eventual cooperation when the Japanese attack at last brought America into the war. Incidentally, the rifles went to arm the Home Guard who were growing in numbers and effectiveness rapidly. Altogether, though it was an anxious period the tide of war was already changing.

For my own part, I had missed two more embarkations in my efforts to get nearer to the battle. My third was when the Tunnellers HQ took off for Malta and the fourth was when, shortly after I had left them, 172 Tunnelling Company was sent to Gibraltar, where it spent most of the rest of the war mining under the Rock. Sadly, Major Foss died there of natural causes.

CHAPTER 6

506 Field Company, RE
2nd Divisional Engineers
(April – August, 1941)

After a long drive we crossed the River Ouse at Boothferry Bridge, just north of Goole, and then pushed on another twenty miles or so further north to Pocklington, a pleasant little town in the middle of what used to be the East Riding of Yorkshire. Having located his headquarters, with no great difficulty, I had a fairly short interview with Lt. Colonel Aldous, the commanding officer of 2nd Divisional Engineers. He was clearly a regular officer and seemed impressive, although I barely got to know him then or later. He told me that I was to proceed immediately to Withernsea on the coast and with luck I might get there in time for dinner.

He told me that his command consisted of four companies. Apart from the 506 Field Company, in which I served for the next five months, I cannot remember the numbers of either of the other two field companies, but I do recollect that one of them was a regular army unit and the other was a territorial unit. 506 Company on the other hand, was a supplementary reserve unit, but I do not recall from which part of the country it was drawn. The fourth was the Field Park Company and that I think had the number 21. The other two field companies were also on the coast at Hornsea and Easington but these were only temporary locations while they were all helping the infantry put up beach defences and lay mine-fields. The Field Park Company was apparently at its semi-permanent home at Wheldrake, a small village eight miles west of Pocklington. Having gathered most of this from Colonel Aldous, I met briefly his adjutant and his two field engineers, both 2nd Lieutenants, and then pushed off.

As the Colonel had suggested, I did just reach Withernsea in time for dinner where I met my new colleagues. The Company Commander was a Major Gardiner who, I would say, was in his mid 40's. He was of short and sturdy build and had just a hint of a hare lip, or certainly he twisted his mouth when speaking. He was pleasant and friendly. The 2nd-in-Command, Captain Walker, smiled a lot but yet had a slightly supercilious air. He may have been in his late 30's. He and I did not prove to be soulmates.

The other three were all 2nd Lieutenants. The senior, Eadie, wore the ribbon of the Military Cross, which obviously must have been gained in the retreat to Dunkirk, and I gathered later that it was for his work on demolition of bridges. He was fresh faced with curly fair hair and looked to be some three or four years older than myself. As time went by he seemed to be a slightly solitary person, neither seeking out his seniors' company nor intimate with his younger colleagues. It was difficult to understand, as he was neither stuck-up nor cold and unhelpful when approached.

The next, Allport, could well have been younger than myself but not by much. He was short and slim and very friendly. He also looked and proved to be an efficient young officer who seemed to get on well with his men and have little or no difficulty in carrying them with him. The third, I do not remember at all and I think he left us fairly shortly afterwards, nor do I remember the name of his replacement, unless it was Murray.

I was told that I was to take over Eadie's section and that he was to take charge of the Headquarters troops — the clerks, mess servants and drivers. In this he would help the 2nd-in-Command but he would also be a general reconnaissance officer and assistant directly to the Officer Commanding (OC).

Next day we were on the move, so I did not even see the beach works on which the company had been employed. Nevertheless, I gathered that they had mostly been working on tubular scaffolding anti-tank obstacles and on laying mine-fields. Although I subsequently saw tubular scaffolding fences on a number of occasions I never actually saw a tank trying to get past one. Bearing in mind, however, that they were only meant to delay a tank under fire for a relatively short period while guns were brought to bear on it, they probably did an effective job.

I suppose that, in an actual assault from the sea, naval guns and tank guns would give covering fire to enemy sappers who would, no doubt, come prepared with necklaces of explosives to wrap round the scaffolding to cut a gap. The scaffolding could then be pushed aside quickly by the tanks breaking through. Meanwhile, however, they would have to wait on the beach exposed to counter fire while the sappers would be under intense rifle fire, always provided, of course, that the beach itself was under observation and the moment of attack was in fact expected. These tubular scaffolding obstacles extended around much of the coast of eastern and southern England. The East Riding coastline was now being brought up to the general standard.

We returned to the Company's semi-permanent home while 2nd Division was in East Yorkshire. This was at Menethorpe Hall, two miles south of Malton, in great race-horse breeding and training country. Menethorpe appeared to be in the racing business, but there were only a few brood mares out at pasture. The headquarters staff were located in the Hall and its out buildings while the three sections were scattered around in adjoining farms and hamlets within about half a mile distance.

Each section comprised a lieutenant, a sergeant, a lance-sergeant, a couple of corporals and about thirty five other ranks. The headquarters must have been about the same number, making the total company somewhere in the range of 150 – 170 men.

The first job to be done on arrival was to settle in, but there were still a couple Nissen huts to be completed to house my section. These would not be hard to build providing the concrete floors had been laid down more or less correctly and the holding down bolts for the superstructures had been properly located. Unfortunately, I was no expert on Nissen huts and the matter was urgent. Probably this is why my section was changed over with Allport's. He had built plenty of Nissens and he had a really excellent sergeant. Sergeant Howard held a Military Medal which he had gained at the same time as Eadie was awarded the Military Cross. He was far and away the most efficient of the Sergeants and a first class man to work with into the bargain.

My senior NCOs were Sergeant Cahill and Lance-Sergeant Lambert. Neither of them was in the same class as Sergeant Howard for individual ability and drive, but they were sound enough. We were now located at the village hall in the hamlet of Low Hutton, on the far side of the River Derwent, very close to the railway line, which skirted the river.

The village hall served as a cookhouse and mess room, together with quarters for the senior NCO's. The rest of the section were accommodated in two Nissen huts built just beside the village hall. At least once every week the villagers had back the use of their hall for a small dance — perhaps better referred to as a "hop" — in which the troops joined enthusiastically. As most of the local male talent seemed to have been called up, peace was maintained and a good time was had by all.

Each section officer was responsible for the training of his own section and each Monday we had to submit to the OC our training programme for the week. It is difficult to remember just what we did with all the time. There was a small amount of drill on the road outside the hall and a certain amount of physical training though, as events were to show later, we apparently did not succeed in keeping the men really fit. The only route march we had during my time with the Company was really a complete fiasco, due to the number of men who dropped out on the way. Apart from that we revised our weapon training and did a little bit of work with ropes and spars (poles).

We were, however, allocated a certain amount of explosives for demolitions training. We made Bangalore torpedoes — a length of 2″ diameter steel pipe, plugged at one end, stuffed with ammonal, each fitted with a primer (initiating) cartridge, detonator and fuse and plugged at the top. This was a favourite device for cutting through barbed wire entanglements. In action the tube would be pushed under and through a thick barbed wire fence and exploded when the pieces of tube would be blasted through the fence cutting most of the strands.

Ammonal — a trade name for ammonium sulphate — was a low explosive and, in fact, it is still used commercially as a fertiliser. It is hygroscopic and picks up damp very readily. It was supplied by the army in black tins about one foot cube and with tight fitting lids. These "torpedoes" were much used in the First War.

We also make Cordtex nets. Cordtex is a commercial high explosive and we used it in the form of a thin cable with the explosive packed within a plastic coat. In demolitions it is usually employed to link up and detonate simultaneously a number of charges placed, for example, on the girders of a bridge. A single cordtex main laid out in a circle can provide simply for detonation at both ends at the same time, thus ensuring that if the main is cut at any one point it does not prevent any of the charges from firing. However, we were experimenting on using the cordtex, made into a net, as an explosive sheet which could be laid on the ground and detonated, thus firing off any mines located below it with relatively little danger to those laying the net. We would be attempting to make a broad path through a minefield. When we had finished our tests we were able to certify that the device worked.

Perhaps some explanation should be given here as to the meaning of the terms "low" and "high" as applied to explosives, where they relate to the speed of detonation. With a given quantity of "low" explosive the detonating wave travels relatively slowly (but still very fast) from the point of origin to the boundaries of the explosive. With a "high" explosive the rate of travel — and consumption of the explosive — is very much faster. Accordingly, a "low" explosive is useful for a heaving effect, such as lifting a load of earth out of the ground to make a crater. A "high" explosive would not do this job nearly as well but it has instead a shattering, rather than lifting effect and is the more useful of the two for breaking iron and steel rods or girders.

I also remember us working with our standard camouflet equipment, of which each section carried a set in its own transport. Again, this equipment used 2″ diameter (but thick walled) steel pipe. A hard steel nose was fitted into one end of the pipe and a heavy "driver" (hammer) was lifted onto the other end. A hole was started with a spade until firm ground was reached or, even without a starting hole, the equipment could be used direct on a hard surface. The driver was then lifted up towards the end of the pipe by two or three men and banged down firmly on the end of the pipe. With luck the bit penetrated the ground and the pipe followed it down.

Typically a hole would be driven down about five feet or slightly more into the ground. It was then possible to lift the pipe a few inches off the bottom and a gun cotton explosive primer was lowered down the pipe on the end of a fuse and the fuse was lit. The explosion of the primer expanded the hole at the bottom to a diameter which depended on the relative softness of the ground. Ammonal was poured down the tube into this cavity which would take several pounds of the explosive. Another primer was also lowered with it and this time, when fired, a large crater would be made right back to surface. This crater might be made so close to the abutment of a bridge that it destroyed that as well and it was, even alone, an effective way of destroying relatively small bridges without any great expenditure of time. Alternatively, a road on a causeway might be effectively blocked by two or three overlapping craters.

Fairly soon after we arrived back at Menethorpe we started on a series of regular weekend manoeuvres with the infantry brigades and other arms of 2nd Division. There were two standard plans of campaign which we worked on in co-operation with 1st Division who were defending the coast of Lincolnshire. The picture could be that the Germans landed on the coast of East Yorkshire and 2nd Division made a fighting retreat, demolishing bridges on the River Hull, the River Derwent and the River Ouse on the way back to West Yorkshire. Then, reinforced by 1st Division, 2nd Division re-advanced into East Yorkshire bridging at least one of the rivers on the way back. The alternative scenario was that the Germans attacked on the Lincolnshire coast and 1st Division retreated destroying the bridges over the River Trent on the way. In the counter attack 2nd Division would need to bridge the Trent. None of these are really wide rivers, to compare with the large rivers of Western Europe. The Hull is canalised and, in my recollection, is barely more than 50 feet wide. The Derwent also has locks but is rather wider at most reasonable crossings — up to about 100 feet wide. The Ouse, however, is tidal with a large rise and fall most of the way up to York. When the tide is out there are long muddy banks and when the tide is in the river is up to several hundred feet wide. I believe that the River Trent is not canalised until much higher up its course than the part where we were likely to cross and yet I do not remember anything like the rise and fall of the tide or the steep banks experienced on the Ouse.

The Company normally joined in even the longest manoeuvres on the Wednesday or Thursday and took part, initially, in either the tail end of the retreat or the resumption of the re-advance. We did not rehearse the demolition of any bridges but we still had about two days of grinding

63

along in convoy behind the marching and, theoretically, fighting infantry. Depending on the size of the gap to be bridged we either did three bridges (each one built by a single section), or a single company bridge, the latter usually being a major pontoon bridge. The single section bridges would usually be FBE or SBG (folding boat equipment or small box girder) but, just occasionally, where a heavier floating bridge was required, pontoons might be used on a relatively narrow gap.

The final assault by the brigade was usually timed for first light on the Saturday morning — no doubt to enable the infantry to get their troops back to camp in time to knock off at Saturday lunch time. In such a case the leading infantry brigade headquarters, on the night before, would be one to two miles back from the intended crossing place. If, for example, this were to be over the River Hull in the region of Frodingham bridge, ten miles up river from Beverley, then the brigade headquarters might be looked for either in Wansford, some two miles back, or even at Brigham, less than a mile from the river.

My recollection is that brigade headquarters fitted very comfortably into a large farmhouse or a small country house without inconveniencing the inhabitants too much. The Engineer subaltern, who was to build the bridge, had to attend at brigade headquarters the evening before to hear his orders from the Brigadier. The Engineer's key questions were, firstly, at what time could the bridging vehicles be moved up to a meeting point about a mile from the river? Infantry were usually sensitive about the noise made by the bridging vehicles moving around, indicating to the enemy too clearly the actual crossing place. Secondly, at what time could he start his personal reconnaissance of the bridge approaches and the width of the gap? (so that the infantry might not be too jumpy with a strange officer moving around in the middle of the night). Then, thirdly, who would tell the bridging officer when he could commence actual work on the bridge? Namely, how soon would the infantry think they would have the other bank just clear enough of the enemy to ensure that the bridge site would not be swept by rifle or machine gun fire? Apart from those three points the Brigadier might have other information which he should make available but he would be the only one who could judge that.

Clearly the bridging officer would want to get his equipment as near the river as soon as possible. His own ability to reconnoitre the site would partly depend on whether there was a moon or not and he may indeed have to wait until the first light. However, working on the old axiom that "time spent on reconnaissance is seldom wasted" he would definitely want to look around as soon as he could without causing too much excitement.

On the great night the bridging officer usually found himself skulking around in ditches — it would be silly to be sent home by an umpire as having exposed himself to the theoretical fire of the enemy too much for credibility. In such an event, of course, the sergeant would carry on instead and hopefully would not do better than the officer himself might have done. Finally, either just before zero hour, or maybe just after, there would come the business of getting out the inflatable boat, pumping it up and launching it to carry the officer and his tape across the river at the likely site.

Usually the site had to be one very close to an existing bridge, because only at an existing bridge would there be good approach roads on both sides. Thus, on manoeuvres, it was usual to be building a bridge very close to the real un-destroyed crossing. It might be that in actual fact the normal place to build a bridge might be where the old one had been destroyed and many of our substitute sites were more awkward than they needed to be. Accordingly, unloading the gear and building the rafts, etc. were usually not done in ideal situations.

We usually did manage to get something built in reasonable time but I do remember one occasion when a folding boat bridge was proving extremely awkward. The infantry, who had earlier crossed the river in boats, had decided the theoretical war was over and were hiking back in bribs and drabs over the genuine bridge on the site. We were getting some derisive ribbing and we were fed up. With the men in this mood, I decided a mug of tea was called for and the quickest way of getting it was to march back to our temporary billets, get the tea and return to the job with renewed vigour. Unfortunately, I had no sooner started to put this spineless plan into execution when we met Major Gardiner walking up to the site to see why we were taking so long. We returned to the job with out tails between our legs and it still took us much too long. Not one of my good days!

Over a significant number of weeks the pattern was the same, out on manoeuvres on Wednesday or Thursday and back to headquarters late on Saturday. In the course of some three months I bridged the River Derwent at Elvington, Kirkham, Low Hutton and Stamford bridge, and the River Hull at Hull bridge (at Beverley), Frodingham bridge and Rotsea. Company scale bridges in which I took part were at North Muskham and Dunham on the Trent and Naburn and Cawood on the Ouse but there must be half a dozen sites I cannot now remember. In the midst of all this formal manoeuvring with all arms we also had the great Divisional Engineers Bridging Competition. In the three Field Companies there were nine sections and I think we all met for this one and only time at Bishopsthorpe on the Ouse. Each section in turn had a try first of all at a Small Box Girder bridge. We then competed on a company pontoon bridge, possibly at Naburn, and finally each section would have a go at a folding boat equipment bridge. My section was not last in the Small Box Girder competition but we certainly raised the Company's average time. The Company did well enough in the pontoon competition but the real question was whether I could redeem myself with a good performance with the folding boats. Fortunately, we were drawn last and I was able to have a sight of where my competitors had placed their bank seats. We finished with a triumphant best time and my credit was establised — most importantly with my own section.

As a side effort, to all this bridging, we had a go at making camouflage bridges. I designed a pseudo small box girder bridge made out of light timber slung on ropes with a hessian covering. The bridge went across the gap well enough but seemed to sag suspiciously and it was quite clear that the criss cross markings we made on the side to imitate the girders would be quite useless and we just had to hope that, if we ever did such a bridge in earnest the sun's reflection off the hessian would be just blinding enough to attract and fool a diving pilot anxious to let his bomb go and get away even from rifle fire.

We thought of the problem of the approach tracks but wondered whether, in a "for real" situation, when we could not get our vehicle across the water, a bridge with tracks approaching it on one side but with none going away from it on the other side would fool anybody. After all the point was to get bombs wasted on a dummy which would otherwise be bombs landing on the nearest real bridging site.

In the days in between the manoeuvres, social life in Malton and Menethorpe continued. Malton was the centre of the 6th Brigade group. Each brigade group consisted, in those days, of three infantry battalions, a field artillery regiment, a battery of anti-aircraft guns, a battery of anti-tank guns, a Field Company RE, a section of Royal Signals and a company of Service Corps transport. In theory this would permit the brigade to live and fight independently of the rest of the division and no doubt it could and would have done.

What it also did was to permit a modest social life for the group. Each of the infantry battalions and the field artillery regiment gave a big party in turn and as each of them had 50 or so officers they could manage to entertain all the other officers of the rest of the group. Being part of a regular division, 6th Brigade had some very distinguished battalions. My recollection is that we had the 2nd Battalion Coldstream Guards (the Guards Armoured Division had not yet been formed), the 1st Battalion of the Royal Scots and the 1st Battalion of the Rifle Brigade.

Their headquarters seemed to be situated in the magnificent surroundings of some of the big houses in the Malton area. All six of the 506 Company's officers were invited. However, when it came to the turn of the Field Company to do some entertaining, we could only manage to cope with a small representative group from each of the battalions — its CO, adjutant, a couple of majors and some "lucky" fellows chosen to represent the subalterns of the battalions and the artillery regiment.

These garden parties were held in the late afternoon on Sundays so very little in the way of tea was served but there appeared to be enough spirits to go around and a good time was had by all. When the guests were all assembled, on our front lawn looking out over the pasture down to the River Derwent, it was all very pleasant indeed. However, our Lieutenants had to bustle around keeping glasses filled and with very little time for conversation or viewing the scenery. I got taken on one side and told off by Major Gardiner for inviting some visiting officer to "have another drink". "Mortimer", he said, "it's never another drink, always ask them if they will have a drink", underlining the "a".

Our relations with the locals were less formal but I have mentioned the weekly "hops" at the Low Hutton village hall. There I met the entrancing daughter of the local farmer whose husband was away at the war somewhere. She was a temptress indeed and I was tempted but not as far as I might have been. This brought me into competition with our 2nd-in-Command, Captain Walker, but he did not seem to attract the lady as much as he would have liked and I appeared to be having the field rather to myself.

She suggested that we went riding and I welcomed this proposal now that I had got a little bit of instruction behind me. I approached the OC and he said he would speak to the owners of Menethorpe about it. This he did and a mount was arranged, a mare, whom the only remaining groom pronounced as being a very mild old lady. So she was. As he let go of her head he clapped her on the backside and she made a spirited move out of the front gate. As soon as she had got around the corner she slowed down to a very mild walk and would produce nothing more for the rest of the afternoon.

We met the farmer's daughter mounted on a lively little horse on which she looked a perfect treat but I had no spurs or whip with which to keep up with her. I kicked my heels into the mare's ribs but this was useless. The farmer's daughter gave my horse another clip on the backside and for a moment we had a slight trot but as soon as the lady pulled ahead again my mount stopped again. So we continued until at last, in disgust, we agreed to abandon the ride. I set out to return to Menethorpe, crossing the river and making my way up the pastures. Just in front of the house the sappers were playing football with a large crowd watching. They turned to watch me briefly so I decided to let them see that the damned horse could go at more than a walk. I dug in my heels really savagely whereupon the old lady put me straight over her head and onto the ground.

I did a complete somersault and landed on my feet, but let go of the reins. There was a restrained laugh from the audience and they turned away from my embarrassment, although a couple did start out to see if I had hurt myself. Meanwhile the mare demonstrated her best canter and took off for the stables like a shot. I picked up my hat and walked after her to find the groom waiting for me in the yard and the mare looking out triumphantly over the bottom half of her stall door. He enquired anxiously and, when I told him ruefully that I had had a terrible ride but had escaped injury, he refrained from laughing. I think he knew what was going to happen as he expressed no surprise at all. Sadly there was never another opportunity to try.

I think that it was on Wednesday during the following week that we were awakened before dawn with an emergency call for the Company to move rapidly into Hull to help out with the aftermath of a severe night's bombing. At this time the Germans were trying out their "Baedeker" raids on key British cities, which combined historic pasts with great modern commercial and industrial activity. The standard pattern was to create havoc in the centre of the city on the first night and to reinforce that by a second raid on the second night in the hope that, by the third night the city's emergency services and routes would have been overwhelmed with, in consequence, even greater damage would result from a third raid.

The essential counter measure, apparently, was to get the streets cleared of rubble as quickly as possible and to make sure that any damaged buildings, which might be shaken down into the streets and re-block them, were demolished by explosives and cleared away before the second night's raid. This was to give the fire brigade and other emergency services as free access as possible to the centre of the city and this was the task on which the 506 and the other Field Companies were to commence. Long before daylight we were on the road in full Company convoy with all our vehicles and equipment, together with our personal equipment and bedding.

On reaching the city we turned into a housing estate where a number of buildings had been evacuated as billets allotted to us. We unloaded our personal equipment quickly and then moved straight into the centre of the city where a few buildings were still burning and a great deal of damage had been done. In the commercial area most buildings had been hit or badly shaken. The fronts had collapsed into the streets and the various floors had all collapsed into the basements. The party walls were all still standing but we worked out that the easiest way of getting these to fall down was to attack the chimney stacks. A few gun cotton slabs, nailed to a plank and then primed and fused, were thrust up the chimneys before lighting.

68

The difficulty was getting the adjoining area clear enough to permit charges to be fired safely. Many of the property holders were trying to do their own salvage, particularly salvage of their safes, most of which seemed to have crashed down from the upper floors into the cellars. The owners were naturally concerned to try to get these out before more rubble was dropped on top of them. Even when the area had been completely cleared and guards put on the approaching streets, somehow the tenants managed to dodge around them and re-enter the building just as we were about to start the fuses going.

The sightseers were also a frightful nuisance. The people who worked in the area seemed mostly to have come in from the outskirts and decided to do the same as usual, even though there was no place to work. Accordingly, there was all the time in the world to wander around sightseeing. They too were having to be rescued from the possible results of their own indiscretions. A large amount of time was being wasted.

Eventually the area would look clear enough, the police whistles sounded and the fuses were lit. Slight curls of smoke rising from the ruins were then the only visible warning of what was going to happen. A few sharp cracks and then a rumble and down came the walls, most of the rubble fortunately remaining inside the line of the former buildings. Gradually the easy buildings were dealt with and the harder ones remained as it sometimes took two or three separate charges to get a wall to move. Clearly we were running out of work and at 5.30 p.m. we were withdrawn, having been on the job about ten hours.

The cooks had also been warned of our imminent return and a meal was ready for the troops. Having seen them served, we officers left and returned to our own mess where our meal was also ready. We all gathered except Eadie, who had had a fairly easy day and was to take charge of a section of men to stand by for rescue duties during the night when the second of the three raids was expected. To pass the evening, Major Gardiner thought that a game of "Cardinal Puff" would be a good idea. For those who do not know it, this game is a slightly dangerous trap. The junior and most unaware member of the party was selected to propose the toast of the health of Cardinal Puff. In doing this he was guided by the most experienced of the party who recited to him and demonstrated, "I drink to the health of Cardinal Puff for the first time". He slapped his left knee with his left hand, his right knee with his right hand, patted himself on the head with both hands in correct succession once only, then raised himself in his seat and bumped himself down, once only and then took one drink from his glass.

This was repeated by the pupil. It was all then repeated as he drank to the health of Cardinal Puff Puff for the second time. He then repeated all the movements twice each and took two drinks from his glass. If the pupil was still surviving he drank to the health of Cardinal Puff Puff Puff for the third and last time and then repeated all the actions three times each and finished his glass in three sips. If at any stage the pupil got anything wrong then he was required to drink his glass to the bottom, have it re-filled and start again. If the tutor did it wrong then he did the same but usually he was too clever to make a mistake, or for it to be noticed. The result was usually that, with a nervous pupil, the poor chap was paralytic before he had finished.

Major Gardiner chose to be the tutor and he selected Lieutenant Murray, the youngest and most callow of the three of us, to be his victim. Murray made a most unpromising start but just then the telephone went and the Major was called to answer it. We could hear him doing so and a long conversation ensued. With him safely out of the way, Allport and I decided we could not let him get away with it, so I filled his beer glass up with gin. When the Major returned he raised his glass, asked who had put gin in it, and then went through the whole routine and drank his glass to the bottom, went to bed and that was the last of Cardinal Puff for that night or any other. We feared the repercussions but there never were any.

On the second day, while we continued to deal with a few unsafe buildings, the emphasis had changed to saving food stocks. Hull had been a major importer of food and its warehouses were full. Before we left the billets the Major warned the officers to be on their watch for any signs of pilfering of any nature, from shops or warehouses, by our men. The first of the remarkable sights for the day was to see Ministry of Food Inspectors around the streets, directing their own working parties, who were actually scraping up butter from the gutters where it had run out from the warehouses during the heat of the fires. One of the other companies had a very tricky job trying to remove the maximum number of full crates of oranges from underneath the wreckage of a warehouse. The outer walls had fallen away and the upper floors had collapsed but were now supported by the stacks of crates of oranges. One by one the crates had to be removed from wherever it appeared safe to do so. By the end of the day some 90 per cent had been saved but the rest had to be sacrificed.

My own trouble was tinned fruit. About the middle of the day I noticed that the camouflage nets, which had been taken off our 3 ton lorries and placed in the backs of them for safety, seemed to have grown unusually large but, on having them removed, I found that the whole back of each of the lorries was stacked with tins of fruit. I had the tins removed and handed over to one of the food inspectors. Then I noticed that we seemed to have been using our pneumatic drills but could not think why. These were normally carried in fitted wooden boxes in the

70

back of our compressor truck but they were stacked on top of the compressor with their hoses draped over them. I had the driver of the truck remove them. The wooden boxes were full from end to end with tins of fruit.

This time, I had all the junior NCOs paraded and I read the riot act firmly and fully. I pointed out that once we started on taking other peoples property there was no telling where it would end and the whole company would be in real bother if one of the inspectors spotted us. One of the corporals had the infernal nerve to say that the inspectors would certainly not examine our vehicles and I left him in no doubt as to what I thought about that observation. The difficulty was that, scattered in small parties around the streets, I could not possibly watch them all, while the senior NCOs clearly saw no harm in what the men were doing.

Their argument was that, if they left the tins where they were, they would soon be buried by the rubble of the buildings we were demolishing. Why then, should they not have the benefit of them. As all the men seemed to see the matter, it would only be just recompense for their troubles. It was difficult to argue with their lack of any moral sense in the matter, but surely my point about the risk of falling foul of the law, or of the army's own discipline should have carried weight. All the NCOs clearly reckoned that the risk of discovery by anyone other than myself was so small that I should condone their actions. In their view looting should be free from penalties. In fact they did not see it as looting at all.

When we got back to the billets, I went, as was normal, to inspect the evening meal. While I was looking around the kitchen of the house being used as the cook house and mess room I opened the pantry door and found that the men had been making deliveries of tinned fruit to their own cook house and, in consequence, the pantry was stacked from floor to ceiling with tins of fruit. Sergeant Cahill had no good explanation to give me and it was clear that he must have been aware of what was going on and no doubt hoped that they could eat all the fruit before I discovered it.

While I watched them, half a dozen of the sappers dug a large pit in the garden and put all the tins in it and buried them. I have very little doubt in my mind that they dug them up again at some later stage, but at least it would have been done in absolute secrecy and it would prevent some future keen gardener from discovering them. I gave the whole section a final warning.

To conclude this story, walking around the planned demolitions the following day, I came to a warehouse where three or four charges were ready to go and the fuses plain to see. It looked a good job. Seated in the middle of the ruins were my two best Lance Corporals calmly eating tinned pineapple out of a large tin they had opened. Sadly, I felt I could do nothing else but put them on a charge and they were in due course stripped of their rank and sentenced to a period of extra fatigues. I am sure I handled it badly somewhere but where I still can't think.

On the third night we were all ready for the expected return of the bombers but they too had had enough of Hull and did not show up. Nor again did they appear during the rest of the fortnight we spent in the city.

On the evening of the second day, when we were still facing a third night of bombing, Colonel Aldous attended a meeting at the City Council and when his turn came to speak he explained that he could not much longer expect the infantry battalions, who had other work and training to do, to continue to supply large working parties for clearing the streets and the City Council would have to supply him with more civilian labour recruited from the many unemployed who were clearly visible around the streets each day. I think he was speechless when some councillor kindly pointed out to him that the next day, being Saturday, would involve payments based on "time and a half" and the following day being a Sunday might even involve "double time". It seemed useless to point out to them that their city was collapsing or burning to the ground around them.

Following the ending of the bombing there was little more for the engineers to do in the centre of the city but, in the outskirts, a lot of minor damage had been done to many houses. Blast and anti-aircraft shrapnel had done much damage to tiles and windows and in some cases doors had been blown off their hinges. Occasionally a small amount of brickwork might be needed to make a house completely habitable again. Accordingly, each section was allocated a complete street to inspect, decide on minor repairs that might do the job, and then to get on with it. Large rolls of roofing felt and kraft paper would do most of the jobs but some putty and a very small amount of glass was also made available.

As a section officer, with my sergeants, I went down the street examining each house in turn; then I wrote on the door of the house in chalk what needed to be done and small working parties of sappers took over each house in turn and did the necessary jobs. A few cups of tea were produced by the thankful citizens but for the most part it was a pretty boring job. The men now felt that this was a job for civilians and that they should be released to go back to their ordinary training. This was particularly so because, in many streets, civilian builders had been commissioned by the occupants or owners of the houses to do the job.

When I choked him off about the tinned fruit, Sergeant Cahill had told me, as a riposte, that the men expected to get some form of bonus from the City and people of Hull when we had finished our work for them. I demanded to know why he thought we would get such a gift and he told me that the City of London had been very generous for similar help. I told him, and was subsequently proved right, that Yorkshire and the City of Hull were a totally different situation and that, in my view, we could expect nothing. Murmuring on the same lines was increasingly common during our time on the streets and the lieutenants felt obliged to report this to the major. We got short shrift for our pains. We were told it was our job to see that this murmuring did not continue and that the men approached their job more cheerfully. The major told us that there was no hope whatsoever of getting some bonus from Hull. However, there was one redeeming feature about the job. It did enable us, for a few days, to give some of the unusual tradesmen that we carried on our War Establishment, such as tilers and glaziers, a chance to work at their real trades, so no doubt they, at any rate, were happy temporarily.

At the end of the second week we received orders to return to billets at Menethorpe and in due course we were all lined up in convoy and took off. When we arrived the major sent for the lieutenants, tore us off a monumental strip for the state of the billets we had left behind, and sent the whole company back to make a real job of clearing up. I make no excuses for myself but on the whole I think this worked out well. If the lieutenants had achieved the same result at first go, even with the support of their sergeants, which was not readily available, the men would have resented it enormously. When they knew that it was the major who had sent them back they realised that they had let the company down and accepted the loss of the rest of their Sunday as fair punishment. Discipline, which had suffered in Hull, was restored immediately.

About this time I was sent off to York on a physical training course. It was held in the Railway Institute near the station. As I had been a PT "Instructor" when a prefect at school it did not teach me very much that was new but it was worthwhile and certainly, like all the others, I got quite fit in a week. Sensibly, we were not introduced to gymnasium work — even though the Institute was well equipped to have done this — because there was no way in which we could have done this back at our units. What we did was the bending, stretching and breathing type exercises which are now called "aerobics".

What I did learn was a series or methods of surmounting obstacles, not so much individually but as a squad group. Most obstacle courses one sees these days essentially require individual prowess; what we were taught was how to do the job with a squad and get everyone over the obstacle at the same time.

Another thing that was attempted without too much success — and the failure was probably my fault — was boxing. The instructor set out to show us how to organise a boxing competition and he decided to have a small ad hoc light-heavyweight contest. He spotted me and my weight was right but my proposed opponent looked to me to be a slight under-match. Although his weight was right, he was definitely shorter by quite a bit and his reach was probably less than mine by quite a bit too.

Nevertheless, the instructor was undismayed and ordered us into the ring. He then told us to advance towards one another and commence scrapping. No doubt he intended us to demonstrate how not to box and then he would then step in and show us the right way. I must admit to advancing with fear and trepidation, not so much at the actual physical contact but in the fear of being made to look silly. I had never been in the ring before in my life and all I knew about was that I should "keep a straight left". As we came within range I decided to straighten my left which I did and caught my opponent what I thought was a light blow in his right eye. At once he collapsed on the canvas holding his eye and making no end of a song about it. I retreated to my corner. Ever since I have wondered whether I did hit him hard or whether he was just funking out. So ended my first and only contest in the ring with a win by a technical knockout.

Another scaring experience was extra-mural when I volunteered to make up a rowing party on the Ouse which I expected to be at a park lake level of skill. It turned out that I had enlisted in an eight and that there was no chance of withdrawing. It was alright when we were paddling upstream but I was frightened out of my skin when we turned around and stroke began to raise the pace.

I was at No. 3 or 4 and just holding my own but the speed seemed terrifying. Still, I caught no crabs and gained confidence. It was exhilarating and I have always meant to try again — though perhaps my luck would not hold next time. My colleagues all voted it a most successful outing but they did not realise how successful and how lucky they had been.

On my return to camp at Menethorpe the major decided to have a route march and the whole Company set out led by himself. The more I think of it the more I wonder why we had never had one before because we certainly needed to have done so. It was an appalling fiasco for the 160/170 men in the Company. Only about ten were excused but only twenty finished the course — valiantly the major struggled through to the last but I, fit from my course, was the only officer to accompany him and Sergeant Howard was the only senior NCO to do so. All the rest had dropped out somewhere and straggled home over the next hour or two. I would have thought that this was, if anything, a case for sending the lot of us back to do it again but I imagine that the major realised that he could hardly do that without doing the distance again himself. Anyway, route marching did not appear on the programme again for the short time that I subsequently remained with the Company.

74

The only other course I attended during my time with 506 Company was one for junior officers at the Northern School of Military Engineering which duplicated the peace-time SME at Chatham. Ripon is a lovely town and the courses at the SME were always interesting and worthwhile. This was a short course but it did, at least, give us a chance to see and have a first go at the Bailey Bridge which was just becoming available at training establishments only. In addition, the visit gave me the chance to see Fountains Abbey which is, of course, magnificent and was only some three miles from the School. Incidentally, at Menethorpe, the ruins of Kirkham Priory, in a beautiful setting, were within strolling distance and Alport and I visited them on a couple of occasions.

The final assignment in which I took part was a really major new hutted camp building project which would test the whole range of our skills in that direction: hut building, water supply, drainage, camp sanitation and road building. We had only built the first few huts and I felt that I was only just beginning to get the hang of it when the major sent for me and told me that I was to be transferred, at least temporarily, to 1st Corps Headquarters as a Stores Officer. I have never imagined that I was chosen for this post because of any particular aptitude that I had had any chance to display during my six months with the Company. Indeed my only conclusion was that he decided that I was the lieutenant who could best be spared without weakening the Company too much and without running the risk that I would fail at the post and thus discredit my commanding officer's choice. My preferred explanation was that the major was concerned lest Captain Walker's and my thinly veiled dislike for one another, and rivalry for the farmer's daughter, should break out into open hostility. If so she did me a good turn.

World news during my seven months with 2nd Division was largely taken up with the Mediterranean and the Middle East. Italy's entry into the war in June, 1940 was not inspired by any belief that Mussolini may have held about his country's military prowess, but rather by the feeling that he would be dealing with a couple of dead ducks (France and Britain) and the wish to share in spoils. With a navy twice the size of the British force in the Mediterranean and and air force eight times the size he should be able to take over the Central Mediterranean and push the Royal Navy back to Gibraltar and Alexandria. Mussolini also had an army of 500,000 in Africa against a mere 100,000 available to General Wavell in the whole Middle East. He therefore felt comfortable enough to take over British Somaliland in East Africa — after it had been evacuated, to invade Egypt and capture Sidi Barrani and to invade Greece and Albania.

This all turned sour on Mussolini very quickly. In November 1940 British naval aircraft had destroyed half the Italian battle fleet in harbour at Taranto. In December, 1940 and January, 1941 a British force of 25,000 men — about half of them Australians — had destroyed 10 Italian divisions and captured the whole of Cyrenaica in 60 days, collecting 113,000 prisoners. At the turn of the year the Greeks were still proving a match for the Italians in the fighting on their borders.

This caused Hitler to intervene. He had not wished to help Mussolini, who had tried to be clever at his expense, but he was planning to invade Russia in the New Year and did not want to leave too much trouble in his rear. He sent Rommell to Libya with the Afrika Korps and reinforced Sicily with strong contingents of the Luftwaffe. The latter, particularly, reversed the balance of power again in favour of the Axis, in spite of British success against Italian heavy cruisers and destroyers at the battle of Matapan at the end of March, 1941.

Rommell also affected the balance of power very quickly. In fourteen days, at the beginning of April, he pushed the British out of Cyrenaica again and British tanks were seen to be sadly inferior to the German machines. Furthermore, British forces sent to Greece were expelled in April, leaving 12,000 prisoners behind and in May German paratroopers captured Crete and another 12,000 British prisoners were left behind but, in the fierce fighting, German paratroop power was largely destroyed.

In some compensation, British troops routed the Italians in East Africa and by May they had occupied the whole of Abyssinia, Eritrea and Somaliland at small cost in killed and wounded. In addition, although free French cooperation was negligible, the British defeated the Vichy French and expelled German interests from Syria, changing the pro-axis government of Iraq without much difficulty.

The various defeats brought some criticism of Churchill but in May, in the House of Commons, he won a vote of confidence by an enormous majority.

Not long after I left them to go to HQ 1st Corps, 2nd Division sailed for India and Burma, where they greatly distinguished themselves in battle with the Japanese. Sadly I heard much later that Major Gardiner was killed in one of these operations.

I missed my fifth possible embarkation.

CHAPTER 7   1st Corps Headquarters
                (September, 1941 – September, 1942)

In the early autumn of 1941 I was posted from the 506 Field Company to Headquarters 1st Corps at Hickleton Hall, some six miles west of Doncaster. This was the ancestral home of Lord Halifax who had been Foreign Secretary in Neville Chamberlain's Government at the start of the war. The main departments of the headquarters were located in Hickleton Hall itself but the Chief Engineer's office was in a shortened Nissen hut in the gardens a short way from the main building. Although I served on the headquarters for at least six months I did not at any time get a really good look around the main building and the only times I ever went into it was about once a month, when my turn came to be Duty Officer. Then I had to get my camp bed fixed up in the "G" office — the general office of the General Staff — and spend the night there in case somebody had an urgent message to give us. To my recollection no one ever did.

This general office was, I think, in the Earl's dining room and certainly there was a magnificent big table in the middle of it which was usually loaded with an indescribable mess of papers which no one ever seemed to put away. Any spy would certainly have had his work cut out in trying to find any particular paper. Almost buried in the papers were the occasional field telephones and the cables serving them were liberally draped over the family portraits of the Wood family which still occupied the walls. I am sure they must have been valuable and it seemed an astonishing risk to take in leaving them out during army occupation of the building. It was a bore doing duty there, because no one ever seemed to feel the need of a Duty Officer's services, but yet it was interesting to wallow in the distinguished background.

The Chief Engineer was Brigadier Harry Genet, a shortish but spruce and efficient looking regular officer with large horn-rimmed glasses. He occupied half the hut and the rest of the officers shared the other half. There were three of us, the senior being Captain the Viscount (David) Hanworth RE. David was a regular officer and was a qualified mechanical and electrical engineer. He was the SORE 3 (Ops), the acronym standing for Staff Officer, Royal Engineers, Grade 3 specialising in engineer operations. As such, David's job was to keep touch with the engineer operational units in the Corps Troops and the divisions and, generally, to co-ordinate their work, keeping the Chief

Engineer fully informed and seeing that adequate records were kept.

In the keeping of records, he was assisted by the Intelligence Officer, Lt. Hoare, another regular and a fresh faced young man — at least as young as myself (at 23). 1st Corps consisted of two divisions at the time, 1st Division was looking after the Lincolnshire coast and 2nd Division, which I had just left, was still watching the coast of East Yorkshire. Accordingly, each division was hard at work erecting tubular scaffolding anti-tank fences and anti-tank minefields on the beaches and cliffs, building concrete pillboxes, preparing bridges for demolition by explosives and arranging to demolish Inland Petroleum Distribution Depots — IDDs for short — when necessary. This all required a tremendous amount of recording and many difficulties were already becoming apparent. In addition, all units were heavily involved in training and frequent, divisional scale manoeuvres. This involved the two regiments of divisional engineers and one of corps troops engineers. These three amounted to some 2,500 men.

I was to be the Stores Officer, but still with the rank of 2nd Lieutenant. My job was obvious — anyone who wanted anything in the way of engineer equipment and material came to me and I had to try and find it. In this work I was assisted by the 105th Corps Field Park Company, which I was later to command. It was stationed at Misson, a village just over the border of West Yorkshire into Nottinghamshire, and about fifteen miles from Corps HQ. Our two or three clerks at HQ 1st Corps also occupied our office and clattered away on their typewriters for most of every day. Fortunately I spent a lot of time out, travelling and getting to know the area and the people. David soon found an extra job for me in training Home Guard in the employment of the Hanworth torpedo, a lethal device which he had invented and on which he was still spending rather too much time. However, he had made sure that it worked and he wanted me to see that the Home Guard knew how to use it. This was mostly done on Sunday mornings.

The device consisted of a simple "gun" and a projectile which could be fired from it. The "gun" was a length of one and a half inch gas pipe mounted securely on a one inch thick board about 3 feet long and 6 inches wide. There was a plug in the back end of the pipe through which a small hole had been bored. Two electric wires passed through this and connected to a detonator buried in a small rubber bag (balloon) full of coarse gunpowder.

The projectile was mounted on a broomstick which fitted loosely into the gas pipe and the projectiles were of two types. One had a single RE anti-tank mine, about the size of a medium cake tin, mounted on the end of the broomstick and was intended to be projected through the air to hit either the upper track or the body of an armoured vehicle.

78

The other carried two anti-tank mines on a little wooden trolley with wooden wheels and was again mounted on the end of a broomstick. The first type was designed to be hidden in the hedgerows of roads along which German armoured columns might penetrate deep behind the British lines. The trolley type would be dug into the grass verges on such roads and was aimed essentially at the lower track or the less well protected underside of the target vehicles. On impact the mechanisum fired the detonater just as it would if a vehicle ran over one of the mines.

A pair of Home Guardsmen would have one of these devices and, with others similarly equipped, would be deployed along a number of roads across a three or four mile front and over a depth of three or four miles. A platoon of say thirty Home Guard might thus deploy fifteen or sixteen devices and a company of one hundred Home Guard would cover an area three times as big. When I joined 1st Corps HQ we had two Home Guard companies allocated to the work and they were drawn from the coal miners of the Yorkshire and Nottinghamshire coalfields respectively. They were very suitable for the task, but at the start we did not have sufficient devices or even dummies for practice to go round.

At this stage the Home Guard as a whole was beginning to become a serious force, but the necessity for it was beginning to disappear. The men all had uniform, steel helmets and gas masks and my companies were fully equipped with rifles and ammunition. Being men in a reserved occupation, they were certainly far from superannuated. They would have given a good account of themselves with or without the Hanworth torpedo but we had reached the time when the British Army was beginning to think of taking the offensive and it began to seem unlikely that the Home Guard would ever be called on to resist an invasion.

The strategic idea behind the invention and its utilisation (assuming an invasion was still a possibility) was to prevent the rapid exploitation in depth of a breakthrough of German troops, such as happened in Poland in 1939 and in the Ardennes and north west France in 1940. At that time, light armoured columns had exploited gaps made by the blitzkrieg attack. Coupled with some parachute attacks as well, they made extremely rapid progress, completely disorganising the rear areas behind the penetrated front line.

Eventually the attack, which originally faced south west, rolled up the left wing of the French army and its British and Belgian allies further west by turning north east in line with the coast. Hence the attempt to devise some form of weapon to counter penetration by these light forces and give a cheap and quick method of defence in considerable depth. It seemed to me that Hanworth's torpedo might just fill the bill because there certainly were not the required number of anti-tank guns available.

As soon as we had a few dummy torpedoes available it was necessary

79

to teach these simple tactics to the Home Guardsmen themselves. One of my companies was based on Doncaster Drill Hall and this one was the more advanced in its general organisation and preparation. The other one was based at Ollerton some twenty miles south, down in Sherwood Forest. The officers of the latter were also colliery managers, (except that the Doncaster company was commanded by a Major Atherton who was a senior official of the Cementation Company's mining wing).

Every Sunday morning we went out from the Drill Hall into the south Yorkshire and Nottinghamshire countryside and dropped off the men at suitable intervals to dig in their little trollies and run their firing wires a hundred yards back from the road to some point of vantage from which the road and approaching vehicles could be seen. At first we used the hired lorries as targets but, as the shooting improved, so did the risk of damage, even though we were only firing the wheeled projectile which kept low on the road.

Accordingly, I searched for alternative targets and eventually made contact with the Reconnaissance Regiment of one of the reserve divisions in our general area. These regiments were mostly equipped with light armoured cars and a few light tanks and were ideal for my purpose. They were about the weight and speed of the light German forces used in France and the vehicles were unlikely to be damaged by the dummy torpedoes.

Nevertheless, I felt it desirable to show the colonel of the regiment and some of his people that this was no game of soldiers we were playing but that we had a really serious instrument of war. I, therefore, set up a live flying torpedo with a genuine anti-tank mine and aimed it at a large but dead tree in some parkland near where we were assembling for the day's exercise.

I explained the strategic and tactical use of the weapon and we fired it off. It far exceeded our expectations. The thing hurtled through the air, a distance of some fifteen yards, with great accuracy, and hit the tree fair and square. With a huge bang and a cloud of smoke the tree seemingly disappeared, although we found the pieces scattered around afterwards. For a while there was silence and then excited exclamations from both sides in the war game. Our collaborators departed to do their drive through the appointed area still feeling, perhaps, that their speed would keep them out of trouble, though I had set a limit of thirty to forty miles per hour.

I think they made the mistake of trying to spot the weapons because they did not in fact drive through all that fast. They did not spot any of them before they were fired but they did claim to have spotted some of the Home Guard jumping around excitedly after they had made their hit. As far as we could find out, in fact, all the weapons secured hits and some of the armoured cars had been hit two or three times. From our point of view it was a great success but the Reconnaissance Regiment thereafter refused to play. The colonel said it was bad for the morale of his men, even to be thumped continuously by dummy torpedoes. I could see his point.

Coupled with this field practice I got hold of a couple of German war films "Sieg in Osten" and "Sieg in Westen" which showed the campaigns in Poland and in France. It was good German propaganda but I think it missed its mark with our lot and they fully understood that my purpose was to give them a clear impression of how the enemy might, in fact, look when seen across the hedgerows in action. There were also pictures of all the various sizes of German armoured equipment which we might encounter if, as seemed increasingly unlikely, blitzkreig ever came to Britain. The excited talk afterwards showed that the experiment had been well worthwhile.

In the meantime the Field Park Company had been slowly accummulating stocks of base boards and war heads so that we could begin to visualise the possibility of providing for a second shot, but vehicles to get out into the field for practice and experiment proved more and more difficult to obtain. Whether we could ever have organised for the company to fire a first shot and then re-assemble to re-arm and get out into the field again for a second shot was problematical and might have required too high a standard of map reading but it was an interesting possibility.

At about this time I was able to secure a moderate supply of condemned explosives, i.e. sticks of dynamite that were so old that there was the chance they would not fire when detonated. I had the rather risky idea that the Home Guard might be taught something about demolitions and booby traps. The risk appeared in a degree of over confidence in men who used explosives in their normal work. In each squad we could be certain of having one colliery shotfirer and a couple or so who had helped in setting charges. This seemed to make them feel that they knew all there was to know about explosives in whatever way they were being used.

Each squad had written instructions as to the particular booby trap they were to erect but they clearly thought that half a stick of dynamite was a rather poor show and fortified substantially most of the charges they set. When firing time came the resultant bangs were very much more than I expected but delighted the participants.

Only one failed to go off. This was a device where a thin trip wire across the road caused an anti-tank mine to swing down out of the foliage of the trees until a short firing wire stopped its fall and pulled the safety pin out of the mine detonating mechanism. Our version of the trap only half removed the safety pin and the mine was left swinging in the breeze. Unfortunately, it was clearly my task to render it safe, although there were plenty of volunteers. Mounted on top of the lorry I was brought under the swinging mine. My past and future passed before my eyes as I gingerly caught the mine and removed the detonator. After that I decided that booby traps and Home Guard did not mix too well and I did not see myself volunteering to disarm any more of their misfires.

Most of this work, as I have said, had been done with the Doncaster Company and I had kept the Ollerton Company informed and they were following the same course, but some weeks behind. Hanworth was pleased to hear of our progress but did not show a very active interest in it. He still battled on trying to get further technical improvements to the torpedo. I thought this unnecessary and counter-productive, but time was running out for both of us. The war was changing.

Had the Germans ever come to England I am sure that tank trapping — as we called it — would have had its place and the Home Guard companies would have performed well. Whether I would have served with them, much as I would have wanted to, was doubtful. Atherton and his colleagues could have managed without me, even though I was still very much their tactical instructor. Indeed, I had progressed to lecturing regularly to various Home Guard companies on such matters as how to prepare a village for defence, camouflage and serious demolitions.

Returning to our headquarters, which was now in a large house in a village near Hickelton, after a weekend camouflage course, we were astounded to see a number of ATS girls leaning out of the windows to view our arrival. It turned out that the headquarters was about to be split into an Operations element, which would be available for service overseas, and a Works element, which would remain in the UK. Among these ladies was one who eventually became my wife.

In talking about the Hanworth Torpedo and the Home Guard, which were essentially evening or Sunday morning activities, I have said little about what we did during the rest of the week, but I have referred to the difference between Works and Operations. Apart from these two main branches of the Royal Engineers' work in war and peace, there are at least three other specialist sections. One is transportation and is mainly concerned with the railway movement of goods and troops. I think this branch also includes Ports and Harbours, where there may be substantial specialist works to be done. Then there is the RE Postal Service which handles all the private mail of the troops. Thirdly, there is the Survey Section, principally responsible for securing the supply of good maps to the forces, either from their own surveying or field revisions (as with the Ordnance Survey in peacetime) or from re-printing from other sources. All these branches have their own distinctive and distinguished histories and traditions, but most engineer officers will have very little involvement with the latter three sections. Most will spend some time on both Works and Operations.

Works is essentially concerned with the housing of the army, whether in permanent barracks or hutted camps, and at a time of rapid expansion of the army or major re-deployment, its work is enormous. New building, conversions and repairs keep a very large number of men and officers occupied. Much of their work is contracted out to civilian companies but part is always done by operational units temporarily employed in a Works role. In war time a large number of units in the Line of Communications area specialise in Works. These are General Construction Companies, Artisan Works Companies, Well Boring Companies and other specialists as the work may demand. Indeed the tunnelling companies, in which I served earlier in the war, and the quarrying companies, into which most of them were later converted, can also be regarded as Works units, as can the airfield construction units. If fortification work was in fashion this too would fall under the Works department, as with the 19th Century works at Dover and around Portsmouth, such as Fort Southwick where I served later.

The Operations side of the work was concerned essentially with field engineering such as bridging, demolitions, minefields, etc. done by field units such as the field companies and squadrons and the field park companies under command of 1st Corps, in the divisional engineers and the corps troops engineers.

A lot of our work consisted of visiting these operational units and that in turn involved some fairly intensive map reading to get from place to place. In those days there were no sign posts directing the way and very few notice boards announcing the name of any village or settlement. We relied entirely on our ability to read the one inch Ordnance Survey maps and indeed for longer distances the quarter inch to the mile edition. Brigadier Genet had his copies made up into bound books which were extremely convenient when travelling by car, but not quite so easy to handle when walking the ground. Nevertheless, we all became experts at using the maps and finding our way. We made great use of the national grid reference system which divides the whole map into kilometre squares. Every officer and most other ranks could give and interpret six figure map references which defined any point or location to within fifty metres in any direction.

I see that this system is still described carefully in the margins of the present ordnance maps but it is my guess that fewer than one in ten of people who use an ordnance map learn to use a grid reference in these days.

Added to the lack of direction signs or any location indicators whatsoever (even the railway station nameboards were removed to avoid giving help to the enemy in any way), the almost complete lack of lighting after dark made travelling even more of an enterprise. Headlamps were cut down to narrow slits, torches were frowned on and street lighting or window lighting of any nature was completely forbidden. We always tried to be on a main road heading for home, or within a well known range of say twenty miles, before darkness and the blackout. Otherwise getting home at any reasonable time at all was liable to be a real problem.

The Brigadier was also involved, to some extent, on the Works side in a small way and it was fairly clear that he had a particular interest in that direction, but it did not greatly concern his three juniors.

In December 1941 I completed eighteen months commissioned service. In peacetime a second lieutenant had to serve three years before gaining his promotion to lieutenant automatically, but in wartime this was halved, so my name appeared in Orders and I put up my second pip — the shoulder epaulette device indicating an officer; one pip on each shoulder for a second lieutenant, two pips for a full lieutenant and three for a captain. Within a couple of weeks I was able to put up the third pip on each side, as I was promoted to the rank of captain because 1st Corps was being re-organised. As far as the engineers were concerned, this re-organisation meant that we were to take over full responsibility for engineer Works in our Corps area, namely Lincolnshire, East Yorkshire and, I think, a good part of West Yorkshire. Recognising that the Brigadier would be heavily involved with Works, his three operational juniors were all promoted in rank and thus given more independent authority and status. Hanworth went up to major and I went up to captain. At the same time Hoare was transferred away — on promotion, I believe, and a new intelligence officer, Robin Anderson, was posted in and also promoted to captain. Joy all round! But universal joy was not to last.

At the same time we were given a substantial Works wing. There was to be a deputy chief engineer, a full Colonel Baker — another regular and apparently well known to the Brigadier. Below him was a lieutenant colonel and no less than four or five majors and a couple of captains with a set of staff sergeants, sergeants and corporals to boot, together with a posse of a dozen ATS clerks. To accommodate all this lot we had to move from Hickleton to a nearby village, Bolton-on-Dearne, literally surrounded by pit heaps and headgears. We took over the big house of the village which although somewhat tarnished by coal dust, was surrounded by a fairly large, though seedy, garden and lawns. The ATS could not join us immediately because the huts, partly for offices, but chiefly for the girls' sleeping accommodation, had not been completed. This brings me back to the point at which Major Hanworth and I, returning from a camouflage course, found ourselves being interestedly assessed by the varied grades of beauty leaning out of the main building windows. Life had certainly changed.

Certainly less than two months later, and possibly as little as one month later, the Brigadier decided on — or more likely completed his negotiations for — the removal of Major Hanworth. Whether this was done amicably or not I do not know. One sad feature was that David had just been introducing his new viscountess, Rosamond, an ATS officer, to his colleagues. It was many many years until I met her again, when she was a JP and served with me on the Surrey Police Authority Committee. Anyway, all I knew was that David suddenly disappeared and I was summoned to the brigadier's presence and told that I was promoted to major. I remember thinking that having held four ranks, albeit briefly for two of them, within three months must constitute some kind of a record.

In handing over to me, the Brigadier made little or no reference to my predecessor but I just got the impression that he was well aware of the time that David had been spending on the torpedo and that this had resulted in him depending rather too heavily on the intelligence officer and myself to carry the operational responsibility that should have been David's. Even more clearly I got the impression that the Brigadier wanted to hand over to me as much of the operational work as possible, so that he could concentrate on the Works side. I was only too ready to take on that assignment and I threw myself into it with enthusiasm.

When the ATS arrived they had a corporal in charge and I felt myself entitled to call on her for my letters, as we had received no clerical reinforcement on the Operations side. However, with two other senior officers at least calling for her attention, she felt entitled to pass it on to one of the other girls. Accordingly, a Miss Connie Dodd was detailed to attend to my business, such as it might be. Shortly afterwards we started playing tennis together in the evenings at the village tennis club and the friendship ripened. She was a dark pretty girl who kept herself and uniform looking extremely smart. She was a well educated grammar school girl — which most of the other ATS were not. We soon began to attend the village dances and the friendship became a nine days wonder.

Now that we had quite a large establishment of other ranks, the Brigadier decided that we should pay some attention to the Army Council Instruction (ACI) about disseminating the material set out in the publications of the Army Bureau of Current Affairs and he clearly looked to me to do it.

Accordingly, every month I had to face up to a gathering of male and female soldiers who appeared to be only faintly interested in what I was saying to them. Actually, they were not as bad as they looked and most of their questions were moderately intelligent. The publications ranged over a lot of the political questions of the day and largely related to the prospective immediate post war period. Although appearing to be only moderately critical of the Government's political record, the writers conveyed a faintly socialist view of life and affairs. This was moderately in tune with my own feelings at the time, though I am bound to say that I have greatly changed them since. I think I presented the pros and cons fairly but discussion with the troops was slightly stilted and restrained by the difference in rank between us.

Another area that fell to my responsibility was that of any form of military training for the men and, indeed, for the ATS. Ammunition, which had been in short supply for all the war so far, had suddenly become more readily available and I was able to get a fair quota of time expired ammunition, which we were able to fire off at will. Close to Bolton Hall were some old open cast workings — presumably for coal but possibly for clay — and we fixed up a firing range in these where the men and the girls were able to fire off a dozen rounds or so each. Whether they regarded it all as a joke I never found out and Connie was no independent observer.

"Andy", as I now knew Robin Anderson, was very busy still with the recording of minefields and demolition arrangements. It seemed a never ending task and I too spent a lot of time on it. I fear that some of the minefields were not accurately recorded by their planters and some of the demolition charges just disappeared — much, I imagine, to the frustration of post war searchers. 1st Corps headquarters as a whole was beginning to shape up to an overseas role and we began to have radio and coding exercises and to face up to running a mobile headquarters. Here I found myself at a disadvantage compared with my colleagues in other branches who had all had considerable practice with the use of radio and its procedures. Accordingly, on exercises, I took my chances to get in some practice and tended to hog the air a bit. One of my "G" colleagues protested on the air on one occasion and I, as hotly, defended myself by claiming that I had just as much right as anyone else to get the practice while I could, which they had all had in regimental work before joining the headquarters. I wonder what the monitoring German listeners made of that one.

Suddenly Brigadier Genet fell ill and a replacement chief engineer arrived. He was a Brigadier Godfrey and his regime did not look like suiting me as well as Genet's. Firstly, he seemed far less interested in Works than Genet and was prepared to leave it all to Colonel Baker, who did not seem to welcome it either. On the other hand, Godfrey was

*142 Engineer OCTU – Cadets on an "Engineer Exercise Without Troops."
At the right are the author's personal friends Cadets Anstey and Bennett.*

142 Officer Cadet Training Unit – Cadets on an EEWT (Engineer Exercise Without Troops). Planning how to 'improve' a railway embankment to make an effective anti-tank obstacle

142 Officer Cadet Training Unit – Field Works School, building trenchworks to 1914 – 18 war standards

142 Officer Cadet Training Unit – Cadets on a TEWT (Tactical Exercise Without Troops).

142 Officer Cadet Training Unit – Field Works School, erecting sheer legs as improvised heavy lifting gear.

142 Officer Cadet Training Unit — Wet Bridging School, building a standard (pre-war) pontoon equipment bridge.

142 Officer Cadet Training Unit — Lunchtime at the Wet Bridging School, making a folding boat equipment bridge.

142 Officer Cadet Training Unit – Construction training — pill boxes.

142 Officer Cadet Training Unit
Graduating Class No. 6
Officer Commanding (Lt. Col. Binney) Adjutant and Class Officer at centre front flanked by two Young Officers and two Cadets on each side with Class Sergeant on extreme left. All Cadets were commissioned as 2nd Lieutenants June, 1940.

*1st Tunnelling Engineers at Dover. A junction in
completed battery accommodation*

*1st Tunnelling Engineers at Dover.
Defence battery accommodation in chalk cliffs.*

506 Field Company — Training in demolitions.
Making 'cordtex' explosive nets for mine clearance — preferably not smoking.

506 Field Company — Assault training on a course at York.

506 Field Company — Bridging manoeuvres — fraternising with the enemy? . . . .

105 Corps Field Park Company
Author and colleague officers are sitting centre, second row.

105TH CORPS FIELD PARK COY. R.E.

14/2/43.

1st Corps Headquarters — Home Guard Sunday training in tank trapping.
Officer Commanding (Major Atherton) on right.

1st Corps Headquarters — Home Guard training in tank trapping.
The torpedo hits the target.

clearly going to pay intimate attention to what we on the Operations side were doing and my independence was clearly going to be reduced. Secondly, he caught me on the wrong foot, when I was called to his office one day, by choking me off pretty roundly for appearing before him without my battledress blouse. It was a hot day and I had adopted summer order but he seemed to feel that was out of order.

Suddenly the great day came. In late summer 1942 we received orders to separate ourselves — that is the Operational wing — from our Works wing and prepare for overseas service. Unfortunately Andy's health was suspect and he had to leave us. A Captain Melville joined us instead as Intelligence Officer. The Brigadier and I moved down to London to a secret headquarters at the back of the Cumberland Hotel to do the planning for a very hush-hush operation but I thought I must have breached security when I met my mother outside the hotel in the street. However, that turned out to be accidental as she was just out shopping.

I had recently become engaged to Connie, so things were in order there, and we would doubtless receive embarkation leave to get married.

We in 1st Corps were to go to North Africa to fend off any possibility of interference on the flank of the British and American landings in French North Africa in the "Torch" operations. Ours was to be a 1st Corps operation only. 2nd Division had long since departed from the 1st Corps area and had gone off to the Far East to defend India against the Japanese, who had overrun Burma. 1st Corps was now likely to consist of the 1st and 3rd Divisions. I had one other thing on my mind. I seemed to have a wart developing on my tongue. A small operation to excise this might take only a couple of days and it could be advisable to have it done before we embarked, rather than have something more serious develop as time went on, requiring treatment under less satisfactory conditions. I discussed this with the Brigadier and he thought that I should have it looked at immediately at the Millbank headquarters of the RAMC.

I went along and the doctor who examined me said I should certainly have it excised forthwith. He reported this to the Brigadier and must have said something else — possibly a fear of cancer — which threw my chief into some alarm. Accordingly he began to talk about replacing me immediately. I had visions of demotion. Officers promoted in wartime are only promoted to temporary ranks but their permanent rank moves up to the one below the one they are holding. If I lost my post as SORE 2 (Ops.) to 1st Corps, I might revert to my permanent rank of captain.

I protested vigorously but Godfrey claimed that his problems were far more severe, as he had to find a suitable substitute in a hurry and I might not be returning. Fortunately, inspiration came my way. A new commanding officer, Major Priestley, had just been appointed to the 105 Field Park Company, which would be going with us on the operation. This new officer was a regular — which I knew by now would attract the Brigadier — and was known to be keen to get a staff job. I suggested to Godfrey that he might arrange a swop and he jumped at the idea immediately. I went off to hospital but returned to the office the following day as they were not quite ready to operate. Godfrey confirmed the arrangements which left Priestley and me both feeling very much happier. In fact, the tongue operation was only a minor one and no complication was found. The only problem was that for a couple of days I had the greatest difficulty in talking, because of the stitches in my tongue. My sister in the WAAF visited me in the Royal Masonic Hospital and, as she had some deafness, we had a real problem.

On the broad war front the year for which I served on Headquarters 1st Corps contained, recognisably, the greatest turning points of the war. Before them, we were unlikely to lose; after them, we were certain to win. This change was fully apparent at the time.

In June, 1941 the Germans had invaded Russia and their armies swept forward almost irresistibly. Britain was helpless to assist, even though Russia appealed for a second front in Europe to take off the pressure. An early Russian defeat was fully expected but, incredibly, in September their line was still in existence, even if heavily battered. It was clear that the Germans would not reach the Caucasus Mountains that year. The Royal Navy, in the Mediterranean had lost cruisers and destroyers off Crete and Greece earlier in 1941 and then, in the autumn, there were the losses of four capital ships to the German U boats and Italian human torpedoes with further cruisers being lost in minefields. Apart from destroyers little was left to the Royal Navy in the Mediterranean. The Italians still had half of their fleet and the Luftwaffe still had a whole air corps in Sicily and North Africa. The axis reigned supreme in the central Mediterranean by the turn of the year.

On 4th December, the German attack on Moscow was called off. On 6th December, the Japanese crippled the U.S. fleet in Pearl Harbour and the Americans were at war with Japan. On the same day the Germans declared war on the U.S. in support of Japan while next day the British declared war on Japan themselves. Although no formal alliance was set up between the U.S. and Britain, this existed, in fact, in the personal relationship between Churchill and Roosevelt. An early product was agreement that priority would be given to the defeat of Germany, with Japan to follow later. Less straightforward was the American insistence that a supreme commander be appointed for each theatre. They softened this by proposing Wavell for the post in South East Asia which was balanced in mid 1942 by the appointment of Eisenhower to supreme command in the Mediterranean (and later to command in North West Europe). The creation of a Combined Chiefs of Staff organisation — by whom the supreme (theatre) commanders were directed — completed the picture but there were many shocks still to come.

On 10th December the Japanese sunk the British battleships, Prince of Wales and Repulse, off Malaya. In February, Singapore surrendered with the loss of 60,000 British troops. In March, an allied fleet was defeated by the Japanese in the Battle of the Java Sea and they overran Burma. It was feared that they were aiming next for Ceylon and India but, having secured their western flanks, they turned backwards to the Pacific where they were much too busy thereafter to pay much attention to the Indian Ocean.

The shipping position in the Atlantic was still serious, particularly as the Americans neglected convoy arrangements and suffered heavily in consequence. Their losses were faster than their shipyards could replace. This position was not corrected until 1943. Britain went very short of supplies and this was aggravated by damaging shortfalls in coal production, largely due to manpower shortages. Coal rationing was only just avoided.

In June 1942 Tobruk fell with the loss of 33,000 men after an assault by Rommel's Afrika Korps.

Bomber command was beginning to outrun its strength and the value of heavy bombing was seriously questioned. Losses were substantial and the effects on the German economy were barely apparent in overall terms. The argument that Britain could do nothing else effectively began to lose its force as the possibility of an invasion somewhere began to gain ground. However, the Russian (and American) idea of a second front in north west Europe received a severe jolt in August when British and Canadian forces attacked Dieppe — without adequate air or naval support admittedly — and were repulsed with heavy losses. It was almost a case of "back to the drawing board".

With Churchill's persuasion, Roosevelt agreed in late July to an invasion of French North Africa; Alexander took over command in the Middle East and Montgomery took charge of the Eighth Army.

Although 1st Corps was almost ready for embarkation when I left Headquarters in September 1942 (and 105th Field Park Company would be going with them), during the year 1942 there was no chance of my going abroad (other than to India with 2nd Division, to which I have already referred).

The invasion (of North Africa by 1st Corps) appeared to be no more than slightly delayed but when the Anglo American ("Torch") landings took place without interference the 1st Corps operation was cancelled in November and my sixth chance of embarkation had gone.

CHAPTER 8

105th Corps Field Park Company
(October, 1942 – November, 1943)

Although I was taking over the 105th Corps Field Park Company from Major Priestley, he was barely there when I arrived because he had already packed and was set to leave the same morning. We had a very brief hand-over but, as he had only recently taken over the Company himself, he had very little to tell me, except that his predecessor (now a Lieutenant Colonel) C.C. Parkman, was in the village and would no doubt come and see me shortly. As I always favour the briefest possible hand-over of any job I saw nothing wrong with the proposed arrangements. I had, of course, met Parkman before while I was on HQ 1st Corps.

Misson was, in those days, a relatively small village though it did have a fair sized church, a couple of pubs and a post office. It was almost doubled in size by the scattered huts occupied by the 105th Company. With the village seemingly having less than 200 inhabitants and the Company having more than 150 on the strength at that stage, the military presence was certainly all pervading. It was situated about ten miles south east of Doncaster, just over the border from Yorkshire into Nottinghamshire. It was some three miles north east of Bawtry, a small town on the pre-motorway A1.

The village streets were laid out in a square, the road from Bawtry entering at the north west, and the exit road which eventually led to Haxey and Epworth on the Isle of Axholme, leaving from the north east corner. To the immediate south of the village was the River Idle, a tributary of the Trent, but the whole area was criss-crossed by drainage ditches, as it was generally very low lying, with occasional gravel knolls. In general, the area had a depressed look and the rustic inhabitants outside the village appeared to live in what could only be called agricultural slums. It was, in fact, a rather unexciting place to be and, in general, the troops kept to their huts and the villagers to their homes and there was very little worthwhile social life.

The 105th Company was part of 1st Corps Troops RE which was commanded by Lieutenant Colonel "Dickie" Poole. His headquarters were at Barnby Moor, seven miles due south of Bawtry, a ribbon development village, with a fine old coaching inn but little else, and roughly the same size as Misson. There were three Field Companies in the Corps Troops, in the standard way, 102, 103 and 104, and these were located, but not respectively, at Blyth and Ranby on the A1 and Tickhill, a slightly larger historic town, four miles west of Bawtry. The villages were all on the fringe of the new Nottinghamshire coalfield.

The War Establishment and organisational structure of the 105th Company was distinctly awkward, even unbalanced, but such a company had three roles. The first one was to organise and manage depots for stores to be used by the Field Companies, for whatever jobs they might be given to undertake, and to act as a reserve of stores to be drawn on by the Divisions in the Corps, through their Divisional Field Park Companies. The company was totally mobile in that it could carry all its own men and equipment with its own transport and yet the stores section had an essentially static role.

If the corps was advancing, the Corps Field Park Company would try to leapfrog its essential stores forward, picking up whatever it thought it might most need and taking it forward to the new depot, leaving the remnants of the old depot to be cleared up later by the Army Workshop and Park Company. When retiring, the Corps Field Park Company would endeavour to pick up and take with it whatever was most essential in its forward depot and try to destroy the rest. However, it was all too easy to build up a depot requiring a hundred or more vehicles to move it all and sometimes two or more depots could be in operation at one time. The depot or depots were managed by a section of twenty clerks and storemen, with working parties of Pioneers attached from the army labour companies, as necessary. The officer in charge had a responsible managing job in these circumstances and I was fortunate in having an experienced and mature Lieutenant "Freddie" May in the post.

From a training point of view the ordinary day to day work of receiving and issuing the relatively small amounts of stores needed by the Field Companies for the work they were doing in the area gave reasonable practice in the checking and recording of receipts, the recording of issues and the preparing of regular stock lists. The only question was whether the standard could be maintained if the turnover was substantially increased, as it would be from time to time in battle conditions. We had a go at an exercise based on rapidly building up a new depot and running it down again on the same day. The idea was good enough but we really needed to devote large numbers more men and vehicles to make it a really testing and realistic exercise.

The next role was that of the Workshop Section and I suppose this could be described as being prepared to manufacture numbers of small items — an example of this was the Hanworth Torpedo, which I have already described — or occasional large items. Although mobile like the rest of the company, it needed to be static for periods of time, in order to develop any serious rate of production.

91

It had a workshop vehicle which could form the basis of a small machine tool section. Its lathe was permanently mounted in the centre of the vehicle and powered from the vehicle's own engine. I recall that there was a post drill which was also permanently mounted as, of course, was the generator which powered these two machines and others, one or, maybe, two of which were also permanently mounted but others had to be taken out of the vehicle and either put in a building or given some secure standing on the ground. The men in this section were all suitable categories of tradesmen for this manufacturing role and for a variety of repair work.

Much the largest section, representing more than half the company, was called the E & M (i.e. Electrical and Mechanical) Section. I suppose that this was intended for emergency repair work to civilian (and military) installations — possibly damaged in the fighting or by air attack — such as electric power generating stations, water supply plants, drainage and sewage plants, etc., — and their subsequent re-commissioning. It was very difficult to train for its role or, indeed, for the officers like myself to get any relevant training. It is true that air bombing had caused considerable damage to installations of this nature in England. However, they seemed to me to be either so seriously damaged as not to be capable of any repair at all, needing re-building, or, alternatively, the damage was relatively minor and was best dealt with by their own permanent staffs or the maker's representatives.

The trouble was that the sort of situation in which an E & M Section would be required to work in war would be one where the civilian organisation had broken down or disappeared. This, patently, did not apply in Britain and it was difficult to set up any form of exercise or practice in which such a situation could be replicated. One exercise I did lay on was a visit to the Railway Workshops at Doncaster where we set out to find out how we would go about demolishing such a workshops in the event that it was about to fall into enemy hands. Envisaging the damage that we could do, we could perhaps visualise what the enemy might do in a similar situation and what we would then have to do to restore some form of service. It was only partially successful. The only other thing I could do that seemed likely to be worthwhile was to send the tradesmen on as many trades courses as possible and to attach parties of them for short periods of work in public service installations of the sort I have mentioned above. In the main, the E & M Section was used in the company as a reinforcement for the Workshops Section. It was in any event similarly equipped though it did have, obviously, a large number more tradesmen's tool kits.

The company carried on its strength an officer, Lieutenant Munday, who was an E & M specialist — though whether he was trained on the electrical or the mechanical side I was never quite certain — and two staff sergeants, equivalent in rank to the company quartermaster sergeants, i.e. coming between the company sergeant major and the full sergeants. One of these staff sergeants was an electrical specialist and tended to look after the E & M Section and the other was a mechanical specialist and looked after the Workshops Section.

As in any other company, the sergeant major (CSM) looked after the billets, discipline, parades, military training and general good order of the company, basing himself in the orderly room, while the company quartermaster sergeant (CQMS) looked after the rations and cooking, the furnishing of the billets and offices, the men's equipment and all the company equipment, listed in a document called the G1098, or war equipment tables. Naturally, he operated from his stores with the assistance of a storeman. The company's transport and drivers, of whom there were quite a number, and its two motorcycle despatch riders, all came under the transport sergeant, Sergeant Fogarty.

As December approached, so did marriage, but in the end it came faster than expected. The company was told to get on and take its embarkation leave. I cannot imagine now why this came at this particular time. The 105th had been due to take part in the proposed North African operation and they must have had some embarkation leave at that time, which was only back in the summer anyway. The only thing I can suppose is that someone in the War Office had imagined that talk of an early second front to take the strain off Russia, which had been invaded by Germany in mid 1942, would be translated into action very much more quickly than it actually was. Anyway, in November and December the company completed its embarkation leave and, being fully equipped and reasonably trained, it was ready to go anywhere when called upon. It may even be that there was uncertainty in someone's mind whether 1st Corps was being reserved to take part in the Second Front or might be sent out, even temporarily, to take part in some operation elsewhere such as North Africa or the Far East.

As soon as I knew my dates, which was literally at a week's notice, I let Connie know and she got leave at once and took off for her home in County Durham, at Chester-le-Street, to get ready for the wedding which we fixed for 3rd December. My young brother was still at school doing examinations and could not get away so I would be supported by my father and mother and my two sisters. Apparently the war was not quite so urgent in the RAF where my older sister was serving in the WAAF.

I asked Robin Anderson to be my best man and, as he was still working at Bolton-on-Dearne, he had no difficulty getting time off. We went up to Chester-le-Street on the day before the wedding and stayed overnight at the Golden Lion, which, surprisingly, still had some quite good accommodation. The church was only just around the corner on the other side of the main street. My younger sister and Connie's sister were to be bridesmaids. Her relatives turned out in good numbers so we had a fair crowd at the church and all went very smoothly. My father conducted the service in good style.

The reception was a very crowded one at Connie's home which, being appropriately called Brewery House, suffered no shortage of essential supplies. Afterwards Connie and I travelled by train from Newcastle, through an air raid to Carlisle, where we were to honeymoon. The journey took a long while, but we managed well enough as we had a compartment to ourselves. The hotel, the Queen's, was comfortable considering wartime conditions and bliss reigned supreme for the three or four days which was all that we were allowed. The only snag noticeable was that most of the historic buildings in Carlisle were in military occupation and were therefore not available for visiting, which was a thing we had rather fancied doing. However, the time was too short anyway. We returned to Chester-le-Street and next day travelled down together to Doncaster and on to Bolton where I delivered Connie to her billet before travelling on to Misson.

Christmas was duly celebrated and, particularly as the Officers Mess was situated in the vast and barn-like vicarage on the outskirts of the village, we decided that we would have to have a formal church parade on the Sunday before Christmas. Connie had secured more leave and we had found some temporary lodgings, with two elderly maiden ladies, the Misses Jones, to continue our brief honeymoon. At least two other wives of fellow officers were also staying in the village for Christmas. We, therefore, had a full front pew in the church. As befitted my rank, I sat on the outside with Connie near the aisle. The other end of the pew was less fortunate as it was immediately under the pulpit and the rather decrepit vicar liberally sprayed them with spittle as he delivered his uninspiring sermon. Furthermore, everyone in the front pews was distracted from attention to his message by waiting to hear the resounding click as his upper denture dropped onto his lower from time to time.

After church the company paraded outside and I took the salute as they marched away to their hutments.

In traditional army fashion, the officers attended at the troops' messroom to serve out at least a portion of their Christmas meal and then transferred afterwards to the sergeants' mess for drinks and a buffet meal with them. This also was in the nature of a farewell party for the old sergeant major, whom I had inherited with the company. He was the only man in the company who insisted on wearing, at all times, his old style, brass buttoned uniform. He was certainly old enough to retire but I am fairly certain that he was not going to do so and that he was following Colonel Parkman to his new appointment.

With the start of the New Year, orders came for the company to move forthwith to a new camp in Scotland, just south of Edinburgh. In a sense, and I think we realised at the time, this move must have been related to a decision to divorce the whole of 1st Corps from having anything to do with the defence of England and to allocate it positively to the Order of Battle for the Second Front and not to a role as a reinforcement to North Africa or the Far East. Furthermore, we were no longer tied to particular divisions as we had been in Yorkshire and Lincolnshire with the 1st and 2nd Divisions or the 1st and 3rd Divisions more recently.

A small advance party under my second-in-command, Captain Paul MacCormack, was sent on ahead and on the day appointed the rest of the company, with all its equipment, but none of the stores from the depot, mounted on every vehicle we had, lined up behind my Humber car around the square layout of the village streets and then pulled slowly out of Misson with some minor tooting of horns but with exact spacing of 30 yards between each vehicle and proceeded down the road to Bawtry and the north, slowly gathering speed to a steady 40 miles per hour on our way to Scotland. Comfort stops were at hourly intervals, the vehicles maintaining their spacing along the road each time we stopped. In the early afternoon we reached our new home which was still partly in the hands of the civilian builders.

The Braids Camp was to be large enough to accommodate all three field companies and my Corps Field Park Company and the headquarters of 1st Corps Troops RE, together with provision for two extra sections to be attached to my company. These two extra sections which joined us during the next month or so were, firstly, a Survey Section RE and, secondly, a Workshops Section from REME (Royal Electrical and Mechanical Engineers). My combined company would now be something over 220 men.

Both these new sections were to be under my command for pay, rations, discipline (in so far as it could not be dealt with by the Section Officer himself) and general administration but in no sense was I responsible for their technical work and efficiency, though I cannot recall ever seeing or dealing with anyone (from their true parents) who was so responsible. Nevertheless, it was a slightly awkward and uncertain relationship, even though the individuals concerned, namely the section officers, were ideal. When the whole regiment was in residence the number of men there under Dickie Poole's command would be somewhere between 900 and 1,000 men. The Survey Section was equipped and manned to do minor amounts of topographical work, that is, field surveying to prepare detailed maps or plans of some minor area or developments not covered or shown on available maps. Then they had a drawing office section which would be prepared to extract portions from available maps to be "blown up" for a specific job or operation and on which could be prepared overlays or overprinting to illustrate military situations or plans in colour. Finally, the section had a small printing division which could produce numbers of copies of any such new survey or drawings for distribution to commanders or troops concerned. In those days, present day photocopiers were not available and what the section had were literally miniature printing presses. It seemed to me not only to be a fascinating diversion but to be potentially an extremely useful adjunct to the services that the Corps Troops RE could render to the whole of 1st Corps. Unfortunately, I never saw it in action and much would depend on the quality of the briefing and the suitability of the work they were given to do.

The REME section was essentially a delegation and de-centralisation of the work of a divisional or corps workshops to a series of regimental workshops. Each battalion and each artillery, engineer, signals and transport regiment would have one of these sections allotted to it. Again, this was a much needed and appreciated development and, although I never saw it in full action in the field, I am sure that this worked well and exactly as visualised. In our case, in addition to dealing with the motor transport of the whole regiment — more than 100 vehicles and motorcyles — it had to deal, in due course, with the two bulldozers which my company had been promised but which had not yet arrived. Though I had felt happy enough about the general maintenance and minor repair work undertaken by Sergeant Fogarty and his drivers I would not have felt the same in the case of the bulldozers without the reasonably close attention and assistance of the experts.

When the field companies and headquarters arrived there was another change. Two of the companies, and I think it was the 103 and the 104, were withdrawn and instead we were given 19 Field Squadron and another Field Company. It was hard to fathom why we had been given a field squadron because there was very little difference between the establishment, equipment and training of a field squadron and that of a field company. In theory a field squadron worked with an armoured division while a field company worked with an infantry division. Presumably, at some stage, 1st Corps might have armoured divisions or armoured brigades under command instead of just two, three or four infantry divisions. The corps troops engineers were always available to reinforce divisional engineer companies and it was presumably thought that it would be better to have a field squadron in corps troops available and experienced in cooperation with an armoured formation.

The only trouble was that 19 Field Squadron may have brought with them some of the elitism and superior attitudes of the cavalry and the rest of the armoured formations. Major Neale, its officer-in-command, seemed pleasant enough, as did his officers, but their relationships with the 105th Corps Field Park Company may have been slightly different — though I observed nothing — from their relations with the 102nd and the other field company but somehow there was an air of resentment and suspicion, which was unfortunate but always seemed to be present when the field squadron and companies were in camp together.

It was perhaps fortunate that it was only for a relatively short proportion of the total time that all the regiment was in the Braids Camp at the same time. Even my own company was slightly depleted by detachments serving away in the west of Scotland. In particular, nearly half the stores section was away running a small depot at Kilbirnie (or Kilbride?) not far from Glasgow, but I cannot now remember for whose benefit we were running this unless it was for our own field companies, or alternatively for the benefit of Combined Operations Training on the coast of the Firth of Clyde.

Then there was the Tighnabruaich project. In happier times Tighnabruaich was a remote little seaside resort on the western shores of the Kyles of Bute, and it had been chosen to be the venue of major beach landing exercises. The disaster of the Canadian raid on Dieppe had shown that beach landings had to be planned in meticulous detail and that the training needed to be done in a thorough and convincing fashion. It was no doubt chosen because of its relative closeness to the Combined Operations Training Centres at Wemyss Bay and Largs on the mainland just west of Glasgow.

On shore it appeared that we were to provide and construct a series of pseudo-resistance points to represent the guns and strong points of the defence that our troops would encounter as they approached the beaches, landed and advanced inland. At each of these points, I assume, there had to be a number of explosive devices and lights to represent heavy and light gunfire for the supporting guns of the fleet, the tanks when they landed and the infantry to fire at. As there was no electric power, each of these points had to be battery powered.

Presumably, there also had to be timing devices to bring each point into action on a programmed basis. Everything was done in complete secrecy and no one ever told me exactly why we had to draw some fifty or more car batteries from ordnance depots, charge them up to full capacity and deliver them to Tighnabruaich. I still do not know whether my guessing was accurate in any way but it seemed to me the only logical explanation.

97

I decided that the charging up of these batteries should be done under field conditions. Not for me the simple course of handing them over to a reliable civilian garage to have the operation done professionally and completely satisfactorily. My staff sergeants assured me that our two workshop trucks had ample generating capacity so I took a substantial proportion of the company out on a twenty mile route march, nearly to Gullane, where we met the workshop trucks and the cooks and settled down for a night in the open while the generators purred away.

I had some qualms as I knew that Dickie Poole would not approve of what I had done but the staff sergeants were confident and provided our luck held and the trucks did not break down we should complete the job satisfactorily and I could no doubt ride out the storm. I certainly did have a slight fracas with the Colonel when I told him how his precious batteries had been charged and he bawled me out for a couple of minutes. Eventually he conceded that no harm had been done, fortunately for me, and we had better go ahead and deliver the batteries to Kilbirnie where they would be collected in due course.

I managed to get a pass from somewhere and went to Wemyss Bay, from where I got a ticket and embarked on the daily steamer that did a round trip from Greenoch to Rothesay, on the Isle of Bute, and around the Kyles of Bute before returning via Largs to its home port. It was a delightful trip but as yet nothing was happending on shore at Tighnabruaich and I left not much wiser about the purpose of our labours. Still it was all interesting.

About this time our two bulldozers arrived and also two transferees with experience in driving them. Sergeant Fogarty appeared to be the man to take charge of them and he was highly interested but whether I could quite trust him in this unfamiliar field seemed doubtful, so I warned Munday and his staff sergeants to keep an eye on the situation. Dickie Poole was very proud of these acquisitions to his command and there would clearly be trouble if anything went wrong. Sure enough something did. One broke down and negligence was suspected.

Accordingly, I was instructed to hold a Court of Inquiry. Dickie Poole lent me one of his two Field Engineers to be the other member of the court. As neither of us had any practical experience whatsoever of bulldozers we had to be supported by one of the staff sergeants as a theoretical "expert" though he had no practical experience of bulldozers either. It was all a matter of "the blind leading the blind" and we made a terrible job of it. What should have taken about five minutes took the best part of five hours as we all built up our knowledge of bulldozer maintenance.

It would have helped if there had been a proper handbook for the damned machine telling us where required lubricating and when. In the end, I think, we drew up some form of maintenance schedule and decided that while, theoretically, someone should have done so some while ago, we all felt in part responsible and managed, after about five pages of foolscap report on our Inquiry, to decide that no specific blame attached to anyone in particular but we should all do better in future. It seemed to satisfy Dickie Poole anyway — although his mind may have been on other things.

At the Braids Camp we were having regular church parades to the Church of Scotland at the Fairmilehead junction, a mile from camp and four miles from the centre of the city. It was a pleasant church with a pleasant minister although our parade services were normally taken by the regiment's own "padre", a member of the Corps of Chaplains, who was attached to Dickie Poole's headquarters. After giving us some stern moral address, or words of homely comfort, he would watch briefly while we re-assembled the troops outside the church before he strode off quickly himself to get back to barracks and seize the mess copy of the News of the World before the rest of the officers had returned from church to challenge his right of first perusal.

Church parade once in a while seemed to me to interest the men more as a change in the normal routine than as a needed and valued spiritual exercise, but regular church parades, I am sure, began to seem onerous and unnecessary for them. Accustomed, as I was, to regular church going I found it comparatively welcome, comparatively challenging and comparatively harmless but nine out of ten of the men were not used to it and basically did not like it. I dared to challenge Dickie Poole and the padre together on my view that regular, compulsory church parades fulfilled little Christian purpose and we had a heated argument for several hours in the mess one night. In the end, Dickie produced the unanswerable argument that, "as long as I am Colonel of this Regiment, there will be compulsory church parades and the men will like it or lump it".

Shortly after that, however, the Colonel ran into serious marital problems. He had been conducting an intimate courtship of a lady friend for some while past and suddenly his wife's case for divorce came through, almost at the same time as his "fiancee" was released from her obligations to her husband. They both fancied a splendid wedding in St. Giles Cathedral and the padre was instructed to make the arrangements. He demurred strongly and said that in no way could he see this being possible in view of the church's attitude towards divorced couples, particularly, to be frank, where they were both the offending parties. He was told to get on with it but returned fortified by the Bishop's opinion that, whatever might be possible in England, it was not so in Scotland.

Within a couple of days the colonel transferred his headquarters to the West of Scotland where at least two of the companies were working on the Tighnabruiach project. The unwilling padre was dragged along with him and sent off to consult the Bishop of Glasgow who, after some argument, gave the same ruling as his Edinburgh colleague. In due course the headquarters returned to base and the happy couple were united in a Registry Office and we never had another church parade compulsory or voluntary.

Suddenly Connie arrived in Scotland, on posting to Dalkeith where she had done her initial training on joining the army. She was to do a short — three weeks, I think — pre-OCTU training course before proceeding to the ATS OCTU in the centre of Edinburgh itself where she would do a three months course. At once she investigated the possibility of getting "sleeping out" passes and, as our relationship was strictly moral, legal and natural, these were readily granted and we had a succession of weekends at various hotels in the south of the city, including one appropriately named the Braids Hotel. We had a delightful time looking at the shops in Edinburgh, attending the theatre, especially one called The Kings which put on a patriotic Scottish show with rousing tunes, and she came to the mess for tea and coffee on a number of occasions. In return we entertained a number of my colleagues to dinner from time to time. One fine occasion was her 21st birthday when my colleagues from the 105th and from headquarters did her proud with a charming gift — I believe it was a Scottish rug.

Sex reared its head in other ways too. The Army Council decided that officers commanding units should be more sensitive to the domestic problems of their troops and should be mindful of their duty to advise them where necessary. Strong reference was made to the fact that many of these problems arose from their marital and non-domestic sexual relationships and that unit officers should be on the lookout for such troubles as the cause of other disciplinary problems. We were required to make ourselves available at "surgery-like" sessions at which our men could come and see us without appointments at set times. As a young married man just gaining real experience, I approached the possibility of such consultations with a mixture of interest and trepidation.

Before any of the company could consult me, however, there arose the case of Corporal "C", a handsome and apparently intelligent young NCO. One evening the sergeant major produced a civilian who wished to see me. The CSM said that he was accompanied by his wife but wished to talk to me first. The husband complained that Corporal "C" was making rather too free use of his marital bed. Asked how he knew this was so he said that he had found the Corporal's cigarette lighter in his bed with his initials on it. I then asked if these irregular relationships had taken place anywhere else other than his house and he said that his wife had told him that they were also conducted in the cinema. My mind boggled at the question of how this was achieved.

I asked then to see his wife, imagining some rather glamorous piece, but when she appeared she was a comfortable little body who looked sheepish, rather than defiant or smug. She corroborated her husband's statements frankly in a slightly embarrassed fashion with only a touch of remorse. It appeared that Corporal "C" was quite a performer and she was in two minds whether to settle for her relatively assured position in life or to seek the excitement of a continued relationship with my Corporal. I sent them home with my assurances that I would think of something to do to settle the matter one way or another.

Next I saw Corporal "C" and it was a guarded interview. He was totally brazen about it all and admitted the truth of his cuckold's complaints, but he seemed to have no regard for his lover's feelings and not to care much whether the affair continued or not. I longed to ask him how he achieved union in the cinema, was it on the floor, between the seats or in the aisle or were they double seats? But sense of propriety intervened. He seemed to me to be completely amoral — a man with whom no woman could be safe and I am sure he had a list of conquests a mile long. The best thing seemed to be to get him out of Edinburgh as soon as possible. I thought of Kilbirnie but decided to send him to Tighnabruaich where the competition for any likely lady would be too severe even for him. He departed next day. I saw the wronged couple again, read them a lecture on mutual forgiveness and hoped for the best.

Fortified by my success in the Corporal "C" case I approached my first consultation with some confidence. One of my sappers had recently married an ATS girl and now, less than two months after the wedding, they wished to divorce. Again the couple arrived to see me.

The girl was no oil painting, but shapely enough, and he was fairly plain. It was very difficult to get anything out of them except that they had decided it was all a mistake. After long and circuitous discussion I decided that there was something wrong with their sexual relationship. As far as I could judge he was completely inexpert and she was completely unprepared, but it was useless to think of my trying to counsel them out of my relative ignorance.

Nor, to the best of my knowledge, did anything like today's marriage guidance counsellors exist in Scotland. The only source of guidance and instruction in those days was the family doctor. I was not sure even that the army medical officer who visited us would be the man for the job. Furthermore, I was not sure that my diagnosis was right. In spite of their desire to have a divorce they seemed to have some regard for each other and all I could think of doing was to tell them to go away and think about it a bit more. They were by now hopelessly embarrassed and sorry they had ever come but I never heard from them again so I assume they sorted things out somehow.

Either the rest of my company were blissfully happy or word got around about my frank interviews and the rest took fright, but no one else visited my surgery.

Driver Donaldson was my only disciplinary case. He was one of the two despatch riders we had on our company strength. He was brought back to camp one night by the military police who had arrested him many miles from camp on some form of unauthorised expedition on his motorcycle. I consigned him to the guardroom and we started to prepare for a court martial but Driver Donaldson absconded from the guardroom, after knocking the sentry over, and disappeared.

Within a week he was back in Edinburgh again, this time in the care of the civilian police, charged with stealing a motorcycle and using it to make a long journey to the Glasgow area. The case came up in court with commendable speed and I was summoned to appear to give evidence of character. His record was far from clean as he had had a number of minor charges but they dated from before my time. I suppose I should have made a plea in mitigation of his offence to which he pleaded guilty. Sadly I was not as forgiving as I might have been. I quoted his record and said that I did not particularly want him back again. While true — he had no friends in the company and we were better without him — I should not have said so. I think he got a three month sentence and he returned to the company just before I left. I feel that was an unfinished problem I left behind me.

The principal item of training with which I was concerned personally was that of fitness. Physical training each morning before breakfast was on the programme whenever there was no strong reason against it and I led it myself. I was also a great believer in route marches, not that I ever really expected that the company would have to move on its own feet or carry its equipment on its own backs but just that walking at a steady pace is excellent exercise anyway and forced marching — 100 paces running and 100 paces marching — really put fitness to the test when kept going for several miles. I am quite sure the company did not love me but at least I did it all myself with them.

On one occasion when we passed near a long deserted stretch of beach I thought that some sea bathing might be the thing so, acting on the impulse, I ordered the company down onto the beach, to strip off and take to the water. Half the company were too shy or modest to remove all their clothing. Some took to the water in their underwear but some

102

appeared likely to refuse to do even that. However, with a bit of urging I got the lot into the water and gave them about quarter of an hour or so lying about in the pale sun to see if they could get their underwear dry enough to put on again. It did surprise me that grown men in their early twenties were so bashful but then no other opportunity came to find out whether they could overcome this with time.

My own training continued and at one time or another during my year with the company I was sent on three courses. One of these was to the Combined Operations Centre at Wemyss Bay. This was a very short course of about three or four days but it gave a general review and awareness of the special problems of a beach landing operation. Clearly 105th was not going to be leading an assault but, nevertheless, if 1st Corps was in the lead, then its Field Park Companies would have to handle all sorts of special equipment and stores.

Then I was sent on a Germany Army course run by the Intelligence Corps at Cambridge. We were quartered in a theological college where, coincidentally, the Principal was a Rev J.S. Whale who was an Old Caterhamian, having been at my old school just before the 1st World War. I had met him before and we enjoyed a pleasant evening together. The course covered an outline of the organisation of the German army and descriptions of its uniforms and equipment that we might either encounter in battle or its aftermath. The theory was that any unit may take prisoners or be first on the scene at some place where the enemy had retreated and left evidence of occupation behind.

Quite apart from documentary evidence as to the identity of the units concerned there might be such things as cap badges, regimental insignia, discarded uniform or many other things which carefully gathered and classified might be of great assistance to the Intelligence Corps.

The third course came fairly early in my time with the company; it was my Company Commander's course, for three weeks at Ripon. In peacetime the Royal Engineers' training centre is at Chatham but as most of my service in England was in the north of the country I had no opportunity to go there. Instead the Corps had built a second School of Military Engineering for Northern Command and Scotland at Ripon, largely for the training of officers but also for some NCOs. For example, all E & M staff sergeants and field works quartermaster sergeants instructors received long (three months) training courses at one or the other of the SMEs.

I had already been to Ripon once for a junior officer's bridging and field works course and the Company Commander's course covered much the same ground, but from a different viewpoint, and with quite a lot of other material added. The most important change, however, and the most time was spent on this, was the introduction of the Bailey

103

Bridge. This was now coming into full production and was beginning to be issued to units (such as the Bridging Companies RASC).

The atmosphere of the course was also different, being almost competitive, which reminds me of the standard army aphorism: –

Lieutenants are friends
Captains are colleagues
Majors are competitors
Colonels are adversaries
Generals are enemies.

Most of those on the course were newly appointed company commanders (majors) but a good proportion were presumably seen by their colonels as having potential for promotion and any report which came back afterwards would no doubt be carefully studied.

The Bailey Bridge was of course a matter of great interest and great keenness to make sure we each understood it intimately. Accordingly, we laboured earnestly at putting a variety of combinations together and stripping them down again. The bridge had enormous flexibility and is still widely used throughout this country and the world.

The standard panel measured $10'0'' \times 5'0''$ and with a single panel on either side of the bridge carrying and bolted to two transoms going from one side of the bridge to the other it might be said that one unit of the bridge had been built. Other units were added on at the back and a light bridge could be constructed with relative ease. Two other panels could be added on each side, outside the first, and to go even further three more panels could be added on top of the first three on each side. This built up the strength of the bridge progressively. On the other hand the longer the gap to be spanned the weaker the bridge for any particular combination of panels. Thus, with single panels each side a $40'0''$ long bridge might have strength enough to carry light loads up to, say, 5 tons but a double triple bridge with six panels each side in each unit would probably be able to carry 40 tons or more over the same span.

The Bailey Bridge was also extremely easy to build and use in combination with pontoons and the standard British army pontoon could be closely enough spaced below a Bailey again to carry 40 tons or more at reasonable intervals. The standard equipment packed readily enough into ordinary 3 ton or 5 ton trucks but pontoons needed either the special trailers or a crane to handle them. By this time Field Park Companies were mostly equipped with excellent mobile cranes of which the best known was made by a firm named Coles.

All this we learned on the course and much much more. We took back to our companies with us enough duplicated paper with extra information to fill a couple of large files. It was an excellent course manned by first class instructors and thoroughly enjoyable as well, especially some of the evening expeditions to Harrogate, which was only five miles down the road.

Officer supply remained a problem for the army and the Army Council laid down that every commanding officer of regiments or officer commanding an independent company had, every month, to nominate one per cent of the strength of his unit to go to a WOSBee to be put through the officer selection process. However, it was obviously useless to send someone who was determined not to be an officer and the men who should have been sent, namely our sergeants, were the most reluctant. As one of them pointed out to me, all he would be doing was taking on much more responsibility for little or no more pay and exchanging the comfortable and familiar atmosphere of the sergeants mess for the more competitive atmosphere of the officers mess with exactly the same rations.

It was true enough, particularly if a man was prepared to look no further than his first appointment. A 2nd Lieutenant's pay was 11 shillings a day plus RE Corps pay of 2 shillings a day. A sergeant who was a class B tradesman in the RE got almost exactly the same pay. I considered this a short sighted view and indeed an unpatriotic one. I would have recommended half my sergeants without hesitation, plus the CSM, the CQMS and the two staff sergeants but not one of them was anxious to go though I think two of them eventually did.

In my time with the company I only supplied half the number required for and practically all of them eventually got commissions. Perhaps if I had had more experience outside the army I would have been in a better position to advise and convince some of these excellent men that it would have been in their own long term interests to take the chance. Maybe more of them did before the end of the war.

One other interesting development on much the same lines was that, towards the middle of 1943, an Army Council Instruction came through inviting temporary officers, as practically all of us were, other than the few regulars around, to apply to be put on a list for consideration for regular commissions in the peacetime army after the war. It needed careful consideration in my own case. I was now 24 but I had never held a civilian job — other than my work experience in University vacations. In the army I had flourished, becoming a major nearly two years previously when I was barely 23. Admittedly, I could expect to have to drop back from major to captain when the army reduced to its peacetime size, unless I had in the meantime reached lieutenant colonel, in which case I could expect to start a peacetime career as a major which would be comfortable enough and offer me a fair certainty of advancement in time to at least full colonel or brigadier. My army career had been a good one to date and I might reasonably hope for twenty to thirty years of further advancement after the war. In summary, the regular army offered me the chance of a good, assured and interesting career in a field where I had already done well.

On the other hand, I was still interested in being a mining engineer in the international field. Nothing the army in peacetime was likely to offer would be anywhere near as challenging and dynamic. Furthermore, in the army, I would be working and training for something I had little or no expectation of seeing happen. Namely, another major war. It might all seem rather pointless. I visualised that, unless I reached the very highest levels — which could not be relied on — I would have little to do with policy and time might hang heavy on my hands.

I decided that I would take my chance in the civilian field and I did not reply to the invitation to apply. One of my Field Company colleagues, and I think it was Major Hughes, did apply and got a peacetime commission. I met him ten years afterwards at Long Marston, the leading engineer depot, and found that he was still a major at that stage. He seemed neither happy nor fulfilled and he certainly seemed to have an excess of time on his hands, while I was just beginning to rise significantly in my career on the mines in South Africa and had plenty of challenges to cope with.

The weekend sleeping-out passes at the Braids Hotel brought the inevitable result. Connie became pregnant. She was delighted although I had very slight reservations as I had hoped to see her commissioned but there were compensations for me and certainly for her. The rules were, however, that as soon as pregnancy was confirmed she was discharged, reasonably enough, so after a couple of small farewell parties she left Edinburgh and went back to stay with her parents in Chester-le-Street.

My training exercises for the company were getting more ambitious. We marched long distances and ventured to the south of Edinburgh as well as to the east, penetrating on a couple of occasions up into the Pentland Hills, which were delightful country and offered some fairly strenuous cross-country forays. This was real fishing and shooting country and we should have perhaps cleared our way with the land owners first. Their gamekeepers (or gillies?) were concerned about what we might do to the birds but on the whole they were relatively easily re-assured.

We also tried one or two night marches around the two golf courses which lay to the north of our camp. I scraped together a dozen or so compasses and sent the men out in small squads on relatively short courses. Unfortunately, just about all of them got lost and those that did do the round trip seemed to take all the time in the world about it. As

106

initiative training it was hardly successful. Worse still, my second-in-command, Captain Paul MacCormack, getting tired of following their slow progress, decided to complete the course on his own. The moon had gone and it was now dark. He sat down on the edge of what he thought was a small depression and threw a stone over to test its depth. It sounded to him to be shallow enough so he decided to jump off. It turned out to be twenty to thirty feet or more and he dislocated his shoulder. He was confined to hospital for two or three weeks. Fortunately none of the men did the same.

Of all my experiences with the 105th Company I suppose that the most striking and perhaps the most salutory was the great morale report. Looking through my incoming mail one morning I saw one letter from Scottish Command Headquarters reminding me that my "morale report" would shortly be due for completion. This was a completely new thing to me and I had never seen anything about it before so I summoned the sergeant major to explain. He expressed surprise that I had never heard of it and said that it was due every six months or so and he would get me the file. This he did and I was astounded at the questions which I was expected to answer. I realised that I did not know how the men thought that the high command of the British army compared with the high command of the German army or how they thought their weapons, equipment, rations and clothing compared with those of their opposite numbers. I did not know either what they thought about our training programme, other than that I was sure that they would rather lie on their beds with their feet up than go for route marches. Indeed, I realised for the first time the tremendous gap in thought between the man in the ranks and his commanding officer.

I had been conscious though of the gap between a commanding officer, such as myself, and his second-in-command and lieutenants. I already suspected that one could not expect to get any honest advice, even from thinking men, in a military situation, as they had all largely become accustomed to the dictum that: –

"Theirs not to reason why, theirs but to do and die."

Accordingly, an invitation to one's second-in-command or even the sergeant major to discuss a suggestion was more like a game in which the junior tried to guess what the senior was thinking or which alternative he actually preferred before being committed irrevocably to the wrong answer. I did not, in fact, believe that I would get any sound assessment of the mens' views by asking my junior officers or the NCOs. They would watch me to see what I thought before they expressed any opinion and I was not prepared to play that game.

Opinion polls were things which had just entered the national consciousness and it seemed to me that the right way to get the right answers to what seemed to be fair questions was to hold my own "opinion poll" of a representative fraction of the company. I told the sergeant major to select for me fifteen of the sappers and drivers, including the company communist! I also asked him to nominate one lance-corporal, one corporal, one lance-sergeant and one sergeant and to add himself to the list. I nominated Lieutenant Munday to take part as well. This party were to assemble in the NAAFI before opening time, after church parade on Sunday. Meanwhile, I had prepared a list of questions which could only be answered by "yes" or "no" but which covered the field of enquiry on which I had to reply.

On the set morning the men assembled, clearly viewing the matter with some trepidation but, in due course, with considerable interest. They took their slips of paper and applied themselves earnestly to thinking about the fifty questions. When we had finished, the company communist demanded to know what they had said. I saw no harm in trying to answer so I scanned through the twenty one papers and discovered remarkable unanimity; there had clearly been no copying or consultation. I briefly summarised their views and they went away satisfied. Now came the difficult part, to convert my summary into a formal report to the colonel. This I did and sent it down to his office.

Almost within five minutes he was on the telephone. "Mortimer, what's this has just come down to me?".

"My morale report, Sir."

"I know that man, come down here at once," he replied.

I grabbed my hat, pulled my uniform together, and stepped down the fifty yards or so as quickly as possible. I knocked and entered his office and saluted smartly. He was still reading the report.

"What's this then," he growled.

"My morale report, Sir. Is there anything wrong?"

"Yes there is. Where did you get all this stuff from. Look at this bit: —

'The men respect but don't like their officers
They like but don't respect their NCOs.' "

I remembered it well. My recollection was that 19 had said "yes" to the first proposition and two said "no" and to the second there were about fifteen "yes" and six "no". Furthermore that was almost exactly what I would have prophesied. I certainly did not intend to convey the idea that the men disliked their officers, they just did not feel close enough to them to like them. They almost saw them as remote and they did not know them personally or intimately. It might have been enough

108

to have said something a little more expansive, such as; "The men respected and had confidence in their officers but did not know them personally well enough to have any closer feeling such as liking." and with regard to the NCOs I might have said "The men liked their NCOs well enough and had no complaints but they did not feel that the NCOs were so much cleverer than themselves, or even more experienced. They were prepared to tolerate them and were not particularly frightened of them." In a sense they saw the NCOs as keeping the show ticking over but they saw all initiative as coming from the officers.

I replied cautiously, "Yes Sir, that's what the men think".

"Of course it isn't. How do you know what they think?"

"I asked them, Sir." and I explained the "Opinion Poll" procedure I had followed.

The Colonel was getting red in the face at all this heresy. "You are not supposed to ask them what they think," he roared, "You are supposed to write down what you think they think." He banged the table in finality.

I tried for the last word. "Sir, I didn't think that it was my morale which was at stake, my report is what my men actually do think themselves and I believe that is a true picture. I would have written the same but with less confidence if I had not asked them."

"Get out!" he said.

I did see his report later. It did not look anything like mine.

At the end of August, 1942 Rommell had made a last attempt, to get through the Alamein lines, which was defeated. Montgomery continued steadily to build up an overwhelming number of guns and tanks and the battle of Alamain began on 23rd October. By 4th November the battle was over and Rommell began his retreat, against Hitler's orders, and on 7th November Anglo-American forces landed at Algiers and other points in French North Africa. What was left of the French fleet at Toulon scuttled itself to escape being taken over by the Germans, who had entered Vichy France.

It took six months and the assistance of Montgomery's Eighth Army to overwhelm the resistance of the French, Italians and Germans still remaining in North Africa and on 12th May the final groups surrendered, making a total of some 80,000 Germans and 170,000 others taken prisoner.

The Allies were embarrassed by political intrigues over French leadership but these were concluded — not entirely satisfactorily — when Admiral Darlan was assassinated by a French royalist and de Gaulle established his ascendency over General Giraud.

War policy was finally clarified when Roosevelt defined it as "unconditional surrender" by all three Axis partners — Germany, Italy and Japan. This would give the victors a free hand and the partners would lose all their conquests and colonies and all would be fully disarmed.

It was clear that no massive invasion of France would be possible while supplies were still being sent to North Africa in large quantities. There was much argument between Churchill, who represented the British wish to avoid the huge casualties they expected from an invasion of north west France (and thus preferred alternative routes to victory, particularly by way of Italy), and General Marshall, representing the American viewpoint, which preferred a head on clash with the Germans as soon as possible. Nevertheless, as a compromise, the Americans agreed to make plans to invade Italy provided Churchill agreed to an invasion of northern France on 1st May, 1944.

Sinkings by "U" boats reduced to a quarter of earlier levels and destruction of "U" boats tripled between March and July, 1943. Germany's only battleship, the Tirpitz, was put out of action in September and its only battlecruiser was sunk in December. The war at sea had changed decisively and British imports increased greatly. Indeed, many of Britain's politicians were turning their thoughts already to the world after the war and a Minister of Reconstruction and a Ministry of Town and Country Planning were created.

In the absence of any other clear and practicable method of operation the British and American bomber commands went ahead with indiscriminate destruction throughout 1943 and this was huge. Nevertheless, it did not do much to slow down German munitions production, which doubled in the two years, 1942 and 1943.

In July, 1943 allied forces landed in Sicily and on 7th September the Italians signed an armistice. The Americans agreed to land in Italy but they insisted that the "Overlord" plan for north west Europe be given priority. The plan, prepared by General F.E. Morgan (under whom I had served in 1st Corps) was approved and orders given that it should go forward. My part in "Overlord" was the next stage in my career.

After the abandonment of the North African invasion, to which I referred in the previous chapter, no proposals emerged during my year with the 105th Corps Field Park Company which involved any likelihood of embarkation for me. Even so, there were many rumours and it was by no means absolutely certain to us that we were positively destined for the Second Front in north west Europe. While I would like to suggest that, somewhere in the process, I lost yet one more chance of embarkation and, indeed, thought so at the time, I now feel that there was no such chance coming until we finally took off for "Overlord" and Normandy.

CHAPTER 9
Headquarters "X" Force
(December, 1943 – February, 1944)

Sometime in the late autumn of 1943, I was summoned to attend at a headquarters somewhere near Kilbirnie, in the south west of Scotland, for interview by a Brigadier John Stone. My colonel, Dickie Poole, was not particularly helpful with further information except that Stone was an engineer — like ourselves — and that he might be looking for someone to fill a staff job. That had me worried because I had no particular wish to return to the staff — I had done a staff job for a year and prospered with it but, not only was I finding my appointment as officer commanding a Corps Field Park Company still gratifying and fulfilling, but I knew well that my personal (and personality) development ought to benefit by a more prolonged period of exposure to company command type responsibilities involving "man management" and, particularly, the building up of sound personal relationships at all levels where I knew I could do better and would eventually need to do so in civilian life.

So, without any high hopes, I travelled to Kilbirnie across the width of Scotland, found the headquarters and was duly ushered into a large and comfortable office, but which was clearly only a temporary home for its current occupant. The officer who began to rise from behind the large desk, while I saluted as smartly as I could, was broad, burly and increasingly tall but, more strikingly, he was white haired and possessed impressively bushy eyebrows. He also displayed, if I remember rightly, the ribbons of the CB (Commander of the Order of the Bath), the MC (Military Cross) and the Africa Star. Clearly a man of status and great ability. Not only that, but he shook hands across the desk warmly and with a very friendly sparkle in his eyes. As we sat down, I noticed that he had a gammy leg — presumbly from a war wound. I have to say that this initial excellent impression only increased day by day of our long association and friendship — but we still had to talk!

He started with a few routine questions to which I could see he already had most of the answers on papers in front of him — Degree (BSc Mining Engineering — First Class), Rank (major for the past 18 months), Age (25 years and one month), Military experience (not very impressive really and certainly no active service, though I had nearly made it to France, Malta, Gibraltar, India and North Africa — I had done a year in the ranks — in the RA, the RAOC and, of course, the RE

OCTU. Then there had been about nine months with the Tunnellers, five months with 2nd Division, thirteen months with 1st Corps HQ and twelve months with the Corps Field Park Company).

After all few troops then in the UK had yet served abroad. I realised gloomily that my story was beginning to add up to rather too good a recommendation for my purposes. The next question was likely to be the clincher one way or the other.

"Now, Mortimer, what do you say then to the possibility of coming back to the Staff again? Brigadier Godfrey has recommended you." The last part was both flattering and a surprise. I had not imagined that we had parted on such a basis of respect. Indeed I had thought he had been as glad to get rid of me, as an awkward and obstinate cuss and a non-Regular soldier to boot, as I had been delighted to get a regimental command. Clearly, I had misjudged this kindly and percipient gentleman. Belatedly I warmed towards him. Nevertheless, I replied that I would rather not rejoin the Staff saying, big-headedly, that I knew all about staff work, that I had not the slightest difficulty about coping with any of it and that it had no new lessons left for me to learn. On the other hand, I pointed out, I still had a number of fields to conquer on the regimental side and I expanded eloquently on the thoughts that had been in my mind as I travelled to Kilbirnie. Unfortunately, even to me it sounded rather thin and, indeed, self-centred. The war was still far from won and might still have years to run. Considerations of my post-war career were irrelevant.

The Brigadier had listened carefully to all I had said, even sympathetically, but with a sparkle in his eyes that could have been amusement. He concluded the meeting by saying, "Well, Mortimer, all that is as it may be, but in war we may well find that we are required to do what we do best, rather than what we may feel is best for us, even for our own broader development!"

The interview was at an end. I returned to Edinburgh feeling that the chances might still be even that I would remain with the 105th Company — but certainly no better than that.

For a while nothing happened — except normal company duties, of course — and I began to hope again. Perhaps he had found another stronger candidate, or had dozens more still to interview. But the bubble burst when, a week before Christmas, Dickie Poole recieved orders from the War Office to the effect that:

> "Major G J Mortimer RE will hand over command of 105th Corps Field Park Company RE forthwith and proceed immediately to Castle Barracks, Oxford, on appointment as an SORE2 with HQ "X"Force."

The acronym stood for "Staff Officer Royal Engineers Grade 2" or major, so I was back on the staff with no change of rank. Cold comfort indeed! But neither my colonel nor I could hazard a guess about "X" Force. I would have to get to Oxford to find out.

Handing over to my Second-in-Command took relatively few minutes. He might reasonably expect to get promotion in my place and could be excused for appearing relatively cheerful. Sadly, he did not get it, as the War Office, in due course, sent up the man it turned out that I was superseding and who, seemingly, had not measured up to the standards our Chief Engineer (Stone) was looking for. There was no time to bid any formal (perhaps inspiring!) farewell to the company as a whole. (Perhaps just as well too!) I shook whatever hands were readily available — mostly officers and sergeants and mess and office staff, who all seemed to think my new appointment a matter for congratulations — even if I did not.

Dickie Poole kindly allowed me to make my exit in style in my large and comfortable Humber command car, which certainly saved me a tedious rail journey. Or he may have thought that the "forthwith" and "immediately" in the orders required him to despatch me by the most direct and expeditious means possible. I never argued with military orders that suited me.

Castle Barracks, Oxford, did not look particularly inviting on a damp late afternoon at the end of December. It also looked to be virtually deserted until I eventually found the orderly room where a lance-sergeant and a couple of clerks were putting on a modest show of busyness. The latter examined my orders slip and identity card with great care, comparing them with documents in front of him until —, presumably satisfied that I was indeed the Major Mortimer I had claimed to be and that I did have a right to move into Castle Barracks — he opened up a little, suggesting that many other officers had yet to report, that the "troops" were mostly off duty and down in the town, that dinner in the officers' mess was probably at about 1930 hours and that "things" in the whole headquarters were not really due to begin until Monday, even though some of the seniors had "of course" been around rather longer. I got the message. The rest of the evening was going to be a dead bore and dinner rather worse, that I had reported at least two days earlier than I need have done, and that even "things" on Monday could be a bit of a shambles.

The sergeant then said that he would hand me over to the RSM (Regimental Sergeant Major) who would know about my accommodation, messing arrangements and so on.

This distinguished functionary, when he eventually arrived from some distant hideout, immediately revealed by his attitude that he had worked out that SOsRE2 and others of equivalent rank (all majors in fact) were going to be ten-a-penny on HQ "X" Force, were all going to need to seek his favours for batmen, cars, accommodation, etc., and could be treated accordingly. He larded every sentence with at least one "Sah" but did so with a faint and almost indiscernable insolence that left me in no doubt which of the two of us he regarded as more indispensible to the organisation.

However, as we walked along he did reveal various helpful bits of information which began to fill in my picture of the organisation I had joined. Firstly, it was large, possibly close to a thousand. Secondly, although currently occupying this single sprawling camp, it was divided into two parts: Main HQ (clearly much the superior half in the RSM's view) which would deal with "operations" in the field, and thus needed to be in close contact with the "G" (General) section of the Staff, and the "much inferior" Rear HQ which would deal with matters of supply (petrol, ammunition, rations, spares) and behind-the-front services such as prisoners, reinforcements, road repairs and routemarking, transport, equipment recovery and repairs, medical services and all the many other such matters which were the general province of the "A" and "Q" (Adjutant General's and Quartermaster General's) sections of the Staff. While the two halves were now in one camp, they could be expected to be a few miles apart in the field — which seemed to have the RSM's wholehearted approval.

With this and other matters we had now reached what appeared to be the officers' quarters. The RSM instructed my driver, who had been slowly following us in my car, to unload my gear. I thought it a hell of a liberty — after all, I might decide I wanted to view some alternative apartment! — but weakly chose to acquiesce and followed the RSM into what looked like a First War wooden hut. It was divided into an number of good sized rooms and the one into which he led me was clean, apparently weather-proof and furnished in Spartan style, with two made-up beds (no sheets), two plain wooden chairs and one folding barrack-room table. I protested at the lack of any facilities for hanging up clothes and was assured that a man would knock a few nails into the wall the very next day (which did happen).

I also claimed that I had not shared a room since I became a captain and trusted I would not have to do so now. The RSM assured me that he would do his utmost to preserve my dignity and privacy (and filled the vacant bed two days later). He did, however, produce a tolerable batman, who added a degree of personal cheerfulness, a further table and some better chairs. He spread my personal belongings around in a way that somehow created a slight air of homeliness as the long, dull weekend progressed and I gradually overcame an overpowering sense of

114

home sickness which had commenced when my car and driver disappeared after unloading and the last link with the Braids Camp and Edinburgh was broken.

The Mess, to which the RSM also conducted me, was, if anything, even more depressing than my personal quarters. It was large and deserted and was, I gathered, intended to serve the "middle rank" officers, namely the captains and majors on the headquarters (I later discovered that there were very few lieutenants on the establishment anyway). One end was designated as the Dining Room and was fully equipped with folding barrack tables and forms which could all do with a good scrub. The other end was presumably the Ante-Room and seemed to have been supplied with its quota of sofas, easy chairs and occasional tables entirely from the rejects of long past Oxford jumble sales. The bar was a large and very securely padlocked hatch in the wall, which seemingly did not open on Fridays.

I ate a lonely dinner, the one waiter assuring me that all my colleagues were no doubt dining out in Oxford and explaining that the incredibly poor standard of the meal was no doubt due to the probable fact that the kitchen staff were all now drinking out in Oxford too.

My room mate arrived on, I think, the Sunday and turned out to be another RE major, Ted Hutton, an airfields construction expert. At first we viewed one another with some hostility, both, I judge, having been assured of sole occupancy. Thereafter we shared rooms, tents, billets, offices and a batman happily for practically the whole campaign and have remained friends ever since.

On Monday morning just about all the Main HQ RE staff assembled in the Engineer Office — another large First War wooden hut with two small private offices at one end for the two senior officers. Brigadier John Stone, to whom I have already referred, was there as Chief Engineer and his right-hand man was Lt. Col. Otto Phibbs, the SORE1 (Operations).

Otto was a tall, handsome "regular" — he had also passed his "jsc" (Junior Staff College — a short wartime course for promising middle grade officers — mostly regulars who could be considered for senior "G", "A" or "Q" staff appointments). He looked energetic and intelligent, every girl's ideal of a soldier, yet I could never quite weigh him up. Naturally, I was never present at any private discussions he had with the Brigadier, when he may have been a ball of fire and contributed magnificently. Nor did I attend any specifically "Ops" section conferences where he may have shone in the chair, but I do not recall that they ever held any without calling in one or all of the rest of us. In over a year of working together I cannot remember Otto ever saying anything really constructive or original but he was a good chap and I was

115

very happy to serve with him but I feel that he would have been far better suited as a regimental officer and that his staff post with us was redundant.

The SORE2 (Ops) was Bob Moodie, a middle-aged territorial — red-faced and rather over-weight but sound and hard working. His SORE3 (Ops) was Captain Colin Williams, a bright young historian who had interrupted a Cambridge course to join-up.

The SORE2 (Intelligence) was Allport-Williams: I think he had been recruited direct from the staff of Liverpool University, where I believe his speciality was architecture. He always seemed terribly harrassed, which was hard to understand because all the information he ever supplied to us, his colleagues, was all derived from a number of large tomes provided for him and kept up to date by some central intelligence agency in Oxford or Cambridge and which really did include massive detail about, for example, every conceivable river we might wish to bridge — widths, depth profiles, bank conditions and profiles, approach roads, water speeds, and so on. To be fair, I suppose such original work as was needed to design a future air strip from original air photos may have come his way from time to time. This would have been a rather hard task but I don't suppose there was even much of that which had not already been done by the central agency.

There were also two SOsRE 3 (Intelligence) who were captains. One, I remember, was a Captain Matthews and he stayed with us right to the German surrender. The other was a bright boy from the Inland Revenue Surtax Department who had many interesting stories to tell about financial high jinks and was clearly right for intelligence work.

I have already mentioned Ted Hutton, who was our SORE2 (Airfields) Ted was, in fact, already a high flyer in the Civil Service in the road construction section of the Department of Transport. He played a lone hand with his department, keeping the Chief in touch, of course, and dealing with me when his stocks of material needed replenishing, but his main contacts were the RAF and the three or four Airfield Construction Groups of about 1000 men each who worked for him. At a later stage we recruited a colleague for him in Jan Roberts who was very much an expert on large scale earth moving and whose title was SORE2 (Mechanical Equipment). The Army, after all, was just beginning to move out of the pick and shovel era and few officers had much idea how to use and look after bulldozers. That still included me.

The Chief Engineer also had a junior officer, Chris Baker, an SORE3 (Personnel), to coordinate the many promotions, demotions, transfers and decorations he had to recommend, endorse or reject.

That left only the Stores section, of which I was the SORE2, the man in charge, with the duties of endeavouring to forecast what engineer stores, big and small, the forward troops might require in the near future and getting them up to forward dumps so that they could be drawn on at will and short notice. Then I would have to stand ready to secure from somewhere, at even shorter notice, all the major demands the forward formations might devise when battle was imminent. This would normally be for bridging equipment, road materials and airfield planking. All these items would come up from base depots by rail or road to a principal forward depot or even, by convoy, direct through to the forward areas. However, there were frequently "specials" which had to be manufactured individually in forward workshops. A very varied job!

I had an SORE3 (Stores) but found we did not suit and I succeeded in changing him for a better man before we finally went overseas. The twelve of us remained close colleagues for most of the coming campaigns, as I shall describe. Looking round that morning, I felt happy about the prospects. The Braids and Edinburgh began to fade.

In addition there were a dozen or so RE clerks on our establishment. Most of them could type and set out documents pretty well, some even did shorthand. My section had two. Sergeant Swift was unflappable and a veritable tower of strength throughout the campaign. His first junior I do not recall, as I soon managed to replace him by Corporal Henshall, purloined from my old company because I knew his worth. He was not as bright or quick as Swift, but he was steady, accurate and reliable.

Then there were the Brigadier's and Otto Phibbs' drivers and three others for the office caravans. These were all from the RASC. At that stage the rest of us all relied on the RSM's car pool and counted ourselves very lucky whenever we could get a car for a day. Finally there were the batmen — officer's servants or orderlies — and as most of them looked after two officers there must have been about six of them. Thus we comprised a total team of about thirty five. Clearly, one knew well the two or three "other ranks" one worked with directly but the rest, I fear, have largely faded from memory — even when I look at the group photograph of us all, taken at the end of the campaign.

The Chief Engineer referred briefly to the role of "X" Force and its possible future. He had to be brief because all he could really say was that, in due course, we would undoubtedly be known by some other name, when an undisclosed number of troops and formations would be allotted to us and we would be given a role to invade some undisclosed part of the world. We were left to speculate where that might be. Stalin was pressing for a second front against the Germans, to reduce the pressure on the Russian front itself. That seemed the best bet but where would we aim? On the Mediterranean side, the Balkans, Italy and Spain were all possibilities but they all had snags and Montgomery was already trying to do something in the area of Sicily and Southern Italy. On the northern side of Europe, the terrible failure of the Dieppe raid seemed to be an effective warning against trying for a short sea crossing while invading Holland, north Germany and Denmark seemed to involve taking on the German Navy where, small as it was, it would have maximum advantage and possibilities. Then there was always the Far Eastern front — not just Burma and Indonesia, but perhaps the Japanese mainland itself — but that would be a colossal gamble. Altogether, the choice seemed endless, the terrain highly variable, the size of the likely force also a wide question. Whether we would be working with Allies or not was problematical too.

The Chief must already have given this talk before to some of the earlier arrivals. He said that, in spite of all the vagueness, our present job was to think about and make whatever plans we could as to the affairs of our respective departments. These would have to cover a variety of what we might consider to be the more likely of the possible scenarios for an "X" Force assignment, chosen for example from those I have mentioned above.

As the meeting broke up and we moved towards our respective desks, Colonel Phibbs beckoned me into his office and said that he had a confidential document which might be of some help to me. He unlocked and relocked a variety of filing cabinets, most of which seemed fairly empty, and eventually found an envelope from which he extracted a dog-eared and rather faded and folded piece of paper. This he handed to me with firm instructions to preserve it from all harm and enemies, as it was the only copy available in "X" Force HQ. Furthermore it was for my eyes only!

I took this document to the desk allotted to me and prepared to study it carefully. It was an extract from a paper given a few years before by a Major-General Inglis to some fairly powerful inter-service committee. General Inglis, I already knew, was now Chief Engineer of what I imagined was our next senior headquarters and he was therefore John Stone's immediate professional superior. It was very brief and contained little more than a simple statement that between June 1917 and June 1918 the British armies on the Western Front, numbering some 3,000,000 men in all, consumed some 1,000,000 tons of engineer stores.

At first glance this information, while of general interest, was unlikely to be of immediate relevance in the circumstances of 1944. After all, in 1917/18 the vast bulk of the expendable material was likely to be trench "furniture" — duckboards, "A" frames, revetting material, dugout timbering and the like plus incredible quantities of barbed wire and stakes for securing it. How could I possibly assume that we would need per 1,000 men the same tonnage, for example, of pierced steel planking

118

(for fighter field runways and standings) as our predecessors had needed for the trench "furniture" we were most unlikely to be using. I locked it away as commanded and, although I assured myself I would find some future opportunity to take it out and ruminate upon it, I felt sure it really did have nothing to say to our war.

Strikingly enough, however, it did come up again when the various departments had to bid for tonnage space on the ships to convey everything we needed — rations, ammunition, engineer stores, ordnance spares and the like — to our ultimate destination. Inglis' figures then gave a strange validity to the estimates I had made by other means and added to my confidence in arguing for them. Incidentally, I would not attribute to General Inglis any of the actual figures I have quoted above. After this length of time they are in no way the product of memory but rather of some dim broad picture which still remains in my mind — and a lot of imagination — but the general context is correct.

However, I had filched from the 105th Company's library a copy of the newly issued catalogue of all engineer stores obtainable from central depots. Not only did it list every item but it also listed the weight of each and in addition the weight of any standard pack in which they might be supplied. A most useful book and almost my bible from now on but it took us a long while to obtain copies from any other source for the use of "X" Force HQ. I decided, in fact, that a practical approach to the conundrum set us by the Chief was, in effect, to devise a standard theoretical 1,000 ton pack of stores for all purposes. Each pack might, for example, include ten paint brushes, 100 gallons of assorted paints, ten claw hammers and half a ton of assorted nails, 100 infantry shovels and 40 picks, 500 standard rolls of barbed wire, a 120 feet Bailey Bridge with 10 pontoons, 100 barrells of road bitumen and 10,000 square feet of pierced steel planking for aircraft standings, together with a few odd machines not included in unit equipment (for example, road rollers, tar sprayers and so on) and a host of other minor items. Such a pack might theoretically provide for a brigade group of 6,000 men for six months. Clearly a simple multiplier could adjust for a different size of force or a different period of time and a simple assessment of the actual terrain or of the enemy to be encountered might lead to some switching or augmentaton or reduction of the major items: some increase in bridging and some decrease in defensive stores, for example.

I think I discussed this approach with my juniors in the hope that they might develop it further. For myself a problem of much greater importance and urgency intervened when the Chief Engineer passed me a memorandum he had received from the Army Chaplains' department to the effect that: –

The Chaplain General (War Office chief of the whole department, world-wide) has recently returned from a visit to North Africa, during which he observed with grief and concern the very poor standard of marking and naming of the graves of British soldiers, when buried where they fell. The majority of such graves he saw were marked by flimsy crosses, hastily knocked up out of pieces of ration boxes, which were clearly far too weak to resist even the wind. They were equally unsuitable to bear any proper record of the man's name, number and regiment. Even less satisfactory devices were also frequently seen. In contrast, enemy graves were marked in a dignified, more lasting fashion. In particular, German graves all appeared to bear very solid wooden crosses of a uniform design and general specification.

Deputy Chaplains General have therefore been instructed to discuss this matter with their respective Chief Engineers to see whether some more satisfactory system of supply can be arrived at.

Can you help, please?

        Sgd ---------
        Major CF
        Deputy Assistant Chaplain General (DACG)

Across the top the Chief Engineer had red-inked: –

Mortimer — Yours I think! J.S.

Knowing what I know now, I should merely have asked six or seven of our RE workshop companies to produce a couple of samples each within the next twenty four hours and then lined up a dozen or so assorted padres and invited them to nominate the three best crosses in each of their opinions. A simple count would then have indicated the three best in order of merit, subject only to my own right to eliminate one or more for essentially practical reasons like over-elaboration of the method of manufacture or too much use of non-standard timber sizes.

I would even have been prepared to nominate 50,000 as the right size for an initial order and to put it out for ordinary commercial competitive tender even though I well knew that many of our own RE workshops could do with a good scale exercise in mass production of anything, however simple. However, I had already had one telling off for too deep an essay into market research and democratic choice, so I decided to play this one the strict Staff way.

Accordingly I responded smartly to the Chaplains:

DACG   Crosses, grave
re yours of yesterday's date to CE

The Chief Engineer accepts that it does seem the best arrangement for this department to take on responsibility for the manufacture and supply of crosses for temporary graves but would be grateful for any advice as to the design that you feel able to give.

Sgd. G J Mortimer Major RE , SORE 2 (Stores) for Chief Engineer

A reply arrived even more promptly:

SORE2 (Stores) Crosses, grave — yours of today's date

Thank you for your letter. I am sure my department will have the greatest confidence in your arrangements for the manufacture and supply of the crosses but I hesitate to advise on design in the absence of the Deputy Chaplain General who is at present on tour in the north. He expects to return within three weeks and I will make sure that he sees your correspondence as soon as he arrives.
Sgd. -------------- Major CF DACG
for Deputy Chaplain General

There seemed little more progress to be made in this direction for the present, but it did seem worth trying to get an answer on the numbers side. After all, I might be able to make a start with organising the supply of the material needed, even if I could manage little more yet than making an application for a licence for the appropriate number of standards of soft wood required. One standard was 165 cubic feet and the precise dimensions of individual pieces would not need to be specified at this stage.

Accordingly, I wrote to the DAAQMG (Deputy assistant adjutant and quartermaster general — who I believed to be of the same rank as myself) supplying him with copies of the correspondence to date and asking him give me some sort of lead as to the proportion of killed in action or died of wounds or accidents or sickness we might expect in a reasonably large campaign. I assumed — but tactfully not in writing —

that his department had access to the records of innumerable actions from the Battle of Hastings onwards. My big mistake was to send him the earlier correspondence. No doubt he noticed that no reply would come from the Deputy Chaplain General for at least three weeks and assumed similar licence for himself. In due course, after more than four weeks, the latter eventually replied with thanks for my letter and apologies for his own long and unavoidable absence. He added:

> However, I do have to say that the responsibility for the design of crosses (and Stars of David) for marking the temporary graves of soldiers buried where they fell or elsewhere, and for the design of headstones for permanent resting places, is entirely that of the Directorate of Graves Registration. A new senior officer for this department has now been selected for appointment to this HQ and may be expected to arrive in this country shortly from North Africa where he will have gained much experience. I am sure he will have his own views and feel that the whole matter should now await his arrival.

> Sgd. ----------------- Colonel Deputy Chaplain General

In view of what the Chaplain General himself (and others) appeared to have had to say about grave markings in North Africa, I felt no confidence in his Deputy's recommendation, little willingness to wait any longer and a strong temptation to produce my own design. First, however, I felt I should apply some personal pressure to the DAAQMG so, on the telephone, I suggested that, if his other methods of estimation appeared to be failing him, perhaps he could try a pin. My attempted sarcasm passed straight over his head and he replied blandly that I had indeed set his department a difficult problem which had had their constant attention and was even now involving a couple of his seniors in fierce debate. Nevertheless, he promised me the definitive answer within the next couple of days. I did not believe a word of it but could do nothing but wait!

No one was more surprised than I when it did arrive exactly two days later even though I did not like the contents at all. It read:

> SORE2 (Stores)   re your letter and recent telephone call
> concerning crosses, grave.
>
> ---
>
> Having considered this matter most carefully the Deputy Adjutant and Quartermaster General is of the opinion that it would be most inadvisable for him or members of his staff to

issue such an estimate of casualties as you have requested for your purpose. He is sure you will understand that, if details of such an estimate became known, they could have a most undesirable effect on the morale of troops shortly to be placed under command of "X" Force.

Sgd. -------------- Maj. RA for Deputy Adjutant DAAQMG and Quartermaster General

At first reading it did sound rather like a veto on the whole project; as if no crosses should be produced before the campaign and the killing started. I certainly took it as that and dropped the whole project. However, a few weeks after the campaign commenced, I found the carpenters' shop section of the 174 Army Workshop and Park Company RE (my department's principal facility) set up in the middle of Bayeux, hard at work producing white wooden grave crosses as fast as they could to catch up with the initial demand, following the landing itself.

They continued to do so intermittently throughout the whole campaign, as did many of our other workshops. Still, both for manufacture and distribution, it was not really efficient nor the best use of our field workshops.

Looking again at the DAQMG ruling, after nearly 50 years, I do wonder whether it was really not meant to be read as a complete embargo on pre-campaign production. Perhaps I was really meant to choose my own figure, keep it to myself, spread the work over three or four separate workshops and leave only the organisation of distribution to all fighting units until immediately after the landing. Perhaps there would have then been rather fewer "known only unto God" inscriptions had I done so.

The War Office had the last word. Right at the end of the campaign — we had, I believe, actually arrived on Luneburg Heath — we received an Army Council Instruction headed "Crosses, grave". It told us that crosses, grave would henceforth be an item of Ordnance Corps supply. They would be carried in unit transport of front line units on a scale of 12 crosses for every 100 men and further supplies would be available from Ordnance Depots. Scales for other units would be issued in due course. I could not help wondering whether this arrangement would have any less effect on the morale of the fighting men than would the one I had in mind.

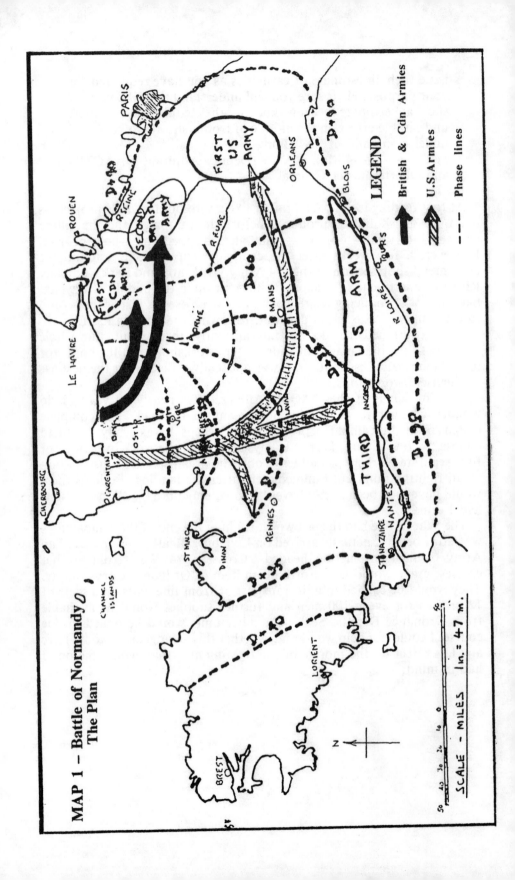

MAP 1 – Battle of Normandy,
The Plan

LEGEND

British & Cdn Armies

U.S. Armies

Phase lines

SCALE – MILES 1 in. = 47 m.

MAP 2 – Battles of the Beach-Heads

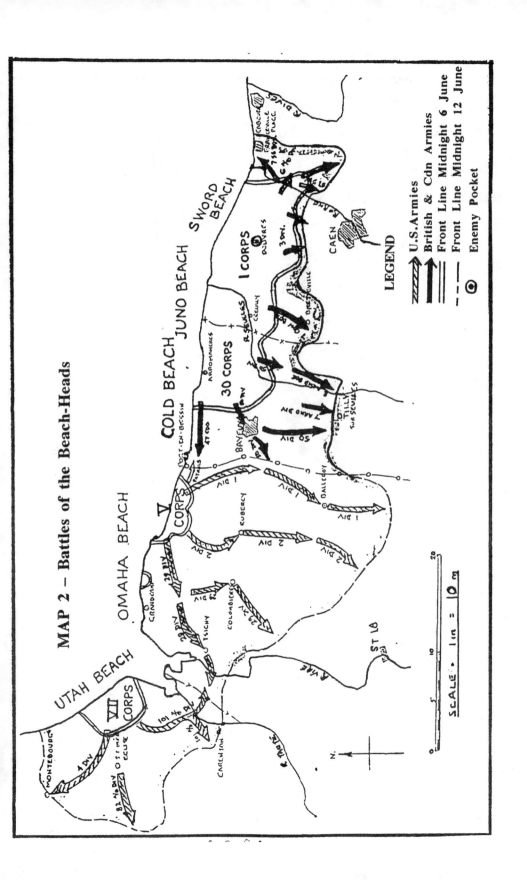

LEGEND

U.S. Armies	
British & Cdn Armies	
Front Line Midnight 6 June	
Front Line Midnight 12 June	
Enemy Pocket	

SCALE: 1 in = 10 m

MAP 3 – Battles of the Breakout – German Deployment

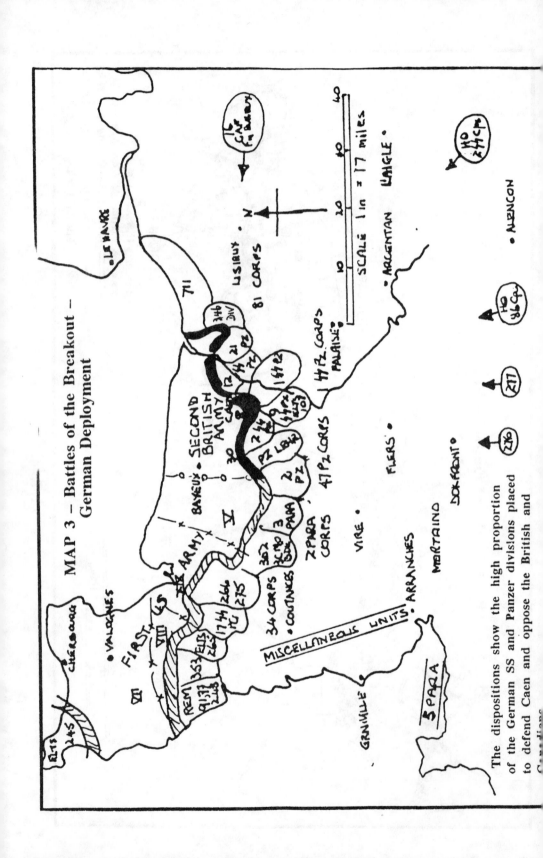

The dispositions show the high proportion of the German SS and Panzer divisions placed to defend Caen and oppose the British and Canadians

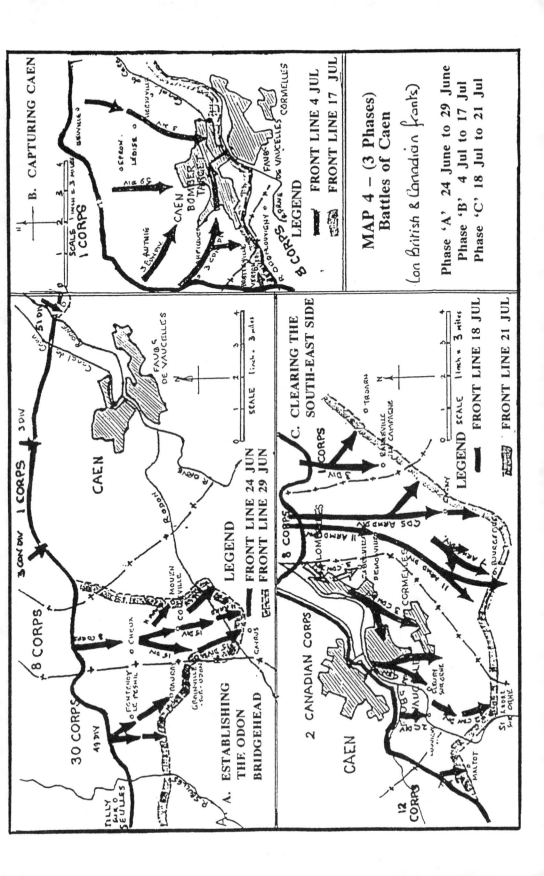

B. CAPTURING CAEN

SCALE 1 inch = 3 miles

N

1 CORPS

8 CORPS

CAEN BOMBER TARGET

LEGEND
FRONT LINE 4 JUL
FRONT LINE 17 JUL

MAP 4 – (3 Phases)
Battles of Caen

(on British & Canadian fronts)

Phase 'A'   24 June to 29 June
Phase 'B'   4 Jul to 17 Jul
Phase 'C'   18 Jul to 21 Jul

30 CORPS   8 CORPS   1 CORPS

CAEN

FAUBG DE
VAUCELLES

LEGEND
FRONT LINE 24 JUN
FRONT LINE 29 JUN

SCALE 1 inch = 3 miles

A. ESTABLISHING
THE ODON
BRIDGEHEAD

C. CLEARING THE
SOUTH-EAST SIDE

8 CORPS   CDS ARMD DIV

2 CANADIAN CORPS

CAEN

12 CORPS

LEGEND   SCALE 1 inch = 3 miles
FRONT LINE 18 JUL
FRONT LINE 21 JUL

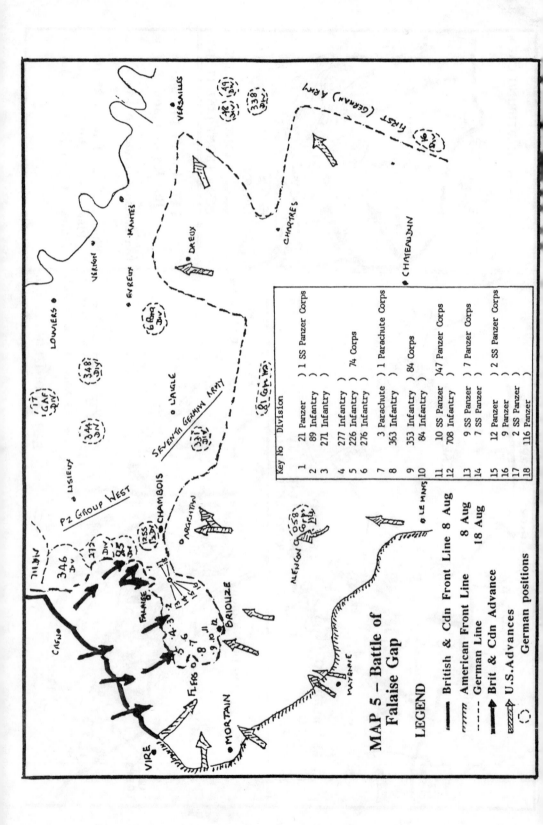

MAP 5 – Battle of Falaise Gap

LEGEND

——— British & Cdn Front Line 8 Aug
~~~~~ American Front Line 8 Aug
– – – German Line 18 Aug
⟹ Brit & Cdn Advance
⟹ U.S.Advances
◯ German positions

Key No	Division	
1	21 Panzer	) 1 SS Panzer Corps
2	89 Infantry	)
3	271 Infantry	)
4	277 Infantry	)
5	226 Infantry	) 74 Corps
6	276 Infantry	)
7	3 Parachute	) 1 Parachute Corps
8	363 Infantry	)
9	353 Infantry	) 84 Corps
10	84 Infantry	)
11	10 SS Panzer	) 47 Panzer Corps
12	708 Infantry	)
13	9 SS Panzer	) 7 Panzer Corps
14	7 SS Panzer	)
15	12 Panzer	) 2 SS Panzer Corps
16	9 Panzer	)
17	2 SS Panzer	)
18	116 Panzer	)

MAP 6 – Battle of Normandy - Review

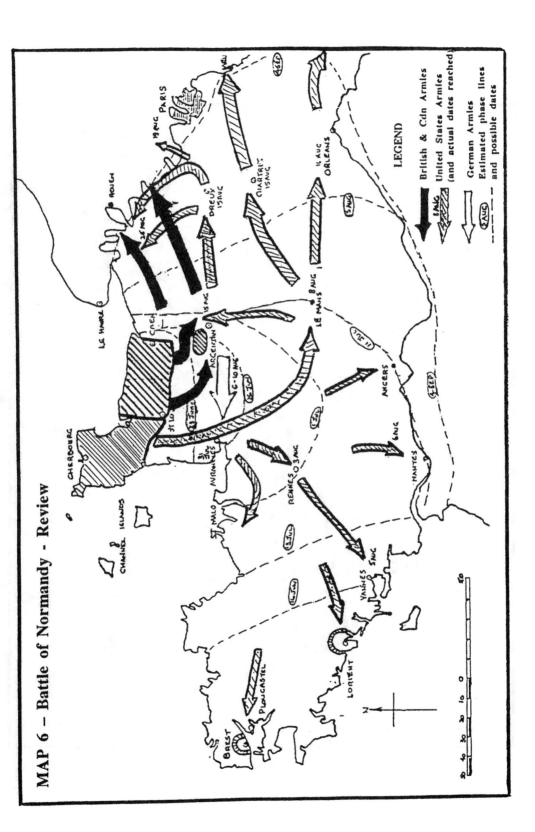

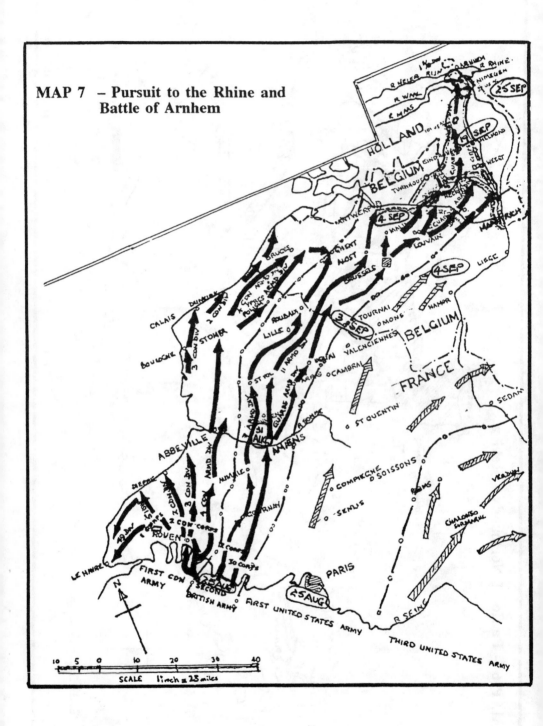

MAP 7 – Pursuit to the Rhine and
Battle of Arnhem

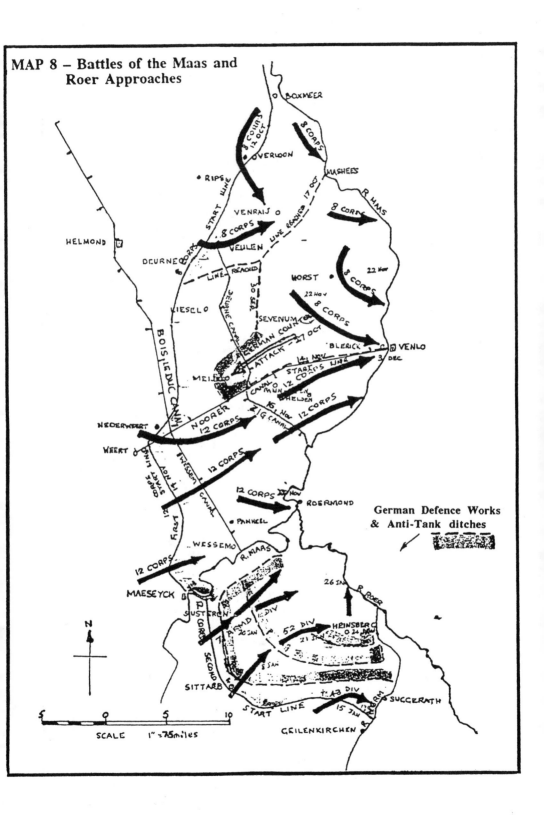

MAP 8 – Battles of the Maas and Roer Approaches

German Defence Works
& Anti-Tank ditches

N

SCALE   1" = 7.5 miles

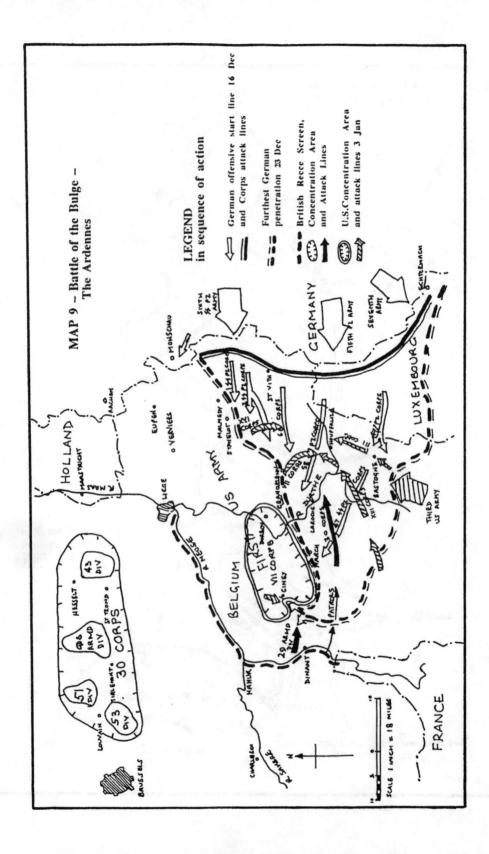

MAP 9 – Battle of the Bulge –
The Ardennes

LEGEND
in sequence of action

German offensive start line 16 Dec
and Corps attack lines

Furthest German
penetration 23 Dec

British Recce Screen,
Concentration Area
and Attack Lines

U.S.Concentration Area
and attack lines 3 Jan

SCALE 1 INCH = 18 MILES

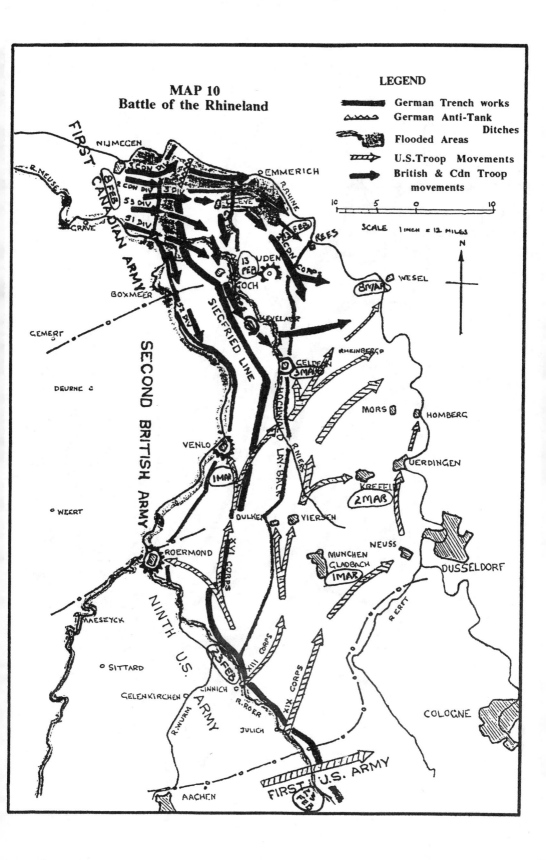

MAP 10
Battle of the Rhineland

LEGEND

German Trench works

German Anti-Tank Ditches

Flooded Areas

U.S.Troop Movements

British & Cdn Troop movements

SCALE 1 INCH = 12 MILES

N

FIRST CANADIAN ARMY
NIJMEGEN
R.MEUSE
GRAVE
EMMERICH
R.RHINE
2 CDN DIV
3 DIV
8 FEB
CLEVE
53 DIV
51 DIV
8 FEB
BOXMEER
13 FEB
UDEN
GOCH
REES
FEB
30 CDN CORPS
8 MAR
WESEL
GEMERT
SIEGFRIED LINE
52 DIV
KEVELAER
DEURNE
SECOND BRITISH ARMY
GELDERN
3 MAR
RHEINBERG
MORS
HOMBERG
VENLO
1 MAR
R.NIER
UERDINGEN
KREFFL
2 MAR
WEERT
DULKEN
VIERSEN
NEUSS
LAY-BACK
XXXI CORPS
ROERMOND
MUNCHEN GLADBACH
1 MAR
DUSSELDORF
NINTH U.S. ARMY
MAESEYCK
SITTARD
23 FEB
XIII CORPS
LINNICH
GELENKIRCHEN
R.ROER
R.WURM
JULICH
XIX CORPS
R.ERFT
COLOGNE
AACHEN
FIRST U.S. ARMY
FEB

MAP 11
The Final Battle – from the Rhine to Denmark

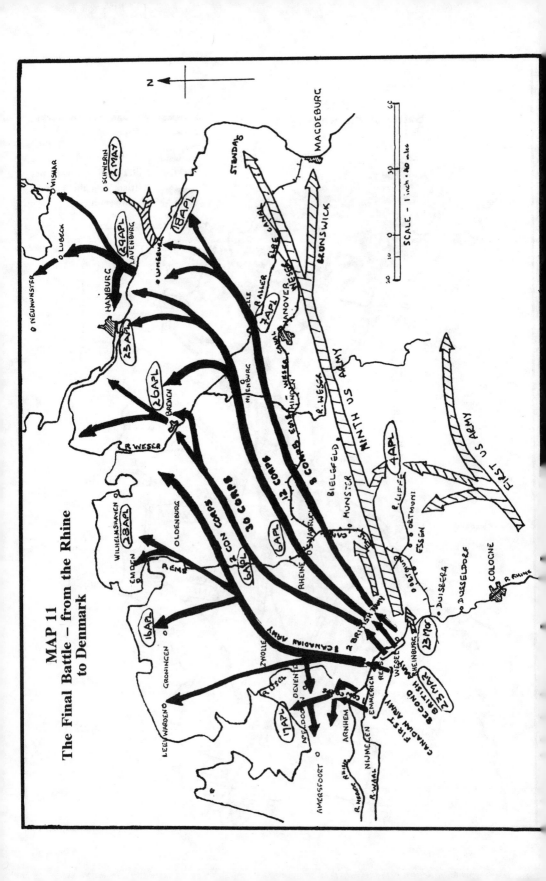

CHAPTER 10 Headquarters Second Army — Planning "Overlord" (March, 1944 – May, 1944)

I had joined Headquarters "X" Force just before Christmas 1943. We were well aware that we were due to be nominated to take charge, probably as headquarters of an Army, of a major invasion project which could be the Second Front that the newspapers had been talking about for a long time past and which the Russians were demanding of the western allies with increasing stridency. An Army is the next higher formation above a Corps and an Army HQ would be provided whenever there were to be two or more Corps to command and co-ordinate.

The work we had been doing could not really be seen as important except in the light of an attempt to prepare ourselves for the major work ahead. The trouble was that we had no real idea of what sort of a plan we might be called upon to fulfil, or where. However, we were getting to know one another and our colleagues in the other departments, with whom we would work more closely when we had something into which we could really get our teeth.

The Staff with which a general works and directs the formations and units under his command — the latter are collectively known as the Order of Battle — is basically and historically divided into three parts.

The senior part is the General Staff — the "G" staff for short. The head of this group at army level is the Brigadier General Staff (BGS) and his department is divided into two main sections — Operations (Ops) and Intelligence (Int) each led by a full colonel. (The Colonel on the Operations side was Selwyn Lloyd, who later became Speaker of the House of Commons.)

Intelligence, obviously, is concerned with the enemy, his strength, his organisations, his dispositions and his intentions. The information flows from many directions. Some might be called basic knowledge available from records and history. A lot flows down from the UK and is the product of espionage, codebreaking, interrogation of prisoners, electronic surveillance and other sources. This mass of information is accumulated, assessed, correlated and disseminated by a host of secret agencies and offices scattered around London and elsewhere.

Other information flows in from the front line, in daily contact with the enemy, and I have described how I learned about this process on a "German Army" course I attended at Cambridge. Other detailed information of this sort comes from refugees and the civilian population who, when the enemy is retreating, will have much valuable information about recent movements and the identification of enemy formations. Liaison with allied armies on the flanks can also yield valuable information; for example, if an enemy formation has been identified in full on one front, then it is unlikely to be also on another front at the same time!

Air reconnaissance also yields information, particularly in photographic form. All this adds up to the total picture of the enemy which is the essential starting point in any appreciation of one's own situation and potential plans.

The Operations section takes on from there and considers the various options open to the commander. Their liaison officers with allied armies and adjoining formations will have knowledge of the other formations' likely plans and these must obviously be taken into account. The state of our own forces would clearly be relevant. Their leadership, strengths, losses from recent battles, sickness, morale and equipment will all be known to "G" "Ops", either directly or through reports made in a routine way to other departments such as "A" and "Q" — the Adjutant General's department and the Quartermaster General's department, which follow hereunder and are usually closely integrated.

They will take advice from the specialist branches: from the Brigadier Royal Artillery (BRA) if a special artillery effort is required, from the Chief Engineer (CE), if river crossings and bridging or minefields are involved, from the Chief Signals Officer and even the Chief Medical Officer. These senior officers and their staffs are mostly situated at Main Headquarters in close proximity to the "G" staff but some would need to be called up from Rear Headquarters when required.

The tentative options would be the subject of discussions between the BGS and his opposite number at Army Group Headquarters (the next higher formation above an Army) and also with the Army commander who would have his own ideas and some inkling of the intentions of the Army Group commander.

From the North African campaigns and elsewhere the system had developed whereby the commanders (of Army, Army Group and Theatre) lived in semi-isolation from their staffs at very small, highly mobile Advanced or Tactical Headquarters, their only companions on a regular basis being a team of young, and apparently intelligent and daring, liaison officers. These fed the commander with up to date reports and impressions from the front line. The commander too was thus able to be very active himself in direct leadership and contact with the front line troops. He would be visited at least daily by his leading staff officer and, of course, fed with all the latest reports, maps etc.

Throughout the campaign which followed I had no idea at all where these advanced headquarters were, (nor did I need to know) and I am not entirely sure if my Chief Engineer was always right up to date either. His contact was normally with the BGS and I judge that much of that contact was at dinner each evening in "A" (the senior mess).

Eventually, when new orders or a changes of plan were called for, "G Ops" would refine their plans and narrow down their options and the commander would make his final choice. "G Ops" would then convert these into definitive orders and they would be circulated at the commander's Order Group.

The second main branch of the staff was the Adjutant General's department and this was essentially involved with "manpower", to which I referred above but repeat that it was concerned with leadership, strengths, losses, sickness, morale, prisoners, reinforcements, hospitals, graves, the chaplain's department and the military police. I believe it also dealt with questions relating to the civilian population insofar as that concerned the forward troops. It was also directly concerned with the Military Secretary's department, in relation to officers and discipline.

The third branch was the Quartermaster General's department and this again had a multiplicity of sections but in essence these were divided into those concerned with the supply to the troops of most of the things they needed — petrol, ammunition, rations and spares, for example, and those concerned with the movement of troops and their supplies and, on occasions, with billeting and accommodation generally.

It follows that the Royal Army Ordnance Corps (RAOC), the Royal Army Service Corps (RASC), the Royal Electrical and Mechanical Engineers (REME) and the Royal Engineers (Transportation) Section were very much under the direction of the Quartermaster General, except in sofar as units had been delegated permanently to lower formations. The Royal Engineers (Transportation) section dealt particularly with rail, canal and sea transport and was rather more concerned with the line of communication to the sea ports than with the Army area. All these branches, together with RE (Works) operated from Rear Headquarters but their direction came eventually from Main Headquarters.

The single head of both the Adjutant General's and the Quartermaster's departments at Army was the Brigadier "A and Q", supported by a large staff, some of whose titles suggested that they operated in both departments — many of them appeared to be DAA & QMGs (Deputy Assistant Adjurtant & Quartermaster Generals), who were of major's rank and therefore my direct opposite numbers.

I have mentioned the stratified messing system. In "X" force, and when we were in London for the planning, this system was not as fully developed as it became later during the campaign. Eventually, we had five Officers' Messes. "A" Mess was for brigadiers and full colonels — all the gentlemen with red bands on their hats and red gorget patches on their collars. "B" Mess was for lieutenant colonels and majors of the "G" staff and the "A & Q" staff with only one or two from the supporting arms (Armoured Corps, Artillery, Engineers, Signals, etc.) "C" Mess was for subalterns (captains and lieutenants) of the "G" and the "A & Q" staffs.

"D" Mess was for majors and captains of the supporting arms and a selection of odd branches, including camouflage and civil affairs, and a number of secretive officers who came and went at odd times. "E" Mess barely existed but, when it did, it housed lieutenants attached to the supporting arms. The average size of these Messes was about 25 officers with "B" Mess as far the largest and "E" as the smallest.

In part, this arrangement was a good one in that there was considerable inter-branch liaison in an informal way through the mixing of branches, particularly in "A" and "B" Messes but only in part in "C" and "D" Messes. For example, though I had a fair idea what was happening in artillery and signals, I had no direct contact with members of the "G" and "A" and "Q" staffs on this informal level. It did not matter much, however, but it was a pity even though I doubt if it affected my efficiency and effectiveness or theirs. Nevertheless, the system greatly reduced any form of social contact between the stratifications. On the other hand it may just have been good for security. It was not necessary for everyone to know everything.

Somewhere towards the end of February or the beginning of March, the Brigadier and Otto Phibbs were called to London and that evening they sent for Moody and Allport-Williams to join them next day. Almost immediately after that I received orders to pack up the rest of our Main HQ engineer branch office and come down to London as well, reporting to a house in Cranley Gardens, close to the Roman Catholic Westminster Cathedral. It was, in fact, a block of flats which the Army had taken over in its entirety. Incidentally, by now Ted Hutton and I had a new batman — a member of the Black Watch (a largely Glasgow regiment of distinguished history). He was a cheerful but inefficient helper. I did not mind him but Ted thought he was appalling!

The ground floor was swarming with military police and at the temporary desk rigged up in the hallway I had to give in a list of all the officers and men I had brought with me, together with all our identity cards and pay books. I was told that before lunchtime new cards and pay books would be issued to us which would contain our photographs and that we were to be especially careful in looking after them in future.

The engineer branch was on one side of the stair well on about the

127

third floor. On reaching our destination we were intercepted by Otto Phibbs who gave us a very quick briefing and handed out to the officers numbered copies of the "Overlord" plan and maps, for all of which we had to sign. Everything was headed "TOP SECRET" and we were told to settle down and read it and ask questions later.

It was fascinating stuff. It started with a broad outline of the plan which was, as is well known, to land on a front of five divisions, (two United States divisions, two British divisions and one Canadian division), with full naval and airforce support, on a front of 40 miles between Carentan and Caen. The sea landing would be preceded by airborne landings by 6th Airborne Division just to the east of Caen on the left flank of the British and Canadian divisions and by 82nd and 101st US Airborne Divisions on the right flank of the United States Force. **(See Map 1)**

The left hand half of the combined operation to the east of Bayeux would be dealt with by the Second British Army, under command of General Demsey, and the western half would be under the command of General Bradley, of the First United States Army. General Montgomery would be in command of 21st Army Group and in overall control of the operations of both armies.

There followed masses of annexures and tabulations. Particularly interesting were the ones showing the German Army dispositions. In all there were 10 Panzer (armoured) and 48 Infantry divisions overall in Holland, Belgium and France of which 1 Panzer and 8 Infantry divisions were in the Pas de Calais, 1 Panzer and 4 Infantry divisions between the Somme and the Seine and 7 Infantry and 3 Panzer divisions between the Seine and Cherbourg with a further 9 Infantry divisions in Brittany and the Channel Islands. Holland and Belgium held a further 7 Infantry and 1 Panzer division.

Thus, facing Britain and America in the possibility of a 2nd front in north west Europe, there were initially a total of 6 Panzer divisions and 35 Infantry divisions (who would take various times to concentrate), but the latter were of a very mixed quality. Of these Infantry divisions only 13 were genuine field divisions and even they depended on horse transport, rather than being fully motorised like the allied divisions they would be facing. Two of the remainder were training divisions and the other 20 were lower establishment divisions, almost completely tied to the coastal defences and without any transport to give them serious mobility. Some of these were even made up of men from the territories the German army had overrun in eastern Europe and their quality was extremely doubtful.

Probably the most important tabulation, from everyone's point of view in our section, was the one that showed the estimated build up of divisions (allied and enemy) on the Second Army front. On the first day we planned to land most of 1st Corps and 30th Corps plus 6th Airborne Division, on the left flank. With parts of several armoured brigades coming on shore as well but with at least one division of each corps left behind to come next day as the first follow up force, it was indicated that the equivalent of six divisions might be on shore by the first night.

The remainder of those two corps would be on shore within the next couple of days and 8th Corps would follow with 12th Corps possibly beginning to arrive by the end of the first fortnight. When the whole of the British part of 21st Army Group, as originally constituted, had arrived it would amount to some twenty four divisions plus masses of corps and army troops as well, together with large elements of Line of Communication Troops with RAF and naval personnel as well. However, this final state would only arrive after one to two months although it would represent in all nearly a million men ("Corps Troops" and "Army Troops" are reserve units of artillery, engineers, signals, RASC and so on, held by corps and army, in addition to those in the divisions' own strength, and allocated to them — or employed in support of them, as the battle demanded).

Throughout this initial period, whatever the planned figure was for our own build up, the Intelligence Department assessment showed a comfortable balance, in our favour, with more of our own troops landed than the enemy could bring against them, at any time during the build up, even though the Germans would be denuding western Europe of every one of their divisions which was fit to move.

I was informed that the corps headquarters would make all arrangements for their own engineer stores requirements for the first two days and that Army Headquarters would make provision for the rest of the first fortnight. I believe that it was indicated in the plan that between twelve and fifteen divisions would arrive by the end of the first fortnight. Allowing for supporting troops, that might represent in all 500,000 men. My task was to estimate what engineer stores they might need in the meantime but also to allow, if possible, for a further build up of stores to create reserves of resources for greater demands to follow.

This first reading of the plan and preliminary calculations and chats about it had occupied most of my first few days in London. My team had arrived with me and consisted of my staff captain, together with Sergeant Swift and Corporal Henshall and they too had had the chance of taking a look at the plan after due warnings about security.

We worked late every night and the work progressed rapidly, though occasionally disrupted by air raid alarms — mostly, I judged by night fighters as they buzzed around for long enough. Only occasionally did they drop a bomb. One came quite close it seemed. We were having a meeting in John Stone's office and all of us hit the floor pretty quickly. He could not, because of his gammy leg, but he was ready with "sweeties" to revive us when we shamefacedly stood up.

Incidentally, we had all been billeted in other empty blocks of flats close to but slightly separated from the Cranley Gardens headquarters. My accommodation was part of a large flat in a block overlooking the side of Victoria Station in Vauxhall Bridge Road. It was unfurnished and bare, but otherwise fine, except that the trams running outside were rather noisy at night.

For our messing accommodation we had taken over the whole of the old ABC restaurant on the corner close to Victoria Station. It was a bit crowded when we were all there although the top ranks had somewhere more private. For those days the rations were adequate and the cooking satisfactory.

My biggest problem initially, from a stores tonnage point of view, was going to be pierced steel planking which the RAF would need in vast quantities for the fighter strips we intended to put down for them in the beachhead. This material was of thin sheet steel, about one eighth inch thick or less, with large holes punched in it to reduce the weight. It had a slight interlock and sheets were about $3' \times 1'$. It sounded as though we were literally putting a single massive road right from end to end of our forty mile front but that would be an exaggeration. Nevertheless, I recall that the initial plan was for something like twelve fighter stations in that area. I checked quantities like this with Ted Hutton who had come down to London with me and whose Airfield Construction Companies would do the actual laying. Clearly, this was my top priority and it was not for me to argue with it. If the RAF thought they needed that, then they had to have it, even if we got little else. Air cover was of overriding importance.

Gradually, over the following days, I began to build up a picture of what else we might require. Defence stores such as barbed wire and sandbags would feature, however temporary any digging in might be. With 500,000 men and nearly 100,000 vehicles, including tanks and other tracked vehicles, milling around in the beachhead, on our front alone (with enemy shelling as well) there would be damage to roads, however good the weather. We might well need a lot of road construction materials, particularly bitumen and asphalt, although we could hope that the military quarrying companies we were bringing with us would look after the stone element. Fortunately, it did not look as if we would need much bridging equipment to start with. Our initial drive would be from north to south in line with the rivers and only when we turned east, after a month or more, would we need to think about that sort of item seriously. On top of all this there would be a multifarious collection of tools and materials that any army might need. So we began to build up our first bid for shipping tonnage.

During this period I had many conversations with my colleagues at corps level and, particularly, those at Army Group Headquarters. 21st Army Group were situated at St Paul's School, then still in Hammersmith where my contact man was a Canadian officer, Major Hignett. We worked in close liaison for the whole campaign but I think I never actually saw him again after we left London.

Obviously I also consulted with Brigadier John Stone, my Chief Engineer, and with Otto Phibbs from time to time as the work went on, until I was able to hand over my tonnage estimate for submission by the Brigadier to the ''A & Q'' branch. Word came back almost immediately that it was too large.

The Brigadier was asked to attend a metting with the BGS and the BA & Q and took me along as his ''figures'' man. They told us that, with the other big tonnage items, petrol, ammunition, rations and spare vehicles, the total army bid was far more than the available shipping could carry, or the beaches were expected to have handling capacity to accept. They said that they thought they would have to ask all departments to take a cut of between a quarter and a third of their total tonnage and the BA & Q had already asked his people to look at it. We engineers had asked for one of the three biggest tonnages and would have clearly have to bear our share of a cut. They asked us for comments.

In return we pointed out that pierced steel planking for airfields accounted for more than 50% of our total and that we understood no cut could be made in this. The BGS agreed this in principle but said that we would have to see what else could be done. He pointed to our figure for roadmaking stores, which was nearly 25% of the whole. We put our points to him and sketched a picture of the effect on traffic and on vehicles themselves of a massive break up of road surfaces. The best roads ran parallel to the coast, while those from north to south, i.e. the direction we wanted to go — looked as if they might be distinctly second class. He asked whether the weather would have much effect and we said that it certainly would if we turned out to have a period of heavy rain. Finally, he said we would have to assume good weather throughout the first fortnight and said we should halve our road-making stores.

He then turned to our third biggest item, which was defence stores, and represented about 10% of the total. He was inclined to say that none were necessary but here the BA & Q was slightly on our side. In the end it seemed to us all that to take no sandbags and no barbed wire might seem to be an outright gamble, or look to the troops like sheer forgetfulness, and that we ought at least to hold on to 5% of total tonnage for this purpose.

The rest of the whole array of engineers stores, representing nearly 10% of the whole, was too detailed for us to argue about and the BGS was inclined to concede that out of hand, until he saw that all we had conceded so far was less than 20% of our total. He grinned and said, "Well, let's leave it at that for tonight. I may still have to ask you to take out all the roadmaking stuff and all the defence stores too and let's hope that it doesn't rain and that we keep Gerry on the run".

John Stone told me afterwards that I had been lucky about the miscellaneous stores and that I should go through my list with a toothcomb. He was not happy about the heavy reduction in roadmaking stores — principally bitumen and asphalt — but thought that the defence stores cut was a sound, although courageous, decision for two infantrymen to make.

It was perfectly true that I had gone through the catalogue of engineer stores and allowed for taking a bit of everything — just in case it might be needed — but I had the greatest reluctance to leave any of it behind. I had even included a certain amount of Bailey bridging stores. I was sure there would be a gap somewhere that someone would want to put a bridge over but I suppose that in total I provided less than 300 or 400 feet of total bridging. Nevertheless, this combing took three or four days and produced little — rather the opposite. At the end of that time we got word from "A & Q" that a 10% overall cut in engineer stores would be sufficient with slightly more asked for from ammunition and petrol. More shipping had been found, but only at the cost of postponing the proposed simultaneous mounting of an invasion of the south of France with troops from Italy and north Africa. Similar cuts had been imposed on our American allies; it was largely their invasion of the south of France, with token support from the Free French, which had been abandoned — at least temporarily.

Now we were clear as to the total tonnage we could reckon on and as to the main splits of that tonnage which had been approved. The remaining 90% was to be split as to: −

	parts	%
Pierced steel planking	55	60
Roadmaking stores	15	17
Defence stores	10	11
Miscellaneous	10	12
	90	100

Now it was a matter of converting these broad outlines into a detailed list and checking that the total tonnage fitted our quota. The final list then had to be divided up by beaches and tides. The First United States Army front was divided into two sectors; UTAH, which was west and north of Carentan, and OMAHA, which was east of Carentan and stretched as far as Bayeux. On the Second British Army front the sectors were; GOLD for the 11 miles immediately east of Bayeux, JUNO for the next 7 miles and SWORD for the last 5 miles up to the River Orne on the left of the line. For shipping purposes each sector was divided into three beaches but I cannot remember their names. It seemed advisable to split the tonnage to be landed on each tide evenly between the three beaches and relatively evenly between the 12 days, and thus 24 high tides, on which the stores would be landed.

Obviously, there were some variations. Defence stores, if they were going to be needed at all, might be needed quickly to face the inevitable German counter attacks once our first troops had landed. Road making stores, however, were not likely to be required before the second week at the earliest. Much of the miscellaneous stores might tend to get lost. This argued for spreading them widely to avoid too big a share being lost in one disaster. On the other hand, such stores tended to be desirable to the first comer to see them and this argued for making the packets reasonably large. A compromise was necessary here.

I undertook myself the drafting of the landing tables because of all the reasoning — some sound and obvious, some obscure — that was involved. Sergeant Swift was trying to keep pace with the typing on the sheets which were nine columns, one for each beach. Down the page were listed at least half the items in the catalogue and there was one separate list, each of many pages, of course, for each of the 24 tides or more with which we were concerned. Gradually the mass of paper built up until it was eventually two to three inches thick. We were using a Banda duplicator and sheets of paper 24" by 16" in size. A really modern duplicator would have been an absolute boon, but we managed, and Sergeant Swift made a really creditable job of it.

In the meantime, and throughout our time in London, my staff captain and Corporal Henshall were fully employed, and I was frequently involved, in meeting the needs of the corps for various items of equipment and stores for the first two days. These kept coming to their minds as they reviewed and reassessed their plans in the light of every new contingency that occurred. The biggest of these was a report from an intrepid party of sapper and naval officers who had landed one night from a submarine and inspected in detail the obstacles, which the Germans had recently been building, on the beaches. Air photographs had been available and were enough to show the areas that had been obstructed but not close enough to give details of the obstacles themselves.

Most of these obstacles turned out to be made of three lengths of heavy rail or angle iron, welded into tetrahedrons. These were chained to anchors buried in the sand and were combined with anti-personnel and anti-tank mines. Some, however, were simply single lengths of rail or angle iron set in concrete and angled towards approaching vehicles.

There were literally thousands of these obstacles scattered on the beaches on which we intended to land, or the land approaches to them. Other hazards, which had not previously been assessed, were bands of clay present in the sand and occasionally exposed by the tides. These might be very difficult for a wheeled vehicle to cross and might even present a problem to tanks.

The corps and divisional engineers had to devise means of safely removing the rail obstacles and of crossing the clay patches. The tetrahedrons either called for suitable explosive charges to destroy them or for slings so that they could be towed out of the way by tanks and bulldozers in spite of the exploding mines. The clay patches seemed to call for some form of track which could be laid down by a tank itself. The solution to this was to fit a tank with a huge cotton-reel type device on which was wound a substantial length of garage-door-like material. Finding some of these materials was quite a difficult task.

All formations had their own particular needs, but none of them had the range of ideas and essential requirements that we found we were dealing with from 1st Corps. They had acquired a new chief engineer from North Africa, Brigadier Campbell, to whom everything was urgent and immediate. He believed in reinforcing every demand by a personal encounter with the most senior officer he could get hold of, which always seemed to be me.

Time was getting short for the submission of our loading tables to 21st Army Group and from them to the War Office. I was working literally all hours except when Brigadier Campbell demanded my attention. I had to appeal to John Stone for some relief and this he obtained for me by insisting that personal representations from the corps were made to himself. In the process I had made an enemy or at least a rather resentful colleague. That one came home to roost later.

As all this was going on, the chief engineer was paying a series of visits all over the country, either alone or with his Deputy Chief Engineer (works), who was at that time a Colonel Reid, or with one of his junior officers. One day he asked me to join him in a visit to Yorkshire to see the 174 Workshop and Park Company RE who were going to be the operators of the principal Army depots for engineer stores as well as our principal engineer workshops in the field — as opposed to at base. We were to fly from Redhill to somewhere like Goole and were considerably intrigued to find that the RAF were insisting on fitting us out with

134

parachutes. It was, perfectly understandable; a relatively slow transport plane would be an easy target for an interloping German long range fighter. After we had been fitted and instructed — and I had made up my mind privately that, if somebody told me to jump, I would do so — we took our seats and the trip passed uneventfully.

We were met by the officer commanding 174, a Major Hall, a real character and an absolute caricature of what he actually was in civilian life — a used car salesman. In his youth he had been a speedway motorcyclist and still had a great love of speed and speedy vehicles. He demonstrated this by showing us, at a very early stage, his driving licence, which had 32 endorsements for speeding, the list of which fell out of the document like a concertina when he handed it around. He was confident and there was no doubt who was in charge of the company, but I felt uneasy and was interested to find that my two seniors were also not too sure about his potential and his future with us. He was certainly energetic, but sharp too! He had many of the attributes that we needed and was clearly very strong on his knowledge of internal combustion engines. That must be of very great value to someone in the job which he held. On the other hand, we feared we would always be wondering what he was doing when we were not watching him. The nearest type I can think of was Private Walker in the post war television show, "Dad's Army".

When we had sent off our loading lists to 21st Army Group and, through them, to the War Office, we thought we might go, after a few days, to see what was happening about them. This involved first going to Long Marston, the principal engineer stores depot, which was situated just south of Stratford on Avon. All the material was apparently in the depot — we had asked for no strange items on our lists. Consignments were all being sent to the West India Docks and were code marked, in a way we understood when it was explained to us, to indicate the beach and tide where we hoped they would turn up.

The next thing to do was to go, some days later, to the West India Docks to see what was happening there. They presented a scene of high activity in the midst of nothing. The whole area, stretching way outside the original lines of the dock walls, had been devastated by the bombing two years before and the fire storm which followed it, but the rubble had all now been cleared and the dock basins, which all seemed to be in good working order, were now surrounded by acres of nothingness. Most of the dockside cranes had also disappeared but the basins we went to visit were full of shipping, and the trains coming in from Long Marston were alongside. The trains were being unloaded on to lorries and these were shuttling to and from the ships which were being loaded from the lorries. The unloading was largely being done by mobile truck mounted cranes.

The ship loading was mostly being done by the ships own handling gear. They mostly looked to be of coaster size and possibly not more than 5,000 tons dead weight capacity per ship on average.

Producing our copy of the loading tables, we checked some of the stores that we could identify. Everything seemed to be working well. Each ship was marked according to its beach and tide and was thus clearly identifiable. I am glad to say the stores that we saw were all going on to the right ships and appeared to be heading in the right direction. We could do no more, the system seemed to be working and there appeared to be every chance that the ships would all be ready to go long before their appointed day. Some of us also made trips to see something of the preparations for the "Mulberry" harbours and PLUTO. It was very difficult to appreciate what was going on with either, but clearly a vast amount of construction was taking place at the seaports we visited. The Mulberry harbour concept was extremely secret and I knew very little myself, and I have not yet even seen what is left of the one Mulberry harbour which succeeded.

The stretch of the French coast on which we were landing contained no significant ports between le Havre and Cherbourg and these, we could be sure, would be bitterly defended, obstructed and left in ruins. The Mulberry scheme was to produce two artificial harbours and literally anchor them off the coast somewhere near the existing little Port en Bessin and the seaside town of Arromanches. The first was to serve the First United States Army and the other was to serve the Second British Army. They were to be assembled on site during the first week of the invasion and it was hoped they would be in commission by the start of the second week. In essence, T-shaped jetties made of huge floating tanks, with articulated roadway on top, projected from the shore. The whole area, with room for ships to move around inside, was protected from the waves and the sea by long walls of sunken ships acting as breakwaters.

The sea wall to surround each of these new ports was to be made by sinking dozens of derelict ships in suitably connected lines. Inside the protected areas there would be jetties and wharves made largely of Braithwaite tanks, a fairly standard item of engineer stores which I had met at the OCTU. These tanks in their minimum form were 3 foot cubes made of bolted sheet steel but they could be fabricated from the same size sheets to make much larger tanks. Such tanks were often used in water supply projects but, in this case, they were to be used for flotation and the object was to keep the water out of them. The ships for the breakwaters would reach the site under their own steam and I believe that many of them would also be towing large assemblages of the Braithwaite tanks. I have no doubt that the ships also carried the superstructures and roadways for the wharves and jetties. Unfortunately, one Braithwaite tank looks very much like another and that was all we saw on our day out.

We did not see any part of PLUTO, the acronym standing for Pipe Line Under The Ocean. The project was to lay a pipe line from England to France, through which enough petroleum products could be pumped to supply the whole expeditionary force once it got on the move. For the initial phase all petrol, of whatever nature, was supplied in jerricans or four gallon non returnable rectangular tins. These tins formed admirable raw material for a multitude of manufactured products, particularly signboards, that the army made for itself.

Sadly, I never saw either of these great projects in working condition but I was very well aware of the huge difference they made to the outcome of the campaign.

Things in London appeared to be slowing to a halt because there was nothing more we could do that would have any effect. We appeared to be totally committed and as far as we could judge everything was going fine. Towards the end of May, therefore, we abandoned Cranley Gardens and moved into our concentration area. Our area, with 30th Corps and most of 1st Corps, was in the New Forest and the area immediately behind Southampton and Portsmouth.

In beautiful countryside, somewhere in the triangle between the villages of Southwick, Denmead and Waterlooville, a substantial tented camp had been established for Army Headquarters, and there we spent the next couple of weeks in glorious weather.

Working was less pleasure. Each day trucks picked us up and drove us to Fort Southwick, one of the large Victorian forts in the front line of the landward defences of Portsmouth and Gosport. The "G" staff and some of the others, were no doubt comfortable enough and cool working in the casemates or magazines of the fort but the branches, including the engineers, were situated in tents in the dry, hot, and terribly dusty, main ditch. Not that we had very much work to do, but just enough to keep us busy came in from the corps, who were still seeking odd bits of equipment and materials for their various gadgets. That certainly ensured that we spent rather more time than we liked sweltering in our office tents. Lunchtime was a welcome break whether travelling or back in camp.

Ted Hutton used this spell largely to find for himself, and incidentally myself, a new batman. He could never stand Private Lunney's slapdash methods of dealing with our sleeping arrangements and cleaning. The new man who turned up was certainly smarter and appeared, on the face of it, more willing to make himself generally useful. Unfortunately, he did not seem to wish to go to war because one lunchtime, as our truck drew into the campsite we heard a shot and a muffled scream from our tent. On getting there we found that the new batman had shot himself in the foot with my 0.38 inch calibre revolver. He was removed for treatment and Private Lunney appeared, with a large grin and the remark "He didn't last long did he?" I persuaded Ted that this was a sign that fate intended us to go to war in the care of Private Lunney.

We knew, of course, that the invasion was due to commence in the first week of June, although I am not sure that we knew the actual day. Apart from the discomforts of the ditch, the time passed pleasantly enough and, as we had not yet adopted the full stratified messing, we enjoyed getting to know better a number of the senior members of the "G" staff who had a very lively line in conversation. Our batman was duly courtmartialled on our evidence. No doubt he served a month or two in a detention centre, which would be pretty tough going, and then no doubt he returned to his regiment at the front and had to like it. He may have got off comparatively lightly first time but a second time could well result in a death penalty. My revolver never shot anybody else.

Incidentally, the whole of Southern England was allocated to the concentration and marshalling areas of the various corps and divisions which would be taking part in Overlord. Dorset, Devon and Cornwall were allocated to the First United States Army and Weymouth, Dartmouth, Plymouth and Falmouth were to be their principal embarkation points. Their early follow-up divisions were allocated to South Wales with Cardiff and Swansea as embarkation points, and their next corps was concentrated in the Swindon area. For Second British Army, I have already referred to the New Forest-Southampton and Portsmouth concentration area and the rest of 1st Corps was based on the Shoreham, Newhaven area. The follow up divisions of 1st Corps and 30th Corps were in East Anglia and were due to leave from Felixstowe and Tilbury. Finally, 8th Corps was in Berkshire and 12th Corps with 2nd Canadian Corps were concentrated in Kent.

Southern England was one vast military camp, waiting for the off, and tight security prevailed everywhere. Every road was lined with military vehicles of every description but prominent amongst them were the DD tanks (the letters actually stood for Duplex Drive) meaning that the tank could use its engine either to operate its tracks, or alternatively, to power a propellor when arranged to operate as a boat. Adequate flotation for the massive weight was secured by fabric shutters which rose around the tanks' upper works. These would be the first armoured vehicles to get on shore and therefore they were vital to the success of the operation.

In various places too one came across the "funnies" of the Assault Brigade (Royal Engineers), part of the 79th Armoured Division. These converted tanks carried a number of useful devices. One was the cotton

Above *Admiral Mountbatten addresses ship's company. With Rear-Admiral Moody, Captain Cunliffe and Commander Wallis.*

Left *A vivid overhead view of* Illustrious. *Both of her lifts are in the 'down' position* (Imperial War Museum).

Below *Corsairs running-up for take-off to Sourabaya.*

Top right *Corsairs taking off for Sourabaya.* Saratoga's *strike aircraft forming up*

Right *Gordon Aitken returns from Sourabaya. John Hastings batting. Note flaps and arrestor hook fully extended.*

Bottom right *At sea off the north-west coast of Australia. The Fleet is in line astern and has just been passed by* Saratoga *and her attendant destroyers (seen in the right background) bidding farewell to the Eastern Fleet as they set course for California* (Imperial War Museum).

Above *Pilots, Chiefs and Petty Officers of 1833 Squadron, Quonset Point, Rhode Island, 1943. Left to right: Back row—CPO Maddison; Sub-Lieutenants Brynildsen, Starkey, Rogers, Shaw; and PO Geddes. Left to right: Centre row—Sub-Lieutenants Munnoch, Baker; Lieutenant Hanson; Lieutenant-Commander Monk; Sub-Lieutenants Aitken and Builder. Left to right: Front row—POs Edwardes, Coussens, Radburn, Turner, Vincent and Clifft.*

Right *Captain of* Illustrious—*R. L. B. Cunliffe, CBE, RN.*

Bottom left *15th Fighter Wing, Spring 1944. Left to right: Back row—Whelpton, Shaw, Barbour, Graham-Cann, Fullerton, Quigg, Starkey, Richardson (Wing Observer), Millard, Rogers, Maclaren, Facer, Buchan, Aitken, Pawson. Middle row—Seebeck, Baker, Booth, Munnoch, the author, Tritton, Sutton, Cole, Hadman, Brown, Retallick. Front row—Brynildsen, Clark, Ritchie, Guy.*

Amphibious equipment — DD. (duplex drive) tanks. Tank entering the water. The screw drive in rear can be engaged for propulsion in the water.

Mine clearance — Scorpion tank in action with flail of heavy chains rotating in the rear to activate mines.

Short gap crossings – Fascine tank at the front carrying two large chained bundles of poles ready to be dropped in a dry gap or similar short crossing.
Following it is a standard armoured bridge layer with a 20 feet long heavy bridge poised ready for release and dropping over a small-medium dry or wet gap, releasing its tank for other gun operations.

Bridge layers – Bridge about to be dropped over the gap.

Rafting operations – Folding boat equipment.
Class 9 (9-ton load) close support raft carrying Armoured Personnel Truck
(15cwt load White scout car), near maximum safe load for raft.

Rafting operations – Class 50/60 equipment in operation on the
Rhine crossing. This equipment was able to carry the heaviest
tanks in service whether on tracks or transporter.

Equipment bridging – Three-span Bailey Bridge carried on pontoon piers over River Orne canal: Triple-panel single-truss construction for class 40 ton loads. 220 feet overall.

Equipment bridging – At Vernon on the River Seine. Class 9 (9 ton load) in the foreground with a class 40 (40 ton load) Bailey pontoon bridge next to the demolished bridge. The bridges were 694/736 feet long overall excluding ramps.

Pierced steel planking being laid in an airfield construction project.

Damage by German swimmers to the railway bridge at Nijmegen.

(above) Bailey pontoon bridge 'London' at Wesel where Rhine subsequently crossed by American timber-piled railway bridge 1800 feet long.

(left) Bailey pontoon bridge "Westminster" at Xanten. The fact that all pontoons are decked and that the pontoons on the upstream side at the inside of the bend are equipped with bow protectors can be clearly seen as well as the disciplined spacing of the heavier items of traffic. The traffic is advancing from west to east.

(below) Bailey pontoon bridges over the Rhine at Emerich. 'Lambeth' bridge on the left upstream is the southerly, 'Blackfriars' bridge on the right is downstream. The bridges are being used on a one-way system.

The staff of the Chief Engineers' Department at 2nd Army HQ on Luneberg Heath on 6th May 1945 with Brig. A D Campbell CBE DSO MC in the centre. Staff Officers fill the 3rd and 4th rows while the other ranks are clerks, drivers and officer's Batmen in approximately equal numbers. The staff had just been almost doubled by the arrival of a large contingent of officers and men allocated to handle Civil Affairs. The author and his three principal colleagues are 4th, 9th (Lt. Col Phibbs), 10th (Major Moodie) and 11th (Maj Thorpe) in the third row. Other members of the Stores Section are Captain N E Walters (4th in the 4th row), Sgt L D Swift, 12th in the 6th row, L/Cpl C B Henshall, 7th in the 1st row and Private F Lunney, Black Watch, 5th in the 2nd row.

German 'Tiger' tank with infantry passengers. Some 60 tons weight and the most formidable tank in the battles.

Twin 88 mm anti-aircraft guns on the roof of the Zoo flak tower in the Tiergarten. There were three other pairs of such guns in similar emplacements also on top of the same building. Major White is demonstrating their scale.

reel device for unwinding a sheet of garage door material to cross the clay patches on the beaches, to which I have referred. Another carried a folding small box girder bridge for crossing small gaps. A third, instead of an ordinary gun, projected and fired a huge bomb used for demolishing concrete pill boxes and emplacements, yet another carried a rotating spindle in front which flailed heavy chains on the ground ahead of it to detonate mines. This is far from the full list but these vehicles and their Royal Engineer crews played a great part in the successes of the first day and in many subsequent assaults.

Altogether, seeing all this mass of first class material and the earnest, but confident looking men, one could not doubt that the outcome would be successful. All we needed was good weather to start the thing off.

Shortly towards the end of our time in the Assembly Area, Second Army headquarters had a visit from General Montgomery and we assembled in a cinema somewhere to hear an address to the Staff. We were congratulated on our work in preparing the detailed plans and Montgomery reviewed the situation as he saw it, literally days before the date for embarkation. He said "When I came home from north Africa I found that a Morale Report was being prepared. Now," he said, "That was very important and I thought that I should take a look at it, and what did I find? I found that nine out of ten junior infantry officers did not expect to cross the beach alive. That would not do so I set out to alter it by speaking to them as I am now speaking to you, and I have changed that attitude. Now all of them expect to cross the beach alive and I have great confidence in them." All this was said in the typical Monty manner but it was also absolutely true. He had made an enormous difference to the confidence of the army in him and in the outcome of the campaign and relatively speaking, compared even with the much smaller landings in Italy, casualties on our side were light, through significant and sad where they occurred.

CHAPTER 11 Headquarters Second Army —
The Beachhead
(June, 1944)

At last the fateful week arrived and the word was passed round that the provisional date for the actual landings was to be 6th June, give or take a day depending on the actual weather conditions at the time. The actual start would be heralded on the evening before when, at last light, the planes and gliders carrying 6th Airborne Division would fly over on their way to the left flank where they were to be dropped to secure, if possible, the crossing of the River Orne.

Headquarters Second Army was not all going to cross at the same time. The first contingent was to go on "D + 1", i.e., the day after the first beach landings. Others were due to cross on "D + 2" and the main part of Main Headquarters was to cross on "D + 3". Again, I was to lead the principal contingent of the Engineers' department.

On the evening of "D − 1", while we were still in our Hampshire meadow, and just as we had had dinner, there came a great roar of engines and the whole of the British airborne invasion passed overhead at, seemingly, little more than rooftop level. It took five to ten minutes to pass. Presumably they were flying fairly low in order to confuse the enemy's radar. Certainly we had a first class view of our forces, almost to being able to distinguish the men inside the individual aircraft and gliders. It was an impressive, even awe-inspiring sight, but one could not help being conscious of the excitement, apprehension and plain fear that every one of those young men must have been feeling as they passed from England, over the sea to the unknown shore beyond. It was with some excitement too that we returned to our mess in the returned hush of evening to speculate, quite uselessly, on the probable success of their endeavours.

Next morning the radio was full of the great events and announced the successful landings of our troops on all beaches and air landing grounds. That was only partly true at the time. The landings by 6th Airborne Division, 1st Corps and 30th Corps all seemed to have landed without any great difficulty and to be pressing on inland, but the landings by First US Army, although they had reached the beaches, appeared to be pinned down there by a spirited defence by the Germans. There was little news of the American airborne landings.

After breakfast, we travelled to Fort Southwick as usual, but this time

140

we made our first call at the "G" department, where the staff had been busy all night. At the entrance large maps were displayed, fastened to blackboards and standing on easels. They were covered with sheets of plastic on which chinagraph pencil marks showed the positions of British and Canadian troops in red and information about the German army in blue. This visit became a ritual after every meal throughout the campaign. The service was intended for just that purpose — to inform members of the supporting staffs, like ourselves from the Engineers, and also casual visitors to headquarters and, at the same time, to avoid obstructing the work of the "G" staff inside.

The first signs on our front were very encouraging. Surprise seemed to have been relatively complete and quick advances had been made. The American situation was marked on a separate map in green and they seemed to have made very little penetration indeed. **(See Map 2)**

As the day went on, until the evening, advances continued. The final report for the day indicated that 30th Corps had advanced six or seven miles, almost to the Bayeux-Caen road. 1st Corps was advancing a little more slowly and there were indications of very heavy fighting on their front about four miles from the coast and about the same from Caen. 30th Corps had extended laterally four or five miles towards Port-en-Bessin, almost to join up with the American V Corps. The Americans had got themselves on shore but had only moved about one mile from the Omaha beaches and two miles from the Utah beaches. Within the British beachhead everything appeared to be clear except for a pocket of major resistance at a place called Douvres, where some sort of underground headquarters was resisting strongly behind the 1st Corps front. So ended our last day at Fort Southwick. We packed up everything, including our office tents, into the office truck and moved back to camp.

Next day, D + 1, was our last day at the camp and was spent packing up. By this time, presumably, our Engineer advanced party, Brigadier Stone, with Colin Williams as his Staff Captain, was close to landing. Our second contingent, Otto Phibbs, Bob Moodie and Dick Allport-Williams were somewhere in the queue, as they were due to embark that afternoon. Meanwhile, on the other side, fighting continued vigorously; 50th Division on the 30th Corps front captured Bayeux and a large section of the Bayeux-Caen road. 1st Corps advanced slowly and it was already clear that the Germans were going to make an all-out effort to defend Caen, as their armoured divisions were pulled in to protect that salient, namely, the area where the Germans had halted the British advance although, on either side of Caen our advance was still continuing, thus leaving the static sector jutting out into British occupied territory.

All was great activity at the camp as we packed up our personal gear and tents and placed them on board the six trucks which it was my responsibility to lead. After an early lunch the mess staff pulled down the mess tents and finished their loading and just before teatime the first vehicles nosed out of camp and onto the open road leading to Fareham and Gosport. All the military world seemed to be converging on the same points. Somewhere near Southwick we were held up temporarily until our position to join the main queue came along and we took our place somewhere between an anti-aircraft battery and the final contingent of an infantry battalion.

Slowly, slowly, we ground south until just beyond Fareham we came to what we were told was our final halt for that night. We were in the middle of a housing estate and my leading truck was in front of a fairly new house with a small but delightful front garden. I made arrangements with the very willing householders for a couple of the other officers and myself to sleep on the grass, the remaining officers to sleep at other houses. Sergeant Swift and his colleague NCO's were told to make similar arrangements for themselves and the remaining men. Meanwhile, I had shown the way by persuading my hosts to provide cups of tea, while we ate our packed supper of bully beef sandwiches.

In the morning, supplies of hot water for washing and shaving were forthcoming from the houses and we were quickly ready to move again, only to have to wait a couple of hours or more before we ground off slowly, until we suddenly saw the sea in front of us at the seaplane base at Lee-on-the-Solent. A small row of American landing ships was drawn up at the hard with their ramps down. In no time at all the marshalls had waved us on board and we were quickly in position with the American seamen fastening chains from the deck to our wheels. Taking our personal packs we left our vehicles and mounted up to the quarters, which were ample for the relatively small number of troops we had with us, compared with the significant number of trucks and other vehicles which had been loaded.

Dinner, or high tea rather, was being served and we were able to forget the remainder of our sandwiches. We were fascinated by the American cafeteria system, which is now much more familiar in this country. We all voted it a fine meal of sausages and beans with a good solid pudding to follow. We went on deck just as the ramps were raised and we floated off on the incoming tide. Soon we were heading down the Solent, past the Isle of Wight and the Spithead Forts, to the open sea just as it was beginning to get dark.

We had only travelled a dozen or so miles since day began in the front garden and yet we seemed to have done so much, but it had passed in a flash. We were all accommodated in bunks with curtains and the gentle motion of the ship soon put me, at any rate, fast asleep.

Came the dawn, with virtually nothing in sight, except the three or four ships of our small convoy. Returning to the quarters we got on with washing and shaving and generally preparing to disembark after an excellent breakfast. It suddenly occurred to me, however, that I was unlikely to get a good bath for the next couple of months, so I rapidly stripped off and wallowed for nearly an hour. When I joined the others on deck, fully equipped as soldiers ready to go, I mentioned my bath to their intense annoyance, because they had not thought of it themselves, and the coast was in sight. The captain announced that he was not going to wait for the tide but was going straight in. He ordered us to join our transport. Either the other captains had had the same idea, or our man was the commodore, because the others turned into line abreast with us and also pushed on straight for the shore. With a bump we grounded and almost immediately the captain let down the ramp only for it to be patently obvious that we had arrived in ten feet of water, or more. We were going to have to wait. After a short while, the captain allowed us to leave our vehicles below, provided we stayed on the top deck.

We now had time to look around at "the vasty fields of France" but there were none to see. The broad beaches were fringed by a low lying range of sand hills, which with a few bathing huts here and there and a few seaside houses, completely blotted out the hinterland. The beaches themselves were absolutely and totally deserted and there was not a sign of life on shore although at least two miles were visible in each direction, but there were no beach obstacles, concrete pillboxes or gun emplacements, or any sign whatsoever that the beach had been either attacked or defended. Silence was total, except for on-board noises and the occasional sea bird. Faint curls of smoke rose from the stacks of the other ships but they too rapidly took on the somnolent look of the entire landscape. Behind us the sea was empty from horizon to horizon. It was almost eerie.

Slowly, slowly the water receded until it looked as if the depth off the end of the ramp might just possibly be some five or six feet. Clearly, the captain hoped it was less but decided that he could not afford to wait any longer for low tide. We were ordered to join our vehicles and the first intrepid ones advanced towards the ramp.

There was a small cheer as word came that the first one had entered the water and was moving away from the ship. Then when it was no more than twenty or thirty yards away, it chugged to a halt and stopped. The waterproofing of the engine had failed and it was going to get no further under its own steam. Similar fates befell the second and third and fourth but the captain made clear that we were all to get off his ship as soon as possible so before very long, some twenty or thirty vehicles were spread out in a fan in front of the ramp, all halted and all helpless.

Word came that the captain had radioed for assistance for us. He sounded his whistle in farewell, raised the ramp and with a mighty effort his engines drew his ship out into deeper water. In ten minutes he was almost out of sight and no help was yet visible from shore. In the next half hour the water did recede another foot or so but was still over the top of the wheels. We were just making up our minds to get our drivers to have a go at drying out our own engines when suddenly someone saw help approaching.

Gradually, a massive bulldozer, with a very small man at the controls, hove into view from the west. He splashed out into the water, which no way reached high enough to get the driver's feet wet and came out to the nearest of our vehicles. He passed over a chain and hook for the driver to fasten on to his vehicle and with a roar of the engine, he pulled it through the water, up the shore and onto the dry beach. A few minutes fiddling and towelling under the bonnet and the driver was able to start up his own vehicle and drive to the top of the beach. Each vehicle in turn was dealt with similarly and by about four o'clock we were ready to drive off.

According to my map, I judged that we had landed about half way between Arromanches and Asnelles. If so, our objective, which was near the village of Creully, was about five miles to the south. We headed for the nearest exit and as we crested the dunes the land behind became visible. There were at last a few signs of the fighting, shell holes in a building or two and rubble in the road where some wall had been knocked down, possibly by a tank, but otherwise general calm still prevailed. We threaded our way through a couple of hamlets and on to a passable secondary road. We had checked, before leaving camp in England, that Creully had been cleared of the enemy so I pressed on regardless and was soon obviously very close to the map reference I had been given. A bend in the road and a sight of the spire of what must have been the Creully church, and I seemed to be as near as anyone could ask for practical purposes.

We turned into a large grass field and pulled on to the top of a small fold in the ground with a reasonable view in most directions. There was no one to greet us and no sign posts but I was convinced I was right. We had made it and we were the first there.

After a few minutes look around — disclosing no sign of friend or foe, or plain neutral, in any direction — for lack of anything better to do I told the men to cook up their emergency rations. I think we had each been given two or three of these which were each contained in packages a little larger than a one pound box of chocolates. We opened them with great interest and the first item to emerge was a tin of self-heating soup. I

144

stood mine on a couple of stones, lit the fuse and stood back. It did not explode but fizzed away nicely, until the soup was steaming. We all voted the soup course as first class. Next came dry mince, which had to be mixed with a small amount of water from our water bottles, and heated up in our mess tins over some wood chippings and dry sticks we found lying around. In spite of adequate cooking, it seemed gritty to the end and was not so highly regarded, although the reconstituted potato was tolerable. Pudding was a fairly large bar of good chocolate and we finished on cheese from a small tin and a few of the biscuits, which constituted most the rest of our "goodie" parcel. The rest was a small packet of cornflakes, some dried milk, a little sugar and a tea bag and a small tin of bacon, which was clearly intended for our breakfast.

By this time the sun was setting and we began to wonder about sleeping arrangements. However, this was soon settled for us. As the sun went down, so, apparently, the enemy woke up. Overhead came the drone of one or two planes in the sky. I cannot recall whether we had doubts about them or not, but it was very clear that a dozen or more anti-aircraft batteries in the near vicinity had no doubt that they were enemies and opened up with everything they had and for a while we were treated to a first class fireworks show. However, the aftermath was not quite so pleasant. In a couple of moments the shrapnel started to rain down in bits that were thumping into the tilts of the trucks and, more ominously, into the ground around us. We had been standing out watching the show but, as one man, with me only slightly behind, everyone dived for the cover available under the vehicles. That was fatal. After a long day, the warm summer evening and the cessation of the artillery allowed us all to drop off into a deep sleep. I have never ceased since to blame myself for not setting a sentry or two before dropping off and had we been surprised by the enemy during the night, I would have had no excuse. Fortunately the enemy was already three or four miles away and showed no inclination to come back. I got away with it.

Come the early dawn, I naturally needed to get up and was staggered to find that the whole field was now full from end to end with a multitude of trucks like our own. I was naturally relieved to find that not one of their crews had set a sentry on duty either and I was the only man in the camp who was actually awake. During the night the rest of the Army Headquarters had arrived, seen our lonely vehicles, decided we were clearly on the right spot and joined us — a tribute to my map reading no doubt — but not to my sense of military priorities.

No one seemed to be stirring in the other vehicles and our lot clearly were, so I went back to my bed for another half hour until Private Lunney appeared with tea and a mug full of shaving water, and so the day began.

In due course, the Camp Commandant, a Lieutenant Colonel (Quartermaster) of the Grenadier Guards, and members of his staff appeared. We were, in fact, at exactly the right spot that they had intended in their orders before we left England and the actual position that the headquarters was due to occupy was in the next field down the hill. We were shown to our appointed site for the engineer headquarters and unpacking the vehicles and erecting of our office tents began.

Not everyone had offices in tents — the majority did not. The Brigadier had a 3-ton truck to himself of which half of the back had been converted to a fairly comfortable sleeping quarter and the other half to an office. Another caravan/office had been allotted to Colonel Phibbs and two other trucks, with tented side extensions, had been converted to offices, one for the Operations staff — Moodie, Colin Williams and Baker, and one for the Intelligence Staff — Allport-Williams and his two captains. Ted Hutton and I were meant to share an office tent and also to share a sleeping tent, but we decided we preferred the arrangement of each having a joint sleeping and office tent. Other officers, usually liaison officers or flooding experts, from the Belgian and Dutch forces, joined us from time to time — two or three was a good average. They were allotted tents on the same basis as Ted and myself. The standard tent that we used was a square one in plan, 14' × 14'. The side walls were about 2' high and the ridge pole was 7' above the ground. The tent was also fitted with a fly sheet which kept it reasonably cool most of the time, particularly if both ends were open.

By lunch time all the tents were erected and telephones connected and we were in action. Accordingly, we set out to find the mess which was a modest walk away from our section. On the way we looked for and found the "G" Staff tents and caravans. Sure enough the situation maps were outside available for study. It was now "D + 4" but Second Army still had not quite reached all the "D" Day objectives. 30th Corps was now well astride the Bayeux-Caen Road, which we had expected to reach on "D" Day, but 1st Corps was still three miles away from Caen and 6th Airborne Division was still some miles short of its "D" Day objective, which had been the line of the River Dives between Cabourg and Troarn. More and more Panzer Divisions had been identified on the Caen front or on the way to it. All these Panzer divisions had had, or were having, very hazardous journeys to the front. Bomber Command was putting in some surprisingly accurate bombing of the railway lines and, especially, of every bridge of significance. It was beginning to take a week or more for the enemy to travel relatively short distances and their losses on the way were heavy. However, 12 SS Panzer (Hitler Jugend), 21 Panzer and 116 Panzer had already arrived. These were all high quality divisions and were going to be very difficult to budge from their positions. (See Map 3)

At the mess tents, tables were set out in the open for lunch. We were now able to see clearly who were going to be our colleagues in "D" mess for most of the campaign. The engineers and signals made up a large proportion. There were four camouflage officers, also Royal Engineers, although not forming part of our department. The five from the engineer's department were Hutton, Roberts, Williams, Baker and myself. The four signals officers included two majors, Croskin and Withers-Green, and Captain Walker together with another staff captain. Then there was one artilleryman, Major Esmond. There was also a medical major who turned out to be a psychiatrist, together with the camp doctor, Captain MacDonald, and also the camp padre, Major Wansey. There were two other engineers, of the survey department, Major Leishman and Captain Bartlett. Finally, I think, there were two or three gentlemen whose work appeared to be rather specially secret. One was Major Christopher Mayhew who later became a Labour MP and Minister but who later joined the Liberal Party and was created a Life Peer.

All the faces were familiar as we had all been part of the same mess in the assembly area before embarkation. Everyone had stories to tell about their journeys over. Some, indeed, had come over earlier and had been temporarily working at Tactical Headquarters.

There was very little work to do at first, once our offices were established, but it was important to form an impression as soon as possible as to how well the engineer stores were coming on shore. Accordingly, I set out next day to find out. This involved a grand tour of the beaches. Unfortunately, at the time when I went around, the tide appeared to be out and I did not see any ships at all that were unloading, or even parked on the beaches. I gathered that the turn round of the ships was extremely swift. They came in as the tide began to fall, dried out — or nearly so — and went out on the next rising tide, being in for some six to eight hours at most. It seemed that most of them carried vehicles on deck and on top of the heavier stores in the hold. Engineer stores appeared to be mostly near the bottom which was not surprising as there was little fear of squashing the bundles of pierced steel planking, the drums of bitumen and the bundles of sandbags and barbed wire. The main secret appeared to be to have a constant supply of trucks coming out alongside the ship for loading and rapid clearance of the stores. On every beach there were some signs of spillage of the engineer stores but that was presumably from over-full lorries lurching up the beach.

Major Hall, of the 174 Workshop and Park Company, seized his opportunity to get the jeep, which he considered worthy of himself, instead of the small 8 cwt truck that he had been allotted in his war equipment tables and which he considered to be an insult to a driver of his capabilities. Accordingly, one night he took his place in the queue of drivers waiting to pick up the spare vehicles as they were unloaded and drive them to the Ordnance Corps vehicle park. He wore other ranks clothes for the purpose and when his turn came he collected a vehicle but did not take it to the vehicle park. He merely commandeered it for his own use.

"D + 4" was only the third day on which such stores were being landed and there seemed to be some evidence that more engineer stores were being diverted direct to use than were actually reaching the depots. The bitumen had not yet begun to arrive and it was understandable that the defence stores should be drawn out pretty quickly and I believe that, in fact, Ted Hutton had arranged for the beach parties to deliver his pierced steel planking direct to the proposed fighter strips. Accordingly, it was difficult to form a judgement yet as to whether all our consignments were arriving but such evidence as was available was moderately encouraging. It is difficult to remember just why I never visited the beaches again. Presumably I had some work to do though I cannot recall what it would be at that stage of the operations.

Each evening at dusk one or two German planes flew over to a very spirited anti-aircraft reception. We soon took precautions against the falling shrapnel by having our batmen dig shallow pits for us in our sleeping area and put our beds into them. For further protection we moved our tables over the top of them and felt moderately safe. As a matter of fact, the precaution was totally unnecessary. The slightly slack fly sheets of our tents were fully shrapnel-proof. It merely bounced off and never once did I see any sign that the jagged metal had actually punctured the fly sheets. We soon abandoned the pits and filled them in.

We had been in Creully Camp for four or five days when our own private prisoner of war came to light. He had been hiding in a ditch only yards away from my tent ever since the invasion began and he deemed it safer to hide rather than be a hero for the Fatherland. He had lost his steel helmet and his rifle, or had dumped them somewhere, and finally decided the time had come to reveal himself. There was great excitement among our batmen when they "captured" him. They gave him a meal of bread and cheese for which he was duly grateful and haled him off to the Camp Commandant's Office — where he no doubt got fed again — before being consigned to the prisoner of war depot on one of the beaches. A steady trickle of prisoners was passing through these every day as more and more of the enemy decided that square meals in a British Prisoner of War Camp were more welcome than the call of unfed duty.

The daily changes in the "G" maps were relatively small until about the 12th of June ("D + 6") when the Americans made a decisive move forward from the Omaha immediate beachhead and crossed the St. Lo — Bayeux Road in the Foret de Cerisy, near Balleroy. 30th Corps moved up to keep pace with them and captured Tilly-Sur-Seulles and the Caen salient became even more pronounced as 1st Corps was still only able to inch forward. U.S. troops, having overcome their initial difficulties on the beaches, had advanced forty miles in the first week. 30th Corps had moved thirty miles but 1st Corps was still little more than ten miles from the start and six miles from Caen. The northern suburbs of that city were steadily being converted to piles of rubble which increased rather than decreased the opportunities for the Panzer Divisions, and particularly the S.S., to continue their dogged and bitter resistance.

The next week saw comparatively little movement of all fronts and none at all on the 1st Corps front. The only striking feature was that United States forces from the Utah beaches drove right across the Contentin Peninsula to Barneville. This cut off the Germans defending Cherbourg from contact with the rest of their forces.

Gradually progress was falling more and more behind the most optimistic projections of the "Overlord" plans. The main reason for this was due to the weather and the effects that it had had on the Mulberry harbours and thus on the build-up of the incoming troops. A storm on about "D + 4 or D + 5" had completely destroyed the harbour being built on the American front and knocked about the one at Arromanches on the British front considerably. All salvageable material from the first harbour was transferred to the second to make it stronger and slightly extended. This meant that more material had to be brought over the beaches than had originally been intended but mostly it was the arrival of new divisions that was most delayed.

Fortunately the enemy build-up was also delayed but for different reasons. R.A.F. and American Airforce fighter bombers were giving the German army a torrid time as they attempted to concentrate more and more divisions against the British and American fronts. By the 30th of June, just over three weeks after the first landing, 8th Corps, largely made up of armoured divisions, had come in on the British front and VII and XIX Corps on the American front so that something like twenty British and American divisions in all were now present.

However, more than twenty divisions had also shown up on the German side, although a number of these were now represented by little more than badly mauled remnants. Seven of the nine divisions on the British front were Panzer Divisions and four of those were of the particularly formidable S.S. troops. There was no doubt that Second British Army had drawn off and was holding the cream of the German army but this served our purpose ideally as the First U.S. Army was increasingly able to push southwards and begin to swing round to face east. In the last days of June Cherbourg fell but it was to be many weeks before the benefit of that acquisition would be felt by our shipping.

Bitter fighting continued around Caen with 1st and 8th Corps giving the Germans no rest. 30th Corps on the left flank of the First U.S. Army had problems of another nature. They were now fully enmeshed in the "bocage" country. The feature of this area was the large number of small fields surrounded by thick high earth banks with hedges on top and many trees. In June and July the area was literally overgrown with foliage making defence easy and attack almost suicidal. Unsupported infantry could make little progress and armoured progress could best be described as very difficult indeed. Every small advance cost heavy losses and enormous expenditure of ammunition.

Ted Hutton and I thought we ought to go and see this bocage country, which was certainly slowing up progress. It would also give me an opportunity to see whether, anywhere along the way so far, we might have missed any worthwhile local supplies of engineer stores. I was particularly keen to find a local supply of timber but there may have been some other local sources of glass, paint or even bitumen. However, the whole area looked to be entirely devoted to farming, there seemed to be no local road depots and little forestry that we were able to find.

However, the bocage was certainly all around us and it was a totally new experience to the two of us to see the sort of country through which our infantry were having to battle their way. No wonder some of them were feeling discouraged and it was amazing what was actually being achieved. We saw nothing whatsoever either of our own troops or of the enemy as the country gradually closed in on us even more and more. The only evidence of the war was a lone cow which had been shot. It was lying on its back; its body already bloating with decay; its feet stuck ludicrously upwards. Meanwhile, on the hot summer day the only sound was the buzz of insects and the only smell was the sticky smell of the decaying cow.

I was certain that I knew where we were on the map but where we were in relation to the front line I had no real idea at all, except that I thought that we were getting fairly close to the last red lines on the lunchtime map and the first blue ones indicating the enemy. There was no indication whatsoever as to where either party might be. Suddenly, when we had slowed down almost to a stop, a very young looking soldier with a Welsh accent rose out of the ditch beside us clutching his machine pistol.

"I don't think you should go any further Sir" said he, "Gerry is just up ahead round the next bend. I'm the last of our people and I'm just thinking of moving back a bit."

"Good for you lad" I said, "we haven't seen anybody for quite a bit and I was just thinking of turning back anyway."

He grinned at us and vanished into the hedgerow. The road ahead still looked silent and ominous and that was the nearest I ever got to meeting the enemy seriously and certainly the nearest to firing a shot in anger. We would have looked silly getting captured because we expected to see the front line before we hit it.

Long before our first fortnight was up and the final stores I had ordered had been landed, 21st Army Group took over responsibility for the depots from us. By the second week the need for road work was becoming essential, even though there had been no rain, and the Engineer-in-Chief of 21st Army Group, now Major General Eustace Tickell, had decided to hold a regular allocation meeting for bitumen once a week. With my opposite number from First Canadian Army, who had now landed and taken over 1st Corps from Second Army, and our colleague from the L of C (Line of Communications) area we sat down to consider the situation. I thought the theory was that, if it was to be a bidding match, I should make my claim firmly and not hold back. A couple of days later John Stone got a letter from the General complaining about my attitude. Fortunately for me Stone took a relaxed view and merely wrote back that he thought that my arguing must have been based on an excess of zeal.

Pluto seemed to come into action without any trouble at all. At some stage — I think it was in the second week — we changed over and found that no more cans of petrol were being landed on the beach. Instead, somewhere there was a can filling plant and all went smoothly.

The 174 Workshop and Park Company had arrived at about the same time as I had landed myself. It took over the depots temporarily established by the Corps Field Park Companies and the 174's workshops were set up in Bayeux.

The end of the "Beachhead" phase cannot be precisely defined. It would no longer be relevant when it was no longer necessary to land supplies over the beaches, but this did not happen for many months. Alternatively, the "Beachhead" would be regarded as an inappropriate description when the enemy had been driven back so far that no counter attack could be expected to reach the beaches or to "drive our forces back into the sea". In that case it could have almost been ended from "D" Day onwards. However, my own guess is that the first week in July represented the end of beachhead defence operations. In that week the Americans were driving south along their whole front and 1st Corps swept into the northern suburbs of Caen (**See Maps 4A and 4B**). 30th Corps pushed on grimly into the bocage while 12th Corps, with 8th Corps and 2nd Canadian Corps in support, began to push south-eastwards towards the encirclement of Caen. This, to me, looked like the real beginning of the break-out stage.

Towards the end of our time in the beachhead Montgomery called a meeting of all the officers of Second Army Headquarters as a follow-up to the one he had held in the Portsmouth area before embarkation. He reviewed the landings and the beachhead battles. He commended all the army for its achievements and made favourable references to the work of the supporting arms — artillery, engineers, signals and so on. However, he had some reservations about the morale and elan of the infantry. He referred to the fact that, with the exception of the Canadians, the leading troops in the assault on the beaches were all drawn from divisions brought home for the purpose from North Africa and Italy. He said that they had done their initial tasks magnificently but subsequently they had shown a reluctance to get involved seriously in the battles. Indeed, there had been much murmuring that it was time they were let off and that those troops, who had spent the war so far in Britain, should take up the real strain.

Pursuing his theme, he said that the whole gist of war news and of the contents of Army Bureau of Current Affairs publications was that the war was as good as won and it only required a small push more to topple Hitler's Germany. He said that a man would readily give his life in defence of his family, his home and his country when things looked black. "It was," he said, "totally different when everyone was talking about what a glorious thing life after the war would be when we had won and all danger had passed". A man might well question why he should give his life for other people to enjoy these benefits. Accordingly he was not at all surprised at the dissatisfaction of some of the North African veterans.

On the other hand, he now had to question whether those formations were spent forces and likely to be unreliable in battle. We should not, therefore, be surprised to find that, although their names might still appear in the order of battle, certain divisions might in future have no role. Indeed, their infantry could be broken up and used as reinforcements for other divisions and their artillery, engineers and signals, for example, could henceforth be used as Army support groups as AGRAs (Army Groups Royal Artillery) and AGREs (Army Groups Royal Engineers) and so on. He also referred to the fact that Britain was close to exhausting its available resources of infantry. Whether the question of morale or the question of the sheer logic of numbers would be the ruling factor he apparently left us to decide for ourselves. As always, a Monty lecture was a combination of the informative, the stimulating, the thoughtful and the threatening — but very well worth listening to.

CHAPTER 12 Headquarters Second Army —
The Advance to the Rhine
(July, 1944 – September, 1944)

At last the front began to move in a decisive fashion. 8th Corps, which comprised three British armoured divisions, was transferred from the Second British Army front to come under command of First Canadian Army and there commenced operation "Goodwood" in mid July, a three-pronged attack by the three armoured divisions moving southwards around the perimeter of Caen. 2nd Canadian Corps followed with infantry through the suburbs on the right of the armoured divisions. On the left 1st Corps moved forward to reach the River Dives and the Caen salient was virtually eliminated. **(See Map 4c)**

Now followed some weeks of intense excitement and almost constant movement. At first the movement was most marked on the American Army front. On 25th July, the Americans commenced their drive from the Lessay-St. Lo start line. On their right wing, VIII Corps covered nearly 130 miles by 5th August through Coutances, Granville and Avranches to Rennes and Vannes, cutting right through Brittany. Elements of this Corps were now attacking westwards. The remaining German garrisons in Brittany amounted to some six relatively untouched infantry divisions but, by about 10th August, they had been shut into the perimeters of the two naval bases at Brest and Lorient. A further infantry division was cut off in the Channel Islands. These garrisons were left where they were and finally surrendered many weeks later. St. Lazaire, Nantes and Angers fell about 6th August and Le Mans was reached by the 8th.

On the left flank of the United States First Army their V Corps had to battle through the bocage to reach Vire but that fifteen miles by 4th August was progress indeed. Beyond, on their left flank, British 8th Corps conformed, reaching Vire and the road from Vire to Vassy on the same day. In the British centre, 30th Corps struggled up the slopes of Mount Pincon, some ten miles from their start line of 28th July. As every formation turned eastwards a new north-south front began to take shape.

In the German centre, Panzer Group West and the German Seventh Army battled manfully. Not a yard of ground was readily conceded, but their position was becoming increasingly hopeless. An interesting bulge was developing in their front.

From Vire to Caen the British and Canadian front ran north-eastwards, hinging on Vire. From Vire to Le Mans the American front ran south-eastwards and the Canadians at Caen were sixty miles away from the Americans at Le Mans on 8th August. This became known as the Falaise Gap and the Canadians now pressed hard to the south down the Caen-Falaise road, while the Americans drove north up the Le Mans-Argentan road to close that gap.

The delay to the American V Corps and XIX Corps was partly caused by the difficult fighting faced in the thick bocage area but it was partly also caused by the German lack of mobility which prevented them from retreating fast enough to keep their lines straight.

The Germans could have been expected to make immediate efforts to withdraw from the Vire area, thirty miles to the west, before the gap was closed. This would have involved the German army in wholesale retreat to the line of the River Seine, but they might at least have saved their army. However, at this point Hitler himself took charge of the battle. He ordered Panzer Group West to counter-attack with seven of the available nine Panzer divisions with the object of breaking through from Mortain to the sea at Avranches. This would, potentially, cut off the two American corps, which had advanced further south. Some ten German infantry divisions were also committed to the counter attack and holding open the flanks with the support of the crack 21st Panzer division on the north and the redoubtable 12th S.S. (Hitler Jugend) Panzer division on the south.

At the head of the bulge, at Vire and Mortain (40 miles west of Argentan), the German counter-attack made little progress. Their forces began to fall back to escape the closing jaws which were, by 16th August, a mere ten miles apart at Argentan and about the same at Briouze (15 miles west of Argentan). In this double pocket, seventeen German divisions were held in a hopeless traffic jam, with vehicles literally unable to move. 21st Panzer and 12th S.S. Panzer by their efforts enabled large numbers of men to escape but these men had to leave behind most of their tanks and guns and almost all their wheeled transport. It was a defeat of epic proportions.

By 17th August, the American VII Corps closed the gap at Briouze. Shortly afterwards, on 19th August, Polish Armoured Division and 4th Canadian Armoured Division closed the gap at Chambois (near Argentan). Thousands of Germans were trapped in the final pockets which were quickly eliminated. All the Allies now turned eastwards and headed for the Seine, which was reached along the whole front between Troyes, some hundred miles south-east of Paris, and the sea at Quillebeuf, a hundred miles north-west of Paris, by 25th August. (See Map 6)

The Germans had lost nearly 500,000 men, more than half their

154

strength in the west, and were falling back in complete disarray with the way to the German border apparently fully open in front of us. It was a complete debacle of classic scale. The Overlord Plan had indicated to us in London that we would reach the lines of the Seine and Loire by "D + 90" and, although some of the first stages had gone a little slowly, that target of the first week in September had been triumphantly achieved with ten days to spare.**(See Map 5)**

During the month that I have just described, Army Main Headquarters moved twice, the first time from Creully to near Caumont (presumably to keep in closer touch with American First Army during 8th Corps' advance to Vire) and, second, to near Villers-Bocage, when the whole of Second Army advanced, in conformity with Second Canadian Army against Falaise and Chambois. When the whole front turned eastwards and moved towards the Seine, Army Headquarters moved up to Gace. During this month Second Army made small demands for engineer stores and the only dump being used at the moment was the main depot in the rear maintenance area which lay astride the Bayeux-Caen road and was administered by Line of Communication Headquarters under the direct control of 21st Army Group. 174th Workshop and Park Company was in process of handing over responsibility for the engineer dump, ready to move forward.

There was, in fact, very little for me to do except to visit the new areas as they were captured in the hope that somewhere the Germans might have left behind some depots of the materials they must have been using for the construction of the beach defences — although these would largely be in the First Canadian Army area — or one would have expected somewhere to find forestry products or materials of that nature from the industry of the area. I can only say that I found none of either.

For the crossing of the Seine, four bridges were prescribed on the Second Army front but one of these, the lighter one for 12th Corps, was not built as proposed at or near Muids because of intense enemy opposition at the site. Their other bridge, was built at St. Pierre du Vauvray without any particular difficulty. Two bridges were built by 43rd Division on the 30th Corps front, one a heavy floating Bailey, downstream of Vernon, and the other a Class 9 folding boat equipment bridge in Vernon itself. The 43rd Division crossing was made on 25th August. The leading infantry used storm boats with large outboard engines and met light opposition. The engineers were harrassed by distant shell fire which interfered slightly with ferrying and bridging until on 28th August the high ground overlooking the crossing area was clear. HQ Second Army crossed the lighter bridge on 28th or 29th August.

On 1st September the Supreme Commander, General Eisenhower, took over direct control of the land battle. Twelfth United States Army

Group then came directly under his command, rather than being under the operational control of General Montgomery. He retained control of First Canadian Army and Second British Army in 21st Army Group and was promoted Field Marshal. 21st Army Group successively set up No. 1 cushion depot at Falaise, No. 3 roadhead depot near Lisieux, No. 4 roadhead depot near Laigle and No. 3a roadhead close up to the River Seine. Although these intermediate depots had a short life this process enabled longer hauls to be made by the biggest transport vehicles and reduced the turn-round for the smaller vehicles of the operational formations. I cannot recall that the engineer stores were put into these temporary depots and I am sure that much more petrol than ammunition went into them. No doubt the Pluto pipeline was being extended as rapidly as possible.

Army Headquarters made no special arrangements for the supply of bridging equipment to the Seine crossings. They were relatively short and one of the three bridges that were built was done from the assaulting division's own bridging column. The two Bailey bridges were, presumably, supplied by the Bridge Companies RASC. (See Map 7)

Once across the Seine, and when the bridge sites were free of any danger of counter-attack, 12th Corps and 30th Corps pressed on rapidly. The lead was now taken by two armoured divisions with their tanks running on their own tracks while the other armoured division and an armoured brigade followed up closely but with the tanks carried on transporters. The Second Army centre line passed through Amiens, Lille and Alost to Antwerp. On the way, Second Army troops captured such towns in the north-east of France as Doullens, St. Pol, Arras, Bethune, Douai and Roubaix. Crossing the border into Belgium, Courtrai, Ghent, Tournai, Brussels, Malines and Louvain were also captured and 11th Armoured Division entered Antwerp on 4th September. This was a journey of 250 miles from the Seine, in about six days. First Canadian Army conformed on the left capturing such channel ports as Le Havre, St. Valery, Dieppe, Boulogne, Calais, Dunkirk, Ostend and Zeebrugge. First Canadian Army subsequently took over responsibility for Antwerp from 30th Corps in order to free the latter for the subsequent advance into Holland. On the right of British Second Army the First United States Army reached the general line of Namur-Tirlemont and the Third United States Army had also closed up to the line of the upper Meuse from Sedan to Verdun and Commercy. There was now a short pause for the consolidation of the front and the elimination of remaining pockets of resistance.

At this point it is necessary to describe the effects of the great extension of the lines of communication and also the effects of the change in the command structure. The front line at Antwerp and beyond was already some 350 miles from the original invasion beaches and the artificial harbour at Arromanche. Although many ports had now been captured they were mostly far from ready to begin importing material from the U.K. The following tabulation shows that some time had to pass before they were all ready for use and, even after that, further time was necessary to provide rail facilities.

Dieppe	captured	1	Sep.	opened	5	Sep.
Ostend	captured	9	Sep.	opened	28	Sep.
Boulogne	captured	22	Sep.	opened	14	Oct.
Calais	captured	30	Sep.	opened	21	Nov.

Each of these ports was rail served, but the railways could not be opened until the port was opened and in some cases they took even longer. Dieppe was connected by rail to Lille via Amiens by 10th September but Ostend was not linked to Antwerp until 12th October.

It is relevant at this point to mention that Antwerp itself was still 100 miles away from the Rhine which was, of course, the key objective of our forces at that stage. However, Antwerp was still not itself availabe for connection to the open sea, from which it was some 40 – 50 miles distant. Both sides of that waterway were still occupied by the enemy in strength and passage of supply ships into Antwerp from the open sea was not going to be possible until both banks had been cleared. This did not happen until mid October.

In consequence, supplies of all sorts still had to make the long journey from the beachhead to the front, mostly by road, for some weeks to come. Supplies of petrol, in particular, were hard to come by but the demand for engineer stores was rising rapidly and supplies of ammunition and rations had still to be maintained. This last factor had a major bearing on the question of whether the final assault on the Rhine should be made on a narrow selective front or on a broad front.

Montgomery had argued and felt he had made his case that the Second Army was sufficiently near to the Rhine to "bounce" a crossing with the utmost speed before the enemy could re-organise to stop us. On the other hand First United States Army and Third United States Army were equally close and had less water obstacles to face. What was quite clear was that sufficient supplies could not be brought forward to enable three or more armies to reach the Rhine rapidly in sufficient strength to have a real chance of success. Eisenhower therefore decided that all three armies at least should be given equal priority but he did give permission for Montgomery to try to bounce a crossing if he could with his own resources.

Montgomery decided to try and ordered 30th Corps to re-commence the advance on 7th September. 30th Corps was to attempt to establish three parallel routes northwards on a front of some 20 – 30 miles. Guards Armoured Division commenced the centre route by making an assault crossing of the Albert Canal. All bridges had been destroyed, that at Beeringen on 8th September. Guards Armoured then pushed forward via Bourg Leopold, heading for the De Groot bridge over the Escaut Canal near Neerpelt. The bridge was secured intact on 10th September and the bridgehead built up next day. 11th Armoured Division was brought up on the right of the Guards and advanced to Bree, also on the Escaut Canal. On the left of the Guards, 50th Division crossed the Albert Canal at Gheel and 15th Division passed through them and crossed the Escaut Canal to capture Rethy.

Bourg Leopold was a major centre for the Belgian army in peace time and it was chosen immediately by the Second Army staff as being entirely suitable for a major base for our further advance. A site was allocated for an engineer stores depot as well as sites for ammunition, petrol and rations depots. Other administrative establishments were also sited there, including facilities for ordnance stores, REME workshops, medical facilities and a reinforcement camp, as well as a prisoner of war staging depot.

The enemy was becoming increasingly active and was attacking the bridgeheads over the Escaut Canal. In any event, delay was inevitable while stocks and supplies of all descriptions were built up at Bourg Leopold. In order to assist the advance of 30th Corps, with 12th Corps following in support, 8th Corps was grounded. All its second line transport and half its first line transport was made available to help the build-up. In addition, Montgomery had to admit to Eisenhower that Second Army could not manage to maintain the necessary speed in face of evidence of enemy build-up, and secured from Supreme Headquarters extra daily airlift of some 400 – 500 tons per day, together with some American truck companies who would increase daily deliveries by a further 500 tons per day.

At the same time extra assistance had to be given to First United States Army in order to enable them to keep pace on Second British Army's right flank. With this assistance, Montgomery was able to decide to re-commence the advance on 17th September and aim for the Rhine. However, the administrative margin was slight and autumn weather was beginning to give some cause for concern, because of its likely effect on air support operations.

After Hitler's personal and devastating intervention in the Battle of Normandy he had handed back command in the west to the professionals, although Field Marshal Von Kluge had committed suicide shortly after the surrender of Paris.

Field Marshal Model took over command in the west temporarily but handed this over to Field Marshal Von Rundstedt, as Commander-in-Chief, while Model retained command of Army Group "B". These two were a formidable combination — if free from interference.

Between the Escaut Canal, at the De Groot bridge, and the Neder Rijn (Lower Rhine), at Arnhem, there were six main water crosssings to be considered. First was the Wilhelmina Canal (from Tilburg to Helmond) at Son followed by, six miles further on, the Zuid Willemsvaart Canal (from 's Hertogenbosch to Helmond) at Veghel. Then, a further 15 miles beyond, came the crossing of the River Maas (the Dutch section of the Meuse) at Grave. Next was the Maas-Waal Canal, three miles outside Nijmegen, followed by the Waal itself at Nijmegen and, finally, the Neder Rijn at Arnhem. The Waal was the southern and wider arm of the River Rhine which splits into two on its way to the sea just to the east of Nijmegen, the Neder Rijn being the northern and somewhat narrower arm of the Rhine. These six formidable obstacles were all crammed into a sixty miles stretch of a single road and once it became clear that this road was the main axis of a really determined drive by British Second Army (to advance to the Zuider Zee and thus to open up the whole North German plain) it could be expected that every one of the bridges at these crossings would be demolished. The only hope of securing them intact was to capture them by an airborne "coup de main".

The Supreme Commander made available to British Second Army the 101st U.S. Airborne Division to capture the canal bridges at Son and Veghel, the 82nd U.S. Airborne Division to capture the bridges at Grave and Nijmegen and the British First Airborne Division and the Polish Airborne Brigade to capture the Arnhem bridge and to help with the capture of the bridges over the Waal at Nijmegen.

Looked at objectively after nearly fifty years, and being wise after the event, to have expected to capture all six of these major crossings seems too much of a gamble. To lose even one crossing would cause serious delays in bringing through ground support to the lightly armed airborne divisions. These were certain to be counter-attacked very heavily indeed. However, the outrageous nature of the gamble was possibly its strongest point and had the whole thing succeeded the gain would have been enormous, and would have almost certainly shortened the war by at least six months, and much bitter fighting could have been avoided.

Second Army Main Headquarters was now established in its last tented camp for the summer season on the heathland somewhere near Bourg Leopold and my department had built up stocks of bridging equipment, including storm boats, at Bourg Leopold depot, in charge of 174th Workshop and Park Company. The question, however, was whether we would be able to get significant amounts of bridging equipment forward quickly, because of congestion on the roads.

The whole of Holland south of the Rhine was low lying and the main road was, in many areas, built up above the level of the surrounding countryside with deep ditches on either side. The road was only wide enough for one column of traffic in each direction. There were also many cross ditches which made it virtually impossible for any parallel, off-road, routes to be developed. Where not completely open, the surrounding country was also heavily wooded with evergreen trees which gave plenty of cover for attacking columns and battle groups to infiltrate near to and onto the road.

On 17th September the great advance began with Guards Armoured Division leading the attack for 30th Corps and advancing out of the De Groot bridgehead. By that night it had advanced six miles and captured Valkenswaard. The 101st U.S. Airborne Division had captured the bridge at Veghel intact, but at Son the bridge was blown by the enemy when the paratroops were only a few hundred yards away. The 82nd U.S. Airborne had captured the bridge at Grave and later secured crossings over the Maas-Waal Canal but its efforts to rush the big Nijmegen bridge failed, although the bridge was not yet destroyed.

The 1st British Airborne Division had landed where expected but was still rather too far from Arnhem for comfort. However, it did appear that some parachute troops had captured the northern end of the Arnhem bridge but were being hard pressed. On the whole, the first day's progress could be regarded as surprisingly satisfactory with the sole exception, perhaps, of the northern end. The difficulty was now to hold on to what we had gained until 30th Corps could link up. For reasons already mentiomed, this was to prove a difficult task.

On 18th September, Guards Armoured Division passed through Aalst without difficulty and attempted to enter Eindhoven but the town was strongly held. Armoured cars bypassed the town and made contact with 101st U.S. Airborne Division who reported the loss of the Son bridge. Bridging equipment was ordered up. Late in the day Eindhoven fell to combined American and British attacks.

Bridging was completed overnight and next morning Guards Armoured Division crossed at Son and pressed on 25 miles in all. It passed the bridge at Veghel, and linked up with 82nd U.S. Airborne Division at the captured bridge at Grave over the Maas. The next bridge, over the Maas-Waal Canal, was found unfit for tanks and a detour was required to another crossing. Parts of Guards Armoured Division were now able to concentrate near Nijmegen ready for an assault on the major bridge.

Meanwhile, 82nd U.S. Airborne was suffering increasing attacks from German forces in the Reichswald Forest, which was, in fact, the northern end of the German defence works known as the Siegfried Line. The presence of the Guards Armoured Division soon relieved this pressure and discouraged the direct intervention of German forces in Nijmegen, which was hindering the assault on the bridge itself.

The through connection, all the way from the Escaut Canal to the Waal, had now been established but it was precarious and, particularly in the area of Uden, just north of Veghel, the road was cut from time to time. It was essential to widen the corridor of country under our control and to get more infantry forward as soon as possible. On the left 12th Corps pushed forward and captured Turnhout and had fair success in widening the salient as far up as the Wilhelmina Canal. On the right, 11th Armoured Division and 3rd Division of 8th Corps were making slow progress but eventually reached the Wilhelmina Canal, capturing Helmond, Gemert and Deurne.

Difficulties still continued at Uden, but every effort now had to be made to capture the Nijmegen bridge and link up with the 1st Airborne Division at Arnhem. Just as the balance of luck had favoured the operations of the two American airborne divisions and the operations of 30th Corps thus far, so there were no favours shown to the 1st Airborne Division. They were endeavouring to concentrate four miles west of the Arnhem bridge, while troops of the parachute brigade held on to a small area in the immediate vicinity of the bridge itself. The first landings on 17th September had been moderately successful but the weather closed in on the 18th and the re-supply of ammunition and food on 18th September was a failure, supplies either falling direct into the hands of the enemy or not being dropped at all.

On 19th September the weather was generally bad and airborne reinforcement and re-supply again failed. In some way the weather was interfering with radio communications and it was not possible to change the dropping zones which had fallen into enemy hands. Only a quarter of the re-supply of food and ammunition reached the troops on the ground and the Polish Parachute Brigade was unable to take off from bases in England. In Nijmegen there was bitter fighting as the Anglo-American forces gradually cleared the town on 20th September up to the southern approaches to the bridge.

On 20th September a joint attack on the Nijmegen bridge was made by troops of the Guards Armoured Division who assaulted the bridge itself while the 504th (U.S.) Regimental Combat Team made an assault crossing of the river about one mile west of the town. The American troops had been supplied with British storm boats in which they had had little practice and it seems, anyway, that the boats and their outboard motors had become separated and, furthermore, because of delays on the road from Bourg Leopold, only sufficient boats had arrived to carry one battalion at a time. The operation was in full view of the enemy and there was little or no cover when the attackers had landed on the far side. Nevertheless, the assault was magnificently successful, although heavy casualties were suffered. The Americans captured the northern end of both the rail bridge and the road bridge. Thereupon the Guards' tanks burst through and joined up with them. There was considerable mopping up and removal of demolition charges to deal with but still no contact with the paratroops.

The final stages of the operation of the airborne troops around Arnhem and the incredible difficulties of trying to join up with them across open low lying ground, with dozens of deep ditches, has been graphically described by other writers and will not be repeated here. Suffice it to say that magnificent efforts were made on both sides of the Neder Rijn but eventually the last 2,400 men had to be evacuated and the attempt to hold a bridgehead over the Neder Rijn had to be abandoned until the Spring.

So ended a magnificent gamble which was, on all the probabilities, fated from the start, and yet so nearly succeeded. Solid gains had been made on the basis of which all the ground in Holland and Belgium, south and west of the Rhine, was won during the winter months ready for the grand assault on the Rhine itself in March. I suppose it can be said that the principal cause of failure at Arnhem was the weather. Had normal re-supply of food and ammunition been possible and had it been possible to land the Polish Airborne Brigade the whole scene might have been different though, even then, it would have been a close thing.

The real joker in the pack was that, whereas light opposition had been expected in Arnhem, it so happened that one fairly fresh armoured division had moved into the area, literally the day before the assault. In addition, there were remnants of another three armoured divisions resting in the area and, with two relatively fresh infantry divisions as well, the enemy was far too strongly placed to make the fight as evenly balanced as expected. However, those are the fortunes of war.

One other casualty that was relatively and personally significant was that our Chief Engineer, Brigadier John Stone, was injured in a Jeep accident on the crowded Nijmegen road. His leg was broken when his car was ditched. He was evacuated to England. The next day we knew that his successor was to be my betenoire, Brigadier A. D. Campbell, until then the Chief Engineer of 1st Corps. Campbell was short and rubicund, with his waistline only just under control. He had short red hair and was generally known as "Ginger", obviously because of his hair, although the nickname did, in fact, describe his style of command extremely well. He believed that a bit of ginger in his relationships with his staff and subordinates was salutary and productive. He certainly frightened me for most of the time that I dealt with him.

We had just moved Main Army Headquarters to Helmond, which had been captured two or three days earlier, as already described. We had moved into winter quarters and the tents were put away until the spring. Our four caravans were parked in the timber yard of a builders' merchant. My department and Ted Hutton's were on the other side of the road in the house of a collaborator who had fled with the retreating Germans. Ted and I were billeted in a very comfortable house indeed at the top of the road on the way to "D" Mess which was in a much bigger house about half a mile out from the outskirts of the town.

Our host at the billet was an elderly retired businessman named Aukes, with a grown up family. I think there were two married sons who we saw occasionally and two unmarried sons who had had great difficulty in keeping out of the hands of German labour recruiters. Their unmarried sister, Carla, ran the house very efficiently and we could see that we were very comfortably placed. Carla still lives in Helmond and I have been in touch with her ever since on a Christmas letter/card basis and I am fairly sure that the letter gets passed around her brothers each year. It think that most of our mess colleagues were similarly well placed and all were enjoying a bit of home life for a while, so the time spent in the mess by most of us was distinctly short.

Ted and I got involved in playing cards every evening with the Aukes family — some Dutch game which seemed to be a mixture between rummy and bridge, complicated by the fact that the court cards all had Dutch names. I remember that the Queen was the "Frau.". We did not learn very much Dutch.

After about three days I could no longer put off an interview with Ginger Campbell as I had to report the state of some of our stocks at the Bourg Leopold depot. I seem to recall that Dannert wire coils came into it. I went to his caravan and found him on his own so I handed over a slip of paper with the relevant figures on it. He put it down on his table and looked at me ominously. "Mortimer", he said, "I believe you are not giving satisfaction to the Corps in regard to the supply of stores."

That was certainly direct but I judged that it was more a matter of style than of truth. I restrained myself from too hot a reply and said, coldly, "I do not know how that can be, Sir, no one other than you has ever complained and that was back in London more than three months ago. Since we landed I have had very few dealings with 1st Corps, particularly since you came under command of Canadian Army nearly two months ago.".

He did not argue, he merely said, "Be that as it may, I shall be watching you closely; the first trip-up and you are out."

Dismayed by this unfair assessment and by the way in which the dice now seemed to be loaded against me, there seemed to be no worthwhile answer at that moment except to say "Yes, Sir" and to withdraw to ponder. I was not prepared to go without a fight and wondered whether there was any advantage in getting in my word first with General Dempsey. The danger was that, if dismissed from my post then I would revert to my substantive rank of Captain, but if Campbell decided to exchange me with another Major I would not necessarily object. A regimental job would still suit me and there was no clear reason why a Company Commander's post should not be made available to me. My case for reasonable treatment seemed to be a strong one and there seemed to be no disadvantage in waiting to see how things developed. Long afterwards I heard that the Brigadier, when reviewing with Otto Phibbs the staff that he had inherited, made quite clear his wish to get rid of me, but Phibbs urged strongly that he should hold his horses. He remembered my predecessor without regret and said that I had a large capacity for work and had never failed so far. In time, Campbell seemed to accept this, but I always regarded him with the greatest of caution and uncertainty. It was not really a happy relationship, but it worked.

The other personal relationship which was giving me trouble at this time was that with Major Hall, the officer commanding 174th Workshop and Park Company. My conscience was worrying me about the supply of engineer stores to the Nijmegen offensive and the Arnhem battle generally. It seemed to me that, while we had been able to answer the call for bridging equipment when it came (we were able to supply from our depot at Bourg Leopold), it still took far too long to get the equipment up to the sites where it was needed. This, in itself, was not our fault. The road was jammed from end to end but we should have anticipated that and had some equipment on wheels as far forward in the advance as possible. Bailey bridging was only needed at the canal crossing at Son and, possibly, for the crossing of the Maas-Waal canal. Nevertheless, I wondered whether, with real anticipation, we could have got more equipment forward more quickly. This problem was even more marked when it came to the assault crossing of the Waal by the 504th U.S. Regimental Combat Team. Had we had the storm boats on the site 24 or even 48 hours earlier, in adequate numbers for at least three battalions, with all the necessary outboard motors, could the assault have been mounted more quickly and with more success and less loss of life?

It may be that it would have made no difference. It may be that the road could not possibly have accepted another twenty or thirty more lorries carrying storm boats, when nobody knew for certain whether they were needed. It may be that we did not even have the numbers of boats, motors and transport required. It may be that the last thing that anybody wanted was yet another staff officer trying to get up to the front to find out the truth for himself. I am not even certain now that talking about storm boats at all is not just a matter of hind sight but what I do remember was that I was uneasy. My uneasiness focused itself on the depot at Bourg Leopold and my increasing lack of confidence in its commander.

I knew that it was wrong in principle, but it seemed to me to be the right thing to do in practice to take over direct command of the depot myself, with my staff captain, Freddie May, on site as my direct representative. In effect I would be taking command of the depot out of the hands of Major Hall and putting it in the hands of Captain May, while leaving Hall to concentrate on his Workshop side. I felt I would get better and more trustworthy knowledge of the broad situation under such an arrangement and could rely on May to act without my needing to hold his hand all the while. Whether this was fair to Hall was an open question. It was what I felt the situation demanded. I got a rocket for it later — No staff officer should really take command of anything direct. In any event, it was really too late to affect the Arnhem battle, though it did no harm.

CHAPTER 13
Headquarters Second Army — Crossing the Rhine (October, 1944 – March, 1945)

With the frustration of our effort to get across the whole of the Rhine barrier at Arnhem, Field Marshal Montgomery re-cast his priorities for 21st Army Group operations during the winter months, in preparation for an all-out assault on the Rhine in the spring.

To the best of my knowledge, he did not say so but I am sure he regarded it as his top priority to hold on to the bridgehead he had established over the Waal and in the country between the Waal and the Neder Rijn. His first active and declared priority was to clear the south coast of the Scheldt estuary and then to capture the Frisian Islands. With some subsidiary clearing up north of Antwerp these operations would open up the port of Antwerp and make an immense difference to the administrative situation of the whole allied front. Until this had been completed, it was not timely to think of mounting any other serious push forward.

The Polish Armoured Division and the 4th Canadian Armoured Division commenced their advance on 11th September. The Poles moved eastwards, completing the capture of Ghent and finishing up at Terneuzen on 22nd September. The coast west of Terneuzen up to Zeebrugge was not cleared until nearly the end of October. East of Antwerp, 1st Corps, also under command of First Canadian Army, commenced its advance on 23rd September, advancing northwards to the mouth of the River Maas, which it reached on 4th and 5th November. On 24th October, the largely sea-borne invasions of the South Beveland peninsula and the islands of North Beveland and Walcheren commenced and were largely completed by 1st November with two sea landings at Flushing and Westkapelle. AVREs (Armoured Vehicles, Royal Engineers) played a major role in the attacks on these islands. My friend, Bennett, from OCTU and Tunnelling days, gained a Military Cross which I am sure was very well deserved indeed.

The third priority was to deal with the remaining German forces south and west of the Maas. The right flank of the Nijmegen Salient had remained on the general line Weert, Deurne and Boxmeer since the end of September but the Germans had been building up in strength in the area left between this line and the River Maas. At Deurne, this enemy area had a depth of nearly 20 miles. **(See Map 8)**

Apart from the fact that, at Deurne, the enemy were uncomfortably close to Helmond and Army Headquarters, this ground would need to be cleared before the spring. Accordingly, at the end of September, 8th Corps began the attack between Weert and Boxmeer while 12th Corps, on their right, extended the line down to Maeseyck on the Maas. On 27th October the Germans counter-attacked towards Weert to gain some ground, but this was fairly soon recovered. On 3rd December, 8th Corps and 12th Corps reached the Maas at Venlo and the whole German bridgehead west of the Maas was now eliminated.

The question now was whether the German army would accept that they had lost the battle west of the Rhine and would now decide to withdraw across that river and set up their defences to resist our crossings and to counter-attack with strong armoured forces wherever we might decide to assault across the river. That would have been the sound plan, but Hitler again decided to take charge, as he was determined not to fall down on his boast to the German people that he would never give up one yard of German soil to invaders.

He therefore ordered Von Runstedt to prepare a massive counter-attack, west of the Rhine in the Ardennes. In this area the First U.S. Army had made good progress and had already reached the line of the German border with Belgium and Luxembourg. To their left (north) was the Ninth U.S. Army, which was temporarily under command of 21st Army Group and Field Marshal Montgomery, and which was holding the line to the right of Second British Army on the Meuse. (See Map 9)

There were assembled for Hitler's purpose no less than four armoured corps, I and II S.S. Panzer Corps and XLVII and LVIII Panzer Corps. Even allowing for the depleted state of many German formations at this stage, this was a formidable force with each corps consisting of two armoured divisions and each of these re-equipped with the latest Panther and Tiger type tanks to a scale of 100 tanks in each division. Late in August, the German armies fleeing from France had been estimated at the equivalent of about 23 divisions. By mid-December, the enemy had admittedly lost the whole of France and Belgium and a fair slice of Holland. However, Germany now had some 70 divisions in the field in the west and was expected to build this up to 90 divisions by the spring. In all, it had seven armoured divisions already involved in fighting and was now prepared to throw in the last eight Panzer divisions. This confirmed that Hitler was not prepared to countenance the loss of the Rhineland but was prepared to gamble again on a win-all-lose-all masterstroke.

The area of the Ardennes is very hilly, even mountainous, country with thick forests and little population. The line was also comparatively thinly held by First U.S. Army which was fully deployed, without having a corps in reserve. The German concentration of troops, armour and artillery was also done with a high degree of secrecy and concealment. The enemy was also assisted by bad weather which hindered satisfactory air reconnaissance. Tactically the offensive, which began on 16th December, achieved complete surprise, starting with the heaviest artillery barrage fired by the Germans in the whole north-west Europe campaign and the dropping of parachutists and the infiltration of saboteurs to spread confusion behind the allied lines.

Sixth S.S. Panzer Army of four armoured divisions was directed at Malmedy and Stavelot towards the northern end of the breach at Monschau and Fifth Panzer Army, also of four armoured divisions, was directed through Luxembourg towards Bastogne, towards the south of the breach at Echternach. Seventeen infantry, parachute and Panzer Grenadier divisions followed them to protect the flanks. On the first two days twenty miles of penetration were achieved, particularly on the Fifth Panzer Army front where Houffalaize was overrun and Bastogne was bypassed but not taken. However, Sixth S.S. Panzer Army was unable to make further progress towards Liege and could not capture Stavelot and Malmedy and turned south-west to reinforce Fifth Panzer army's drive westwards towards Namur. This drive, in particular, got within fifteen miles of Namur, on the junction of the rivers Sambre and Meuse where it would have been only thirty miles from Brussels.

On 19th December Eisenhower ordered Montgomery to take command of the American armies north of the German salient. He immediately took two steps. One was to move the whole of 30th Corps, then four divisions, from the Second Army front between Maeseyck and Geilenkirchen, to take up position between Brussels and Maastricht, ready to counter any crossing of the Meuse. Second, he created a Reserve Corps for First U.S. Army by extracting the divisions of U.S. VII Corps from the line and concentrating them to cover Namur. At the same time, Eisenhower ordered Third U.S. Army to concentrate on the southern flank of the breakthrough and attack towards Bastogne. Meanwhile a British armoured brigade and patrols from 30th Corps had taken up position on the line of the Meuse and this armoured brigade engaged the leading elements of Fifth Panzer Army just to the south of Namur and with VII U.S. Corps halted the German advance. The furthest panzer penetration was achieved on 23rd December and from there on the German line was squeezed steadily backwards.

Fortunately, a period of good weather commenced on 24th December and the allied air forces were able at last to intervene with great effect. The German airforce made a serious attempt to neutralise our air effort by all-out, low-level attacks on 1st January against our main airfields in Belgium and Holland. These caused considerable losses, but they were soon replaced. 30th Corps now crossed the Meuse, south of Namur, and attacked the German bulge head on. VII U.S. Corps was now free to attack from the north and III U.S. Corps and XIII U.S. Corps attacked from the south. The Allies all linked up at Houffalaize on 16th January and this brought the German threat effectively to an end.

It is estimated that the enemy lost some 120,000 men in the battle, together with 600 tanks and assault guns. There were also great losses to the depleted German airforce and to railway equipment. It would have served German ends far better to have saved these fine divisions for delaying operations on the Rhine itself and during the allied advance across Germany. I doubt if we could have attempted to cross the Rhine before March and had the enemy then been able to cause us one month or even two months' longer delay in reaching the Elbe they would have been able to surrender to the western allies thousands upon thousands of those men who were eventually trapped east of the Elbe by the Russians.

Second Army Headquarters, as such, was not involved in the "Battle of the Bulge" (i.e. the German breakthrough and subsequent defeat) except for the temporary detachment of 30th Corps, although we were involved in some of the consequent movement problems. One, I remember, was an exchange of positions between 30th Corps and 8th Corps for some reason. One of them had to travel from south to north and the other had to move from west to east. Their paths crossed at a road junction in the middle of an area of flat low-lying country, much inter-laced with drainage ditches, and there was no avoiding this crossroads. It seemed that it might present the traffic jam of all time and a conference was summoned to debate the possibilities.

Inevitably, someone suggested a flyover and, just as inevitably, our Chief Engineer volunteered to provide one. His staff, were horrified when we heard about it. Both corps included armoured divisions and it was their intention to avoid the wear and tear on their tanks' tracks by having them carried by transporters. A fighting tank on a transporter was a 70 ton all-up load, which was also of significant height, possibly requiring a clearance of fifteen feet or more. Furthermore, such loads would not take readily to an incline of more than one in twenty. Admittedly, the spans required of any such flyover would not be large, but the design problems were tricky and the consumption of material might be significant.

We jibbed and the Chief Engineer granted us a stay of execution while he thought about our objections. Fortunately, by the next time he spoke to "Q" Movements they had thought about it too and made their own plan, which was to place four tar barrels in the road and set up a roundabout. It worked astonishingly well.

Sometime in November my mother wrote to me to say that my young brother, John, was arriving in Belgium shortly as a reinforcement and would I do something about it. I knew what she meant but I was very reluctant to interfere, firstly, because I did not like using influence on a relative's behalf and, secondly, because "playing God" with other peoples' lives seems to me often to encourage disaster. However, I could not refuse and so found out that he had arrived and was in the reinforcement camp at Bourg Leopold. I went there and we met in a rather muddy field, which was at least private. He had been for some while at the Training Battalion RE and had been encouraged to try for a commission. Although he was only 18 they had decided he would be suitable as an officer but, in view of his lack of any engineer professional training at all, they could not recommend him for an engineer commission. He had said, which I thought unwise, that if he could not get an engineer commission he would prefer to serve in the Royal Engineers in the ranks.

All I could say was that it did seem to me that in the immediate future the most interesting job going on in the Royal Engineers would be the bridging of the Rhine. Much of this, I thought, would be done by the AGREs (Army Groups, Royal Engineers) and I would see if I could get him into one of them. When I spoke to "A" Branch my contact was very sympathetic and undertook to do something, if there was a vacancy. Apparently there was not, because the next I heard of him was a letter from my mother, to whom I had reported progress, to say that he was in fact in 52nd (Mountain) Divisional Engineers who, I found out, were right in the firing line. So much for interfering!

Towards Christmas, Army Headquarters moved from Helmond in Holland to Neerpelt, just across the border into Belgium. Here, the Engineer Branch was housed in a Catholic day school but I think the school must have continued in part of the buildings though I have to admit that I never saw any of the children during the time there, but nor did I see many children in Neerpelt anyway. Our four caravans were parked in the school yard, together with our various Jeeps.

Ted Hutton, Jan Roberts — our mechanical equipment expert — Freddie May and I all used a fairly large classroom as our office. Sergeant Swift, Corporal Henshall and my colleague's clerks had another smaller classroom and there was an assembly hall which was used by the various liaison officers we then had with us. The assembly hall was also where we held our morning meetings, just after breakfast, when we had had time to see if there was anything of interest in our postbag. This timing was also before the Chief Engineer went out for the day (he usually returned between 5 and 6 p.m.). We all stood for the meeting which lasted up to half an hour. Each member of the staff, in order of seniority, had to report on the state of his section's affairs.

170

When this run through had finished the Brigadier then selected one of us, usually totally at random, for a spot of "gingering up". The victim had to face up to a quarter of an hour's inquisition, usually partly on the matters on which he had already reported, and partly on other matters which he was thought not to have dealt with as he should have done. Success was achieved if the victim dried up, contradicted himself or revealed his total ignorance some other way. If he proved too tough for the Brigadier to swallow that morning another victim might be selected.

I do not think that I was especially vulnerable, but my report did usually call for supplementary questions because our stocks, particularly of bridging equipment, were either in process of being built up in view of some imminent operation, or in process of being run down, because operations were using up stores faster than they could be replenished. Furthermore, we were usually in process, at the Workshop and Park Company, of manufacturing large quantities of supplementary equipment, such as pontoon covers and bow wave protectors. I usually had some glib answer but it was always an anxious period until the eagle eye passed on.

The people who must have found it most un-nerving were the liaison officers from the Dutch and Belgian armies. Fortunately they had excellent English but occasionally there was some misunderstanding about words. They were expected to be experts on the rivers and their performance, particularly at flood times. As the winter period in the valleys of the Meuse, Rhine and associated waterways was one of continuous and widespread flooding there were bound to be questions for them nearly every morning and they always viewed this with some anxiety.

The Intelligence Section looked sometimes very vulnerable indeed and that of course incited the Brigadier to give them special attention, but the ,man who was most confident, and whom the Brigadier seemed to let off the hook most readily, was Ted Hutton. However, I do not think any of us really liked the inquisition but I am sure it was good for our souls and probably for our efficiency too. Certainly there was always a scramble afterwards to find out the answers to some unanswered question and to prepare a briefing note for the Brigadier to await his return from the field.

The Brigadier's trips into the field, which occupied most of his days, were very thorough indeed. I am not sure how welcome they were to the Chief Engineers of the Corps who were nominally his equals in rank. They could seek the protection of their operational responsibility to their own General, although on technical matters they were strictly answerable to the Chief Engineer of the Army.

An example of this relationship occurred when Brigadier Campbell offered to build the traffic flyover to which I have already referred. His first idea, when his offer was accepted, was to hand the job over to one of the corps and he selected the Chief Engineer of 12th Corps for this doubtful honour. The latter was suspicious and his own staff advised him to decline. Brigadier Campbell tried to insist but was overruled by the General commanding 12th Corps.

During our stay at Neerpelt the "A" Branch found a tame artist among the German prisoners of war. He had offered to do pencil portraits of our staff officers for £5 a time. I think all of us in the Engineer Branch had one done and I have used mine as one of the illustrations to this book.

He called himself Diesex and he was a commercial artist, so whether that was his real name or his pseudonym I do not know. Each picture took him about an hour and a half but it was very good value at the price. Our pictures seemed to flatter us all but we agreed that he made us all look like German officers, though my colleagues said mine looked particularly like me. I did not know how to take that!

In the artistic field our own camouflage department took some beating as they all seemed to be either artists or art critics. They were all Royal Engineers officers but they were answerable direct to the "G" Branch. However, as I have said, they were all in "D" Mess and in Neerpelt the mess was housed in a requisitioned cafe. In fact, the place looked a bit fly blown and devoid of visual attraction so they decided to do something about it.

They purchased somewhere, and brought into the mess, a fairly large piece of modern impressionistic art. Before it arrived, discussion in the mess was desultory, but once the painting was on the wall there was no conversation about anything else. The mess was divided three ways; those who didn't like it, those who did like it but didn't understand it and, thirdly, those who thought they understood it but kept quiet. Certainly our camouflage experts enjoyed themselves and failed to enlighten us.

In Neerpelt also the Brigadier developed his, and therefore our, technique for preparing for battle. Instructions to the staff started with a visit by the BGS to General Dempsey which was relayed to the heads of the services in "A" Mess at or about dinner time when the various chiefs had all returned from the field. When he came back from dinner, Brigadier Campbell would summon Otto Phibbs, Bob Moodie, Richard Allport-Williams and myself to his caravan and give us the outlines of the plan and the engineer aspects. Commonly it was something like: –

"A Corps and B Corps will commence an advance on D Day by crossing L Canal between S and R on a front of two divisions each and each corps building one class 40 bridge and one class 9 bridge. This will be an opposed assault.

On D + 3 they are expected to cross the River M, each on a front of two divisions again, each division to be provided with a class 40 bridge. On D + 7 A Corps will cross the River N and B Corps will cross the O Canal, each on a front of one division. It must be assumed that all existing bridges would by then have been blown and a class 40 bridge and two class 9 bridges must be provided for each division.

All bridging columns must then be re-loaded ready for an immediate further advance.

Storm boats and Class 50/60 rafts are to be provided for all crossings and precautions against swimmers and floating mines must be taken on each divisional front.''

The Brigadier would then ask for any questions and then the three majors would be told to go and get on with the job of producing a plan, with timed equipment schedules, ready for presentation to him the following evening. Later, when we had started on the work, Otto Phibbs would appear to check that we had understood the story, as he recalled it, and to instruct us to report to him before submitting our plans to the Brigadier.

There would be little that I could do on the first evening because it was up to the Intelligence side to suggest the most suitable crossing places and to indicate the profile of the river bed and banks at each recommended point. It was then up to Bob Moodie to work out the equipment requirements for each crossing for relaying to me as soon as possible on the following day. Meanwhile, the only thing I could do was to telephone 21st Army Group, to speak to Major Hignett and to find out if he had the same story as I had and what equipment he expected to deliver to the Army's depot within the time span of the plan. I also needed to telephone the Workshop and Park Company to ensure that they would let me have a really up to date stock position for bridging equipment by the following morning, for their main depot and any subsidiary depot that they were operating. And so to bed! First thing the following morning I would start preparing the working sheets, usually double foolscap in size. The columns would be headed with the various types of loads of bridging equipment we would be using. For example: −

Bailey bridge   — Panel units
                 — Decking units
                 — Ramp units
                 — Pontoon units

	—	other units
Folding boats	—	Boat units
	—	Decking units
	—	Ramp units
	—	other units
Storm boats	—	number
Class 50/60	—	Trailers and loads
rafts		(4 loads = 1 raft)
Special eqpt.	—	Decking for pontoons
	—	Bow protectors
	—	Anti-swimmer nets
	—	Mine booms

Down the left hand side of the working sheets would be: –

Held in Main Depots
    and subsidiary depots
    at start — i.e. on date
    of this first report.
Deliveries expected
    from 21 Army Group
    before "D" Day
    — by train
    — by road
Total available before
    "D" Day
Drawn for first crossings
    on "D" Day or before
Remains in stock after
    "D" Day

This portion of the exercise would be repeated for: –
    Further deliveries and consumption up to D + 3 and further
    deliveries and consumption up to D + 7.

This would lead to a final stock estimate on the morning of D + 8.
    Obviously the hope would be that by "D" Day, which was commonly
about a week after the issue of orders for a major set of crossing
operations, we would have sufficient in hand to start the operation and
that thereafter we would keep pace and would not run out of any key
item.
    The usual form was that, by lunchtime, Bob Moodie was ready to
supply the figures of equipment required for each of the three phases of

174

these typical operations and he and I would then get together to fit his figures into my schedules, as above. If, when the supply and demand programme was set out, as above, it revealed that supply was unlikely to keep pace with demand, I would begin some urgent telephoning, principally to Hignett of 21st Army Group, to see what could be achieved. Usually something could be done. In fact, I do not remember that he ever failed us. In theory, it might have been possible to borrow equipment from First Canadian Army or, almost as a last resort, to alter bridge designs somewhere or to vary the type of bridge to be provided. I suppose that, as a very last resort, we could have postponed part of the operation but I am glad to say that we never had to do any of that.

The worst that I can recall was that we may have had to ask for some speed up of the train scheduling, no doubt with enormous repercussions further back down the line.

The main trouble was that we never seemed to be able to finish our planning and preparations in time to make a spare copy of the schedule and we barely had the time to report to Otto Phibbs before we were all summoned to the Brigadier's caravan. Accordingly, I usually arrived clutching the one and only copy of the schedule. Somehow Otto Phibbs and Richard Allport-Williams always seemed to be able to get themselves excused very rapidly as well, leaving Bob Moodie and I to carry the heat of the day. The opening round was largely fencing, with Bob Moodie assuring the Brigadier that all designs were in order and my assuring him that the equipment would all be available when required. We should long past have got used to what came next, but somehow we never did — there was never time.

The Brigadier would then seize the only copy of the schedule, place it on his blotting pad and sprawl over it, so that it was totally invisible to the two of us standing behind him. He would then ask for an assurance again that everything was alright which I would readily supply.

He would then ask what spare capacity we had and I would indicate what reserve I thought there might be at the various stages. He would then alter the date of "D" Day and ask what effect that had. By rapid mental arithmetic and a feat of memory I might assure him that it was still alright except for some shortage perhaps on the third stage of some relatively unimportant item. He would then alter the date of "D" Day yet again, or the date of the second phase, or both, to tighten up the schedule. He would then perhaps increase the number or size of bridges and would ask for yet further assurance that we could still manage without running out of equipment.

By this time, of course, demand would be beginning to look a little too much to cope with but, provided the strain was not immediate, I would usually claim that we could still manage, even if only just.

175

At about this stage the Brigadier would usually ask for a check through of the figures, phase by phase, while he still held on tightly to the schedule. Somewhere along the line we would disagree and he would start hectoring fiercely. I would stand my ground and Bob Moodie might support me, whereupon the Brigadier would give us a dressing down for insolence and throw us out of his caravan, he still retaining the schedule. The following day the schedule would be returned to me and he would depart to assure the General Staff that the engineers could and would perform!

Fairly early in the New Year the Brigadier took a very short period of leave back in the U.K. and we heard that he had been invited to attend a passing-out parade at the 141 OCTU, where he was to award the Sword of Honour to his own elder son, but we were surprised when the young man returned with him and stayed with us at headquarters for nearly a week. He was a very pleasant youth indeed, slimmer, of course, and taller than his father, but with the same red hair. The Chief was intensely proud of his son and his attitude to his staff completely changed while the young man was with us — I was introduced as "Major Mortimer, on whom I totally depend"! One of the staff captains was deputed to look after the young man and to take him around to the various corps and points of interest. On one of these trips junior succeeded in damaging senior's car — of which the Brigadier was distinctly proud — fairly substantially, but never a word of complaint came from his father. Peace and light and bonhomie continued to reign.

We were all very sorry to see the young man go, when his leave eventually finished and he moved over to The Guards Armoured Division, where he was to start as a 2nd Lieutenant in the Divisional Engineers. The Brigadier was undoubtedly more ambitious for his son than the latter was for himself. Accordingly, he often seemed to have business requiring a telephone call to the local CRE (Commander, Royal Engineers). The Brigadier did not have to ask how his son was doing. The Colonel knew the form well enough to report without being asked. The great thing, though, was that the improved relations with his own Chief Engineer's staff, which the visit had brought about, continued and we all flourished with occasional praise. On one occasion he even expressed surprise at finding me still working at 10 o'clock at night and told me to go to bed as I "must avoid the danger of overwork" but I never tried quoting him back as an excuse for failing to complete anything he told me to put in hand.

Following the German collapse after the "Battle of the Bulge" 21st Army Group was free to turn its attention, as did the American Army Groups further south, to clearing up the whole of the area west of the Rhine. 12th Corps of Second Army, with a proportion of help from

Ninth U.S. Army, was ordered to clear out the Roermond Triangle, north of Aachen, and between the River Meuse and the River Roer, with Roermond, at the junction of the two rivers, forming the north point of the triangle. The area was intensely fortified with earthworks, trenchwork and anti-tank ditches and it took a stiff fight by four divisions to break through and clear out the whole area between 15th and 28th January. Due to the wet weather and flooding, the going was so bad that tanks and the special armour of 79th Division could give little support. When clearance was complete the area was handed over to Ninth U.S. Army.

The area between the Meuse and the Rhine was to be attacked simultaneously, or as nearly so as possible, from north and south. First Canadian Army was reinforced by 30th Corps and by 52nd Division from 12th Corps, for the purpose of the northern attack. 30th Corps commenced the move and had available to it six infantry divisions, one armoured division, three armoured brigades and eleven regiments of specialised armour with enormous quantities of artillery amounting to well over a thousand guns. Enormous quantities of stores had been stacked at the army roadheads and during February no less than 350,000 tons of ammunition and other stores had been accumulated.

In mid-February came the news from home that brother John was "Missing, believed prisoner of war". Obviously our mother would need any news I could get so I managed to locate Headquarters 52nd Division and went down there to the Meuse to see what I could find out. The story, as far as I could gather it from the adjutant of the Divisional Engineers, was that the brigade, to which John's company was attached, had decided to take advantage of a lull in the battle to try to occupy a moated castle which they believed the enemy had abandoned. Accordingly, an infantry platoon had been ordered to make a night attack in the hope of getting into the castle before the enemy might re-occupy it the following day. The engineers had a small supply of rubber boats available and a small squad of sappers were sent along to deal with any mines that might be encountered.

Unfortunately, the infantry did not spot the enemy quickly enough. They charged into the ground floor of the castle, only to find that the stairs had been removed and there were German parachutists waiting for them on the first floor. They were forced to surrender and the parachutists went to find out who else was around. They caught the sappers patiently waiting and raked them into the bag as well. In fact, much of this was supposition, because as far as 52nd Division was concerned, their whole party had disappeared. Only one or two bodies, none Engineers, were found when the castle was overrun by our troops a few days later.

In fact, John was only "in the bag" for about eight weeks and he was liberated by 8th Corps. The Germans had moved the 52nd Division party back rapidly to Flensburg in Schleswig-Holstein and they were only liberated when 8th Corps had crossed the Elbe and were well on their way up towards Denmark. We did not receive official confirmation that he was, in fact, a prisoner of war for some weeks, but, in view of the general disorganisation on the German side at that stage of the war, even that was a fairly good performance.

The weather remained an anxiety; the thaw was beginning and was playing havoc with our communications as was the extensive flooding. There were elaborate deception plans and numerous smoke generators, close to the River Meuse, were kept going for days. The smoke was carried by the prevailing wind over the whole area of the Reichwald Forest. In flooded areas great use was made of amphibious DD tanks (duplex drive), such as had been used in the assault on the Normandy beaches. Amphibious lorries were used to carry forward men and supplies. The whole Reichwald Forest area was heavily fortified and manned by the redoubtable S.S. and airborne formations who fought bitterly, literally to the last man, but they were overwhelmed by the weight of men, armour and fire power thrown at them. It was a terrific struggle but 30th Corps broke through the middle of the forest, captured Goch and pressed on through Weeze and Kevelaer to Geldern. In doing so they were passing down between the second and third rows of the Siegfried Line positions and split the enemy lines into two separate parts. 52nd Division followed up on the right between the first and the second (main) echelons of the Siegfried Line, while 2nd Canadian Corps followed on the left, to break through the third line of the defences and press on to the Rhine opposite Wesel. (See Map 10)

As stated above, it had originally been hoped to commence the attack from the south by Ninth U.S. Army on 8th February, to coincide with the start of the Canadian attack from the north. However, it was not until the 17th February that the Americans could gather together the ten divisions they intended to commit to the battle. By that time the weather had deteriorated badly and movement was intensely difficult but on 23rd February it relaxed sufficiently to start the assault across the River Roer. The Americans advanced in fine style, the weather was fine and the ground was drying, and a large bridgehead was created. From this the Americans surged forward and their objectives for the link-up with First Canadian Army, forty miles ahead at Geldern and Wesel, were reached by 5th March.

The entire west bank of the Rhine, from Nijmegen right up to Dusseldorf, eighty miles away, was now in our hands. Two days later the enemy rearguards had all retired across the river and blown the last remaining bridge at Wesel. Unfortunately, the final days of the operation were unfavourable for flying and hindered the airforces in their attempts to deal with the targets presented at the Wesel bottleneck. On these sectors of the front more than 50,000 prisoners were counted and it is estimated that the enemy lost nearly 40,000 men killed and wounded. Eighteen German divisions had been severely mauled and their failure to withdraw in good time made it certain that, once we were across the Rhine, the enemy would not have the resources to compete with us in battle on any front.

In the meantime American armies in the south were also lining up on the Rhine. On 7th March, First U.S. Army secured intact the railway bridge at Remagen and began to form a bridgehead. Cologne also fell to that army. Third U.S. Army, Seventh U.S. Army and First French Army also closed up to the Rhine. France was now completely freed and all was set for the grand crossings of the Rhine and the drives through Germany to the Elbe and the meetings with the Russians.

By the end of March, on the engineer side, we had been doing a certain amount of detailed planning and a great deal of accumulation of bridging equipment ready for the Rhine crossing. The professional advice available to us indicated a strong probability that, with the melting of winter snow and ice in Switzerland and on either side of the upper Rhine, the river would be in spate well into March. Furthermore, timber and other debris could be expected to be coming down with the river. Even small ice floes were possible. Precautions would have to be taken to protect the pontoons of the floating bridges against these hazards. Quite apart from the separate provision required to protect the bridge against attacks by swimmers, floating mines, boat raids and even midget submarines might be encountered. The 174 Army Workshop and Park Company took on the job of providing this special equipment and carried it out excellently. To protect the bows of the pontoons welded angle-iron devices were manufactured, to be hung from the bows and the bow anchor ropes in order to divert masses of ice and debris past them.

Bearing in mind the heavy flow of water plus the possible impact of ice and debris, extra anchoring ropes would be required, with separate anchors, and indeed a number of heavy naval anchors were provided for each bridge as well as the ordinary quota of engineer anchors.

With the best will in the world, there could be no guarantee that, in spite of the above precautions, pontoons would not get holed. In this case patching would be required and, of course, each pontoon normally carried a small patching outfit of pieces of ply with rubber backing sheets and a screw clamp to hold the patch in place. Unfortunately, these patches seemed to have a great attraction for the Dutch civilian workers

179

in our depots and far too many of them disappeared. It was therefore necessary to have reserves of the standard patching outfits plus some special bigger patches which were produced by the Workshop and Park Company.

The principal protection against swimmers, equipped with aqualung breathing apparatus, was coiled Dannert barbed wire draped from one pontoon to the next and also hung on the bow anchor cables. To catch floating mines and midget submarines it was necessary to have light anti-submarine netting in a curtain right across the river. This netting was provided in 1,000 foot lengths, each net equipped with its own anchor cables, anchors and metal floats. When new and when first fed out into the water this netting was ideal. Unfortunately, it did not survive nearly as well being taken out of the water, rolled up again, transported, put into store and later drawn out again for re-use. Indeed, after a couple of uses little was left but the floats and a couple of anchors, the wire and wire cables having mostly been left in the water. However, for the Rhine we were fortunately working mostly with new nets.

For protection against night attack by boat crews, special lighting was necessary to floodlight the vulnerable area.

Finally, bearing in mind that most of the pontoons were open topped, many of them had to be provided with extra decking to close in the top and extra bow pieces to divert and reject any bow wave that the force of the current might create and which might swamp some of the pontoons.

When it is borne in mind that these bridges mostly had 30 or more complete pontoons in them and that there were in the end something like seven or eight pontoon bridges, the sheer quantity of this variety of equipment can be imagined.

All the special equipment, together with the actual equipment bridging itself, was built up at a new depot at Helmond about five miles out of the town on the Deurne road. Day after day convoys arrived bringing up all this material from rear depots and the railhead. It was unloaded and stacked by mobile cranes and by teams of local Dutch labour and checked and sorted by the NCOs and sappers of the 174th Army Workshop and Park Company. Fortunately, the worst of the spring weather was behind us and the ground stayed fairly firm. Otherwise, even though trackway material had been used for the depot roads, they would have become almost impassible under the heavy traffic they had to bear. The stacked equipment was reasonably spread out so that fire was unlikely to do much damage but, nevertheless, the whole concentration of material seemed to me to present much too attractive a target to the enemy airforce, if there had been one!

Storm boats and outboard motors were now reasonably readily available and stacks of these were also provided but the really new equipment for this part of the campaign was the arrival of the Class 50/60 raft in fair quantity. These rafts were made up of two over-sized pontoons — i.e. they were substantially bigger than the pontoons used on the ordinary floating Bailey bridge. Like them, however, they could be divided into two half pontoons for transport. The four half pontoons were each carried on a specially designed trailer from which they could be lowered direct into the water. The roadway for each quarter of the raft was ready mounted on each half pontoon and they were readily linked together when already floating in the river. A ramp section of the roadway was also provided, so that the raft could be loaded direct from the shore but, from memory, I do not think that these were permanently mounted but were constructed from parts which were carried on the same trailers as the pontoons. I also cannot remember the significance of the double load classification of 50 and 60 tons but I guess now that the 50 tons related to a tank loaded by itself and the 60 ton classification related to a transporter with a smaller tank loaded on it. These were magnificent pieces of equipment and rapidly proved their worth as they could follow immediately behind the first flight of infantry who would have crossed the river by assault boats.

Also to be considered were the semi-permanent railway bridges to be built across the river. Of course, these could not be carried on floating bridges but they would have to be built of timber piled trestle bents. A trestle "bent" consists of a number of piles driven into the river bed at a single location on the line of the bridge, the piles being joined together by diagonal bracing and capped horizontally by heavy timbers, thus forming a sound, rigid pier. These piers would be spaced at intervals along the line of the bridge and might even be high enough above the water to enable a certain amount of barge traffic to continue to use the waterway.

I did not see the final design of the piled bridges it was intended to build but I think that the piers on the Rhine bridges were built at intervals of 100 feet along the line of the bridge and the trestle bents contained from 10 to 20 piles. I am fairly sure the piles themselves were all timber but they could possibly have been made of steel pipes. One of these bridges was to be placed just to the south (upstream) of Wesel on the Ninth U.S. Army front and the other was to be near Emmerich on the Second Army front but very close to the junction with First Canadian Army.

The American Army were to build their bridge, which was slightly the shorter of the two, and, of course, the American Corps of Engineers brought to the task a vast experience from peacetime of this sort of thing. The American Corps of Engineers has overall control in the United States of all waterways and flood programmes and thus, particularly, of the building of piled timber bridges. In comparison the

British Royal Engineers has very little experience of this type of work in the civilian field. I suspect that it was because of this lack of experience that the British bridge was a failure. 21st Army Group, who were directly responsible for the planning and building of the bridge at Emmerich, chose to play for caution. In mitigation I have to say that the story at the time was that the British Army only had one pile driver capable of driving these large piles while the American Army had dozens of them. This meant that the British engineers could only work on one pier at a time while the Americans could afford to mount their pile drivers on rafts which could be moored at each pier site and work on several of them at one time.

The British bridge had to be built progressively from one bank and the bridge had to be cantilevered out from each completed pier to the site of the next one. The pile driver would then be mounted on the unsupported end of the bridge and, in effect, lean over and plant the next set of piles. When all the piles were in for the new pier they would be capped and the bridge extended onto them and beyond, ready for the next lot of pile driving. Whether or not floating pile drivers were quite as quick as a bridge mounted pile driver I cannot say but it is obvious that the Americans stood a great chance of having all their piers built by the time the British had perhaps built two or three.

Obviously the British engineers were aware of this major disadvantage in their system. Certainly we on Second Army Headquarters made our views known to 21st Army Group but there was another factor. During the planning of these bridges we were all, on our side, conscious of the risk of ice and debris coming down the Rhine and perhaps sweeping away the rafts carrying the pile drivers. Clearly a bridge mounted pile driver would be protected against such a hazard and with few, if any, spare pile drivers available within British Army sources, it was argued that it was only prudent not to put our pile drivers at risk, even though the Americans might be able to afford to do so. I suspect that the second argument was only trying to rationalise a bad technical decision which had already been made.

In any event, the American bridge was available and trains were crossing long before the British bridge had reached mid river. In fact, the British bridge could not have been finished before the end of the war when the demand for supplies dropped so substantially that the American bridge was able to carry all the supplies required.

The British bridge was therefore abandoned.

The Second British Army assault on the Rhine was to be made between Wesel on the upstream (southern) side (where Ninth U.S. Army took over) and Emmerich on the downstream (northern) side where First Canadian Army took over. (See Map 11)

The actual assault crossings were to be made by 15th Division for 12th Corps on the right at Xanten and by 51st Division for 30th Corps on the left at Rees. Both Xanten and Rees were the sites of civilian motor ferries which, naturally, were not available for our purpose.

15th Division was to be followed by 52nd Division, 53rd Division and 7th Armoured Division, plus some independent brigades who would press on out of the bridgehead and develop the attack in depth. 51st Division was to be followed by 3rd Division, 43rd Division and 3rd Canadian Division. 3rd, 43rd and 51st Divisions would press on to the north east. 3rd Canadian Division, once across the river, would turn aside to the left and capture Emmerich on behalf of First Canadian Army who would thereafter develop their operations for the liberation of the rest of Holland.

Ninth U.S. Army, after crossing the Rhine on the two division front, would develop their operations to the east and concentrate on isolating and then capturing the whole of the Ruhr industrial area. To ease the advance of both 12th Corps and Ninth U.S. Army two airborne divisions, 6th British and 17th U.S., would be dropped ahead of the advancing British troops once a bridgehead had been established by 12th Corps.

Until almost the very last moment, at the commencement of operations, the Chief Engineer was encouraging everyone to think of any further equipment or modifications they might require. Some we might be able to meet easily, others were more difficult. In particular, at a meeting only two days before the assault, one of the engineer colonels present raised a question of whether trailers were the most suitable way of transporting the 50/60 rafts to the waters edge.

Asked to supply details of how otherwise he thought these substantial and heavy items could be moved up to the Rhine, across the flood plain and over the dykes, he supplied a sketch on the back of an envelope which looked like nothing more or less than a piece of garden trellis work. When the request was passed to me I knew better than to demur in any way. It seemed immediately obvious that to construct even one sledge of the type indicated on the drawing would be more demanding of time and labour than we could afford. Furthermore, we would have to provide one sledge for each half pontoon. All the rafts would have to be brought forward in one go. It seemed impossible but I did not say so. As I walked back to my office a brilliant thought occurred to me. A strong lattice work, for the frame of a sledge, could be provided by two Bailey bridge panels, joined together with standard linking pins, and turned on the flat so that pieces of 9″ × 3″ timber could be bolted to each top and bottom flange to provide the runners. A simple tow bar was easy to provide.

I sent for the officer commanding one of the Corps Field Park Companies available in the area and described my idea to him. He got the point quickly and promised to let me have a sample in four hours. This was real talking because, if the design was suitable, we could readily provide the 120 sledges required, by a bit of intensive work overnight, ready for marshalling on the day before the attack. I quickly arranged for the half pontoon on a trailer with a towing tank to be made available at a suitable test field and when I got there, at the deadline, lo and behold the sledge was standing there hitched up to a tank and ready for loading. It was the easiest thing in the world to wind the half pontoon down the ramp and onto the sledge. It looked marvellous and I could see myself getting considerable largesse for my invention. I gave the word for the tank to start up and with a loud roar its engine burst into action. With a crash of gears the driver took the strain and the sledge nearly moved. Fountains of mud sprayed out in the tanks tracks, cutting into the firm turf. Unfortunately, the sledge did not move forward an inch but the tank's tracks cut down steadily into the sub-soil until the tank bellied, when the tracks spun with a protesting scream, but the driver switched off and silence returned until I burst out laughing.

Neither the proposer of the sledges nor I had given any consideration to the factor of friction. The pull required on the tow bar before the sledge would move was so great that the tank found it far easier to dig itself in than to make forward progress. We hastily packed up and removed the engineering equipment and left the poor tank crew to dig themselves out.

On the way back to report to the Brigadier it occurred to me that, not only was the friction element involved in towing a trailer far lower than in pulling a sledge, but the Experimental Bridging Establishment had almost certainly considered the point and done the calculations. When I told the Brigadier simply that the friction factor was too big he accepted my word without protest and even without asking whether I had tried the thing out in practice. He then said "Mortimer, you have worked very hard indeed on this Rhine project and I think you have provided everything that anyone could conceivably need, now you go and take three days holiday while those fellows up forward get on and use the stuff you have provided". I went off, packed a bag, took my jeep and set off for Louvain and Brussels.

By the time I returned at the end of the week the crossings had all been successful, the enemy was in full retreat and Army Headquarters was just beginning to pack up, move forward and follow them.

CHAPTER 14
Headquarters Second Army —
The Ending
(April, 1945 – June, 1945)

The assault crossings of the Rhine on the 30th Corps front commenced in the late evening of 23rd March, 1945. Four battalions of 51st Division advanced in amphibious trucks with DD tanks and reached the far bank after a seven minute crossing close to Rees. The enemy was thin on the ground and his artillery had been neutralised by counter-battery bombardment.

An hour later a commando brigade crossed the river close to Wesel, while the town was being heavily bombed by the RAF. Three hours later, in the early morning of 24th March, against light opposition, four battalions of 15th Division crossed at Xanten on the 12th Corps front.

Massively protected by fighters of the RAF and American Airforce, both over the bridgehead and deeper into Germany, the 14,000 airborne troops arrived in 1,700 aircraft and 1,300 gliders and were dropped five miles ahead of the bridgehead which 15th Division had just established. Before their arrival the dropping zones had been heavily bombarded by the massed guns of Second Army from the western bank of the Rhine. Losses were light; only 55 transport aircraft and about the same number of gliders were lost in this huge operation. These airborne troops were now well placed, behind many of the German defences, to forge ahead rapidly.

By the end of the month 30th Corps had crossed the River Ijssel and 3rd Canadian Division had surrounded Emmerich, where the division reverted to First Canadian Army. 12th Corps, with the good start given to them by the airborne landings, had progressed some thirty miles and reached the line of Bocholt, Borken and Haltern on the River Lippe. Ninth U.S. Army, on the right of Second British Army, had advanced twenty miles along the northern edge of the Ruhr conurbation. It now reverted from 21st Army Group to control by 12th United States Army Group in order to take part in the surrounding of the Ruhr and to join with the main thrust of the American Armies across the centre of Germany towards the upper Elbe on the general axis from Cologne to Kassel and Leipzig.

First Canadian Army, which was to be substantially reinforced by troops transferred from the Italian campaign, would now comprise 1st and 2nd Canadian Corps and 1st British Corps. It also diverged away from Second British Army and concentrated on the liberation of northern Holland.

Second British Army, now comprised 30th Corps on the left, 12th Corps in the centre, and 8th Corps, which had now crossed the Rhine, had come up on the right of the Army. 8th Corps was now pressing forward towards the lower Elbe with the object of crossing into Schleswig-Holstein and liberating Denmark.

During March the enemy's losses had included 300,000 prisoners of war to which there were to be added, possibly, an equivalent number of killed and wounded. The German army was close to final disintegration and the pursuit across north and central Germany was even more rapid than the pursuit across northern France. Between Bocholt, on the edge of the Rhine bridgehead, which was reached by the end of March, and Lubeck on the Baltic coast, which was reached a mere five weeks later, was an advance of 240 miles.

In the course of this advance our troops had to cross the River Ems, the Dortmund-Ems Canal, the River Weser, and its tributary the Aller, and the River Elbe itself. Very few bridges had been left standing by the retreating Germans on any of these waterways. Every opportunity had been taken to lay many minefields at these bridge sites and elsewhere. In spite of their hopeless position many of the German troops fought hard and bitterly. Particularly difficult were the remnants of SS and other armoured divisions and the airborne divisions of the German airforce as well as some of the ad-hoc battle groups, especially those formed from cadets from the various officer training units. Units of the Volksturm, the German equivalent of the British Home Guard, were numerous as were boys drawn from the Hitler Jugend but these units were not very effective. I honestly believe that our Home Guard would have been a very much more serious proposition had the Germans invaded in, say, 1941 or later.

The continuous demolitions called for an equally continuous set of bridging operations and I was kept very busy arranging supplies of new equipment. Occasionally a bridge put in at the time of an assault would not be needed subsequently. It could therefore be lifted by one of the forward units and brought forward on their own vehicles ready for the next assault. More usually, new equipment was required and, for the most part, this had to be ferried up to the front from the depot built at Helmond for the Rhine crossing. In the very last days of the war a new roadhead depot was opened in the vicinity of Sulingen ready for the Elbe crossing but I cannot recall that we used it for any other operation.

During the advance across the north of Germany I recall that Army Main Headquarters moved forward at least four or five times and sometimes the stay at any one spot was only two or three days. The camp

186

moving drill became quite slick. In the morning I and my colleagues would hand over our office and sleeping tents to our batmen. I would pack most of my papers into my Jeep and push off for a day looking around newly captured areas — again still hoping to find supplies of useful stores and very rarely doing so — and gradually working my way forward, usually with my staff captain, to the given map reference which, surprise-surprise, usually turned out to be the site of the next camp. Provided I did not arrive much before 5.00 p.m. the new camp would have been erected and, after a quick wash, one could go straight to the "D" Mess tent for a drink and dinner, ready to pick up the threads in the office that evening or next morning.

News came to me at one of these stops that Paul Bennett, my friend from OCTU days, had been killed. He had been leading the advance of 30th Corps into the ruined city of Bremen in one of the special tanks of his unit of 79th Armoured Division. It was blown up by a German naval parachute sea mine buried in the street. I had so wished that he would survive the war. We would have seen a lot of one another in South Africa, where I went to work after the war and where he would also have been employed. He was a brave man and a good friend — he deserved to enjoy the rewards of peace.

Equally sad, in a way, was the day when we heard that the Brigadier's son, who had stayed with us at Neerpelt, had also been killed in action with Guards Armoured Division where he was a 2nd Lieutenant in the Divisional Engineers. I do not remember for sure but believe it was in connection with a mine clearing operation not long after the crossing of the Rhine. The Brigadier was very cut up and subdued for a while but he only took a few days off from work, presumably to visit the area and to see his wife and the rest of his family. We were all very sad for him and also for the young man who had been so friendly to us all. His father had been so proud of him and ambitious for his future — perhaps over-ambitious — and he was a great loss to us all. As with Paul Bennett the sadness was increased because the end of the war was clearly so close.

Ted Hutton had his final war adventure, while carrying out his normal duties including, from time to time, reconnoitring ahead for suitable air landing strips near the likely sites of Field Marshal Montgomery's tactical headquarters. From memory, Main Headquarters was at the time near Sulingen and we were still some way short of the River Aller on the 12th Corps front.

The site that Ted was reconnoitring was somewhere near Celle, just across the River Aller on the 8th Corps front, just to the north of Hanover. Unfortunrtely, Ted was rather too quick off the mark and got to the site a little before the Germans had actually evacuated it. Arriving on the site, he was just testing the firmness of the ground and checking the width available for the runway when he was confronted by German infantry patrolling in the woods.

Ted decided to make a fight of it and escape, so he drew his revolver and took a couple of pot shots at the enemy. The enemy responded with sub-machine gun fire and brought Ted down with a shot or two in the leg. He was captured and taken to a German field hospital where he was very well operated on and held, only to be released by our own troops literally while just commencing his convalescence. Ted therefore had a quick trip home to England and out of the war. When he had recovered, he resumed his career as a senior official in the Ministry of Transport where he had for years been a civil engineer.

At our penultimate stop I made my first real mistake with supplies. For the crossing of the Elbe XVIII U.S. Airborne Corps was put back under command of Second Army again on the right of 8th Corps which had 12th Corps on its left. 8th and 12th Corps were to cross the Elbe at Lauenburg while XVIII U.S. Corps was to cross between Bleckede and Darchau. 12th Corps was to turn back to the left after the crossing and prepare to attack Hamburg. 8th Corps was to press on to Lubeck and Kiel and XVIII U.S. Corps was to head east to make contact with the closely approaching Russian Army.

Being on the right of our line XVIII U.S. Corps were the most vulnerable to interference by enemy swimmers and mines at their bridging site. We had already arranged to supply them with the necessary bridging equipment but at the last stage they raised the question of whether we could let them have any of the anti-submarine nets we had used on the Rhine and subsequently. I was consulted and referred to my stock lists to see how we were placed. The lists were very vague and the most I was certain of was that we had enough floats and possibly anchors as well to cope with about 1,000 feet of net. As to the nets the lists were silent but I assumed, too readily, that the nets were with the floats and had not been reported due to difficulties in measuring.

There were no means by which I could telegraph or signal for an early enough clarification. The representatives of the U.S. engineers had trucks with them and wanted to go and pick up the equipment immediately. It seemed best to give them a requisition form and send them off to fend for themselves with the 174th Army Workshop and Park Company. I assured the Chief Engineer that the matter was in hand and I know that he assumed, that the equipment was as good as loaded. The Americans returned next day on their way back to their units with empty trucks. There would be no nets in the water the following morning. When they had arrived at Helmond there were certainly enough floats and a few anchors but not a fathom of wire rope. That was all presumably at the bottom of some river or other. I slunk around for a while expecting a right royal rocket when the Chief Engineer got to know. However, he took it all very philosophically and, as it happened, the Germans had no spirit left to put up any worthwhile resistance. The crossing of the Elbe took place perfectly satisfactorily the following day. Lubeck and Kiel were rapidly captured. The Americans and the Russians met without any accidents or incidents and Hamburg surrendered shortly afterwards.

The negotiations for the surrender of Hamburg precipitated all the negotiations which led to the final surrender. Meanwhile, Army Main Headquarters made its last move onto Luneburg Heath. As usual, members of staff such as myself arrived at about 5.00 p.m. to find all our tents erected and ready and all office/sleeping caravans in place. The only unusual feature was that, at about the same time, a procession of German soldiers of all ranks up to general, some apparently accompanied by members of their families, began to cross the edge of our engineer section site in a steady stream heading for some spot which seemed to be just to the rear, or west, of our camp. None of them were carrying any arms at all, having apparently surrendered those they previously carried at some point further to the front. Their captors had merely directed them to make their way to the rear to a point where they would no doubt be impounded and fed. That was sufficient to keep them moving in the right direction and our forward troops had not troubled to supply them with any form of escort, as they were almost overwhelmed by the numbers surrendering. A trickle of would-be prisoners was still going on late that night and continued for much of the following day.

We went off to find our mess and our dinner, which was not too difficult as all the army messes appeared to be in much the same place, a row of very pleasant villas in a road not very far from the camp site.

Strangely enough, when we were at dinner the following evening, someone came in and announced to the assembled mess that the infamous deputy leader of the Nazi Party, Himmler, had just committed suicide in the adjoining building, which turned out to be either our intelligence headquarters or our police department. He had been picked up during the day and brought in for questioning. During the questioning he had turned away and crunched between his teeth a capsule of cyanide which he had concealed in his mouth. He died almost immediately, thus saving himself from the Nuremburg Trials and inevitable execution. It appeared later that Hitler himself had already committed suicide or did so literally on the same day.

What was apparent to us all was that the Germans were anxious to avoid surrendering to the Russians if they could possibly get out of the war in any other way. A few may have hoped to get terms from the western allies. These might permit them to go on fighting the Russians, but their situation in that regard was just as hopeless, in fact, as it was on the British and American fronts. There was some confusion as to who was in charge on the German side and who was prepared to surrender and who was not, but the situation was beyond German control. Hitler was dead (though we did not know it at the time). Eventually General-Admiral von Friedeberg, representing Grand-Admiral Doenitz, and General Kinzel, representing Field Marshal Busch, arrived at Field Marshal Montgomery's tactical headquarters and signed an Instrument of Surrender of all German armed forces in Holland, in Denmark and in north west Germany, including all islands. This was to be effective on the 5th of May and all forces under their command would lay down their arms and surrender unconditionally. This surrender was confirmed and superseded by further signings at General Eisenhower's headquarters at Reims on 5th May and 6th May and ratified by Field Marshal Keitel, for the German High Command, in Berlin, on 9th May. So ended the German war.

While we were still at Luneburg I received news from home that brother John had arrived in England. The party of sappers and of infantry of the HLI, which he had been with at the attack on the castle, had been moved by the Germans all the way back to a prisoner of war camp at Flensburg on the Baltic coast. On about the 4th of May they had seen from their camp the retreating Germans passing them in large numbers, closely followed by the advance guard of 8th Corps pushing on towards Denmark.

The camp was liberated and the prisoners released. All day long they watched mile upon mile of British vehicles and troops passing them without any visible slow up. Arrangements progressed for the prisoners' evacuation and return to England. On John's actual return he was sent on his disembarkation leave but his release number from the army was very much larger than mine and he had a good year to serve before he was finally discharged. He decided not to extend his service to get a commission as he had already secured a place at a Teachers' Training College. Before his discharge he initially underwent a period of re-training for the Japanese front but when that war ended suddenly too he continued service with the Engineers at Chatham, mostly — it seems — playing rugby.

It was immediately after the German surrender that Brigadier Campbell took two days off and disappeared to London, presumably to the War Office. It seemed that he had already fixed up, or did so then, for his own immediate posting to the Far East to take a similar job, or a more senior one, with our High Command out there. With the ending of the German war all efforts would now be made to reach the same conclusion with the Japanese. At that time we did not know that the atom bomb would be used and all the expectation was that the war would be continued for at least six months to an inevitably very bloody conclusion with an invasion of the Japanese homeland.

Accordingly, after he returned, Campbell summoned all his staff to an informal farewell "parade" outside his caravan. He told us that he was off next day and thanked us all collectively for our services under his command. He then shook hands and said goodbye to each of us in turn. I noticed that, out of the first four or five he spoke to, only to Thorpe (who had come from 1st Corps to take Allport-Williams' place after Neerpelt — when the latter had been transferred to 21st Army Group Headquarters) did he say, "I'll be sending for you later" implying a transfer for Thorpe to the Far East and possible promotion as well. However, to my great surprise, he made the same remark to me in my turn. I thanked him non-committally but it left me in a quandary. We did not know then for sure, although we suspected, that Second Army Headquarters would be disbanded. It seemed unlikely that there would be any other worthwhile work left for us to do. However, someone else might have some interesting job to offer me — though any offer from Campbell, particularly if promotion was involved, would need considering very seriously. In addition, there was the fact that I had already been told my release number (25) which would start clocking up the time for my ultimate release from the army back to civilian life from the date of the German surrender, irrespective of the Japanese war.

As three or four group numbers were expected to be dealt with each month I should have no more than eight months still to serve. I could probably turn down a posting to the Far East on the grounds that there was not time enough to make it worthwhile. I did not know what I would choose.

As it happened, it was only a day or two later that I was told that I was to be posted, personally and separately, to the Headquarters of British Troops in Berlin. That seemed interesting enough and there was no reason why I should not take that one up, as any offer for the Far East would undoubtedly follow me. In the end it did not. The invasion of Japan did not have to take place and I doubt if Brigadier Campbell ever had to recruit any staff for the purpose. I still wonder what would have developed had it ever come about and whether I would in fact have decided to go. Probably an attractive enough offer would have tempted me but I am glad, in the end, that I did not miss Berlin. Still, that is how I missed my eighth and final embarkation.

Since the end of Chapter 8 I have not referred to the progress of the war outside the northern European theatre. By July, 1944 the British nation had largely decided, whether rightly or not, that the war was as good as won. It was true, of course, that very little had still to happen outside the northern European area and the Pacific war zone.

The Mediterranean theatre had lost all significance, although fighting continued in a desultory fashion. Churchill pleaded for reinforcements but the Americans saw the Italian front as no more than a means of pinning down some German forces. At the end of April 1945, Mussolini and his mistress were shot by communist partisans and their bodies hung upside down outside a butcher's shop. Next day the German forces in Italy surrendered unconditionally.

In the Pacific war zone, General Douglas MacArthur launched his promised attack on the Philippines Islands in October, 1944 with 174,000 men of the United States Sixth Army. Fighting was long and hard. Although the Japanese were initially heavily outnumbered they did manage to reinforce the islands to effective equality in manpower. However, they had virtually no airforce as the various island-hopping battles had literally wiped out their strength in fighter pilots. By mid April, 1945 large areas of the Philippines had been re-captured but there were then 200,000 Japanese troops under arms on Luzon. Even so, at the end of the war 65,000 Japanese were still under arms and they had to be ordered by their Emperor to leave.

During the land battle for the Philippines, the greatest sea battle of all times — in terms of the tonnage of ships committed by both sides — took place in Leyte Gulf and elsewhere around the islands. As the Japanese withdrew it is fair to conclude that the Americans had won that battle.

In the Far East also there was intense fighting in Burma. In June, 1944 British and Indian forces won the battle of Imphal and the advance of Lieutenant-General Slim's Fourteenth British Army to the Chindwin River and beyond had begun. The Chindwin was crossed in December, 1944 and Mandalay was captured in March, 1945. The Fourteenth Army went on to capture Rangoon on 1st May and, in the Far Eastern theatre only the final assault on the Japanese Islands and on Japan itself remained before the Second World War would be finally concluded.

There was still to be a final trial for the people of Britain. While they were again enjoying the beaches, which were gradually being cleared of wire and mines, the first flying bomb fell on London on 13th June. These flying bombs were pilotless aeroplanes which came over at all hours with a characteristic drone until the engine stopped and the bomb fell to the ground and exploded. More than 6,000 people were killed, nearly all in London, but, by August, four "doodle-bugs" out of every five were being destroyed, either by anti-aircraft guns on the coast or fighters inland.

By 7th September, 1944 it was announced that "The Battle of London is Over". However, next day the first V2 rockets came over and were a much greater danger than the flying bombs but they were not nearly so alarming because they fell without warning. Fortunately, the launching sites were overrun by the allied armies soon after the attack commenced. The rockets were very expensive to produce and, on average, each one launched killed only two people. Nevertheless, they had been a very severe threat to the future of London.

After the German surrender I only had a few days more at Luneburg. On one of those days two of us and a British nurse, who was stationed in the town, took a day off and tried to make a road journey to Denmark. We got no further than Flensburg where we inspected some of the intense damage by bombing in the harbour area. One small submarine had been blown right out of the water and its wreckage was perched on the edge of a quay. Having looked around even a short distance we saw that we could not possibly hope, in one day, to do much more so we never got to Denmark.

CHAPTER 15
Headquarters British Troops Berlin —
The Road to Berlin
(May, 1945)

My actual posting to Headquarters British Troops Berlin took me first to Brunswick for three days and then to Bielefeld. I had taken Private Lunney with me, hoping to be able to retain him as my batman in Berlin. It was not to be. His own posting back to his regiment, the Black Watch, caught up with us and we had to say goodbye. He urged me to make every effort to keep him and told me that, although we had worked together for less than a year, it was a far longer period than any of his previous employments in the army and out of it. Obviously we suited one another, but he had to go.

Both my new Chief Engineer and his second-in-command were named Brown. The Chief was a handsome man, cheerful and pleasant and his nickname in the Royal Engineers was "Bubbly". I think I understood that was due to his enjoyment of drinking champagne. His deputy looked very much older but I do not know whether he was or not. His nickname was "Freddy". Apart from these two, who were both regulars, the Headquarters team had a distinctly electrical and mechanical look, my appointment as Stores Officer being the apparent exception.

We had nothing much to do except to wait for the Russians to decide that they were ready to let the western Allies take up responsibility for their individual sectors of the city. We were still unable to overfly the city, and we could thus not get up-to-date pictures of the extent and locations of the major damage. This embargo was, theoretically, because of the danger of the Russian anti-aircraft guns opening up on our planes. In practice, I think the Russians had two other matters in mind. Firstly, they had allowed their troops a period of general licence. Other writers have described this period of pillage and rape and the temporary breakdown of their army's discipline. They needed an adequate period to get their troops under control again.

Secondly, there was a certain amount of organised official looting of industrial equipment. There was no agreement yet that was in any way firm and detailed as to whether the Germans were merely to be disarmed or whether this should be extended to include elements almost of reparations. If the latter seemed likely, this might allow the Russians to acquire equipment from the Germans which would replace equipment lost during the German occupation of many parts of the Soviet Union.

The Russians seemed to have decided to anticipate a favourable decision on this point and also to take advantage of the interim period to remove what they could out of the areas of Berlin which were eventually due to be handed over to the western allies whom they, the Russians, saw as not needing such reparations. These matters were among subjects still to be decided at the Potsdam Conference but the Russians believed in "the bird in the hand".

Churchill appeared at the first session in early May as the British representative but then had to fight a General Election at home. On the night of the election, 23rd May, only the actual votes cast in the U.K. itself were counted and it appeared that Churchill had managed to hold on, in spite of the Labour Party making substantial gains. However, when the votes cast by the armies and other forces overseas were counted a couple of days later it was clear that the fighting men had given an overwhelming vote to the Labout Party. In consequence, the Labour Party just won the election overall and for the final sessions of the Potsdam Conference between 17th July and 2nd August a new Prime Minister, Clement Attlee, took the place of Winston Churchill.

It was thus about the 9th or 10th May before it was fixed that an Advance Party could be sent up to Potsdam to make detailed arrangements for the reception of full sized British and American delegations when the Conference should resume. I was told that engineer representatives were to be in this advance party and I was to go, accompanied by a Major White, who had recently joined the engineer section at Bielefeld. A rendezvous near Magdeburg had been fixed for the following morning.

It was still dark when we approached the rendezvous on the east- west autobahn, not far from the destroyed bridge over the Elbe, just north of Magdeburg. The small convoy of the Advance Party for the Potsdam Conference was already there. Drivers and batmen were brewing up and officers were milling around. I reported to the officer who seemed to be in charge and Major White and I were told to "tack on at the back".

We had been briefed the day before by both Colonel "Bubbly" Brown and Lieutenant Colonel "Freddy" Brown and were moderately clear what we thought we had to do. First we had to join this convoy and make our way with them to the accommodation being set aside by the Russians at Potsdam for Churchill's party, when it arrived in due course. White, who was an Electrical and Mechanical Engineer, was to remain and use the equipment we would send him to ensure that Churchill's headquarters was properly provided with electric light and a supply of safe water. We still had no knowledge, in fact, whether Potsdam had been destroyed or not; the guess was moderately hopeful that it had not been badly knocked about. Thirdly, I was to attempt to go on from

Potsdam to Berlin itself and to discover a route which the British main Berlin force could use, which did not involve our using the autobahn from the south west which was reserved for the Americans. This would only be a distance of some twenty five miles but there was no telling yet what bridges had been destroyed and what standard of replacement the Russians had provided.

It has again to be appreciated here that, for some four or five weeks before the Germans surrendered, British planes were restricted from over-flying territory in which the Russian army was fighting. The only news we had, therefore, was largely that which was gathered from refugees crossing into the British zone of West Germany. These were uniformly gloomy, indicating that the whole city was in flames and that the surrounding area was devastated.

At the appointed hour, the tea things were put away and we all sat in the vehicles ready to go, but no word came. At eleven o'clock no word had yet come and it was decided to have more tea. Similarly at one o'clock but, almost before we had finished the tea, a messenger arrived and we were called down into Magdeburg. We took off in a cloud of dust and all went well until we could see — along the city streets, which were largely intact — the Elbe in front of us. A new bridge had been built in the town by the Americans and they had hopefully named it "The Friendship Bridge" but its appearance belied that choice. From end to end the bridge carriageway was stuffed with barbed wire beyond which, on the far bank, we could just see our Russian colleagues, armed to the teeth. We absorbed the fact that early departure was unlikely and, indeed, at our normal teatime we were still waiting. By this time the troops' jokes about shaking hands with Joe Stalin were getting a little thin and everyone voted the occasion "a damn poor show".

It was something like 6.00 pm — more than twelve hours after we had arrived at the rendezvous — before there was real movement. A body of Russian infantry hauled back the barbed wire entanglements and let us advance into their territory. Sallies and ironic greetings from our side were received dourly. However, we imagined that we could reach Potsdam, which was something like fifty miles distant, in time for the evening meal and for a while we drove ahead steadily. Not for long though, as my recollection is that we had no less than seven or eight stops, of at least half an hour each, as we made our way up those fifty miles, which were back on the autobahn again. On the way we seemed to see nothing at all except trees and the occasional messenger telling us to move forward or to stop again, until we reached a built up area which turned out to be our destination.

Somehow, on arrival we were sorted out into small groups, each group of half a dozen officers or so being allocated one villa for accommoda-

196

tion. Fat German women servants were being pushed around by Russian officers and bringing "clean" bed linen and a ghastly brew which may have been coffee. We merely brought in our bedding rolls, put them on top of the beds and got to sleep in no time at all.

The next day was beautifully sunny and the birds were singing very merrily when we woke and looked out of the windows to see that each was guarded by a Russian officer armed with a tommy-gun. Whether they were to keep us in or to keep the starving population out was a matter for speculation but there were not many population visible, except for the Russians who were there in dozens.

When we were ready we went out and indicated to the guards that we were looking for breakfast. The Russians smiled and waved us on our way. We were the only officers in the large conservatory of the house to which we were directed but we gathered from one of the British mess servants that everyone else had breakfasted early and had taken off to have a look at Berlin. However, he informed us, they had not been able to go very far and were all held up at a check point which the Russians had set up on the outskirts of the town.

We were also told, with some relish, that the eight or nine houses we had observed in our own passage to breakfast were all that the Russians had allocated for the entire British and American contingents to the conference. They were sizeable villas but they were not vast and in no way commensurate with the brigade of Guards that Churchill was said to be bringing with him as his own personal escort. Our informant opined darkly, as he left us to fetch our sausages, that Winnie would not be pleased and that Joe had better buck his ideas up.

Accordingly, when we had exhausted the available scuttlebutt, we mounted our own Jeep which we had prudently loaded with all our worldly goods, including our bed rolls, and took off to follow the others. Sure enough they were all standing at a barbed wire obstruction. The front rank appeared to be all Americans who, between explaining to the British that they had "gotten" there first, and arguing and gesticulating at the Russians, who were telling them that no permission to go to Berlin had yet arrived from Moscow, appeared to be getting nowhere fast.

Our experience suggested that if permission had not yet arrived it could well be at least another day before it did. It seemed to me slightly fruitless arguing with the Russian junior officer in charge of the check point so we cast around for an alternative idea that might be more productive. I recalled that on the previous night when we had driven into Potsdam we had passed a number of side turnings after we had left the autobahn. If we took one of those on the left or north west side then, provided it kept going it would be likely, sooner or later, to intercept a highway number 103, coming in to Berlin from the west, and continuing right into the centre of the Spandau district which we knew was due to be part of the British sector of the city.

I handed over the wheel of the Jeep to White and took on the map reading but I was somewhat disconcerted when the road I chose to take, while looking promising at first, appeared to be about to peter out in a wilderness of cabbage fields and small market gardens. However, when we were about to turn around and try again, it gradually began to pick up in size and activity until we found ourselves entering another built-up area.

A new hazard now presented itself when we hit the main road we were expecting. Every so often we came to a minor or major cross roads and the latter appeared to be manned — or rather womanned — by uniformed young ladies who were directing the sparse traffic round the small dais on which each was standing at each of these crossings. They were doing this by waving a pair of table tennis rackets at vehicles and piroueting as gracefully as ballerinas.

Their uniforms were of the same general style and material as those of the troops we had seen at the Friendship Bridge at Magdeburg and, indeed, in Potsdam. The field boots and the khaki cotton summer shirts, buttoned up to the neck, looked the same. The skirts, worn at Western length, did not and a touch of femininity was added by colour — yellow comes to mind — in the neck scarf, worn Boy Scout style, and in the flash of the forage caps which they all wore.

They made charming pictures but we dare not stop to admire or converse. Their welcoming smiles quickly turned to puzzlement and perplexity as they realised that they were looking at some new Army but, fortunately for us, they did not seem to have anyone handy to refer to and their devotion to duty tied them to their stands as new vehicles approached and drew them back to the bat routine.

Signs of war became all-pervading as we approached the centre of Spandau and, in one section, there seemed to be nothing to see except piles of rubble. This looked much more like Allied bombing than the effects of the Russians' final assault. The "Occupying Power" and the population were trying to do something about it. Gangs of women were sorting through the rubble for good, re-usable bricks and then passing them from hand-to-hand across a re-discernible street to be stacked on the other side. Suddenly, to our surprise, a couple of trams appeared, seemingly picking their way through the rubble. Clearly, there was electric power available — as there had been in Potsdam the night before. Things were not too desperate!

Then too, we suddenly noticed the occasional standpipe among the ruins at which German women were filling jugs, buckets and basins with water. Not too desperate there either! I thought of White's lorries

198

standing waiting to be sent up to him at Potsdam with their loads of generating sets and water purification plant but I didn't mention the matter as I did not want to discourage him!

We were now approaching the District of Charlottenburg, which was also to be part of the British Sector, and found our first properly demolished bridges over the River Spree and its adjoining canals and inlets from the Havel Lake. It seemed to have been a thoroughly planned demolition line and was possibly well executed but the gaps looked too narrow to have been more than very temporary obstacles to tanks and nothing to infantry. However, the Russians had made a very thorough job too of the replacement bridges, which were all timber trestle construction.

Incidentally, they all had the look as though these were things that Red Army sappers — and German sappers — could knock up before breakfast and make a first class job of too. We have the finest equipment bridging in the world and know how to use it but our sappers frequently seem dazed when confronted by a piling job or timber construction using locally cut material. Should not a small piledriver be on every sapper unit's war equipment list?

Trying to assess such a bridge, while riding over it in a Jeep without stopping, is far from easy and so I found. For a start the footings were all under water and it was impossible to tell whether the trestle bents had been prefabricated or piled in situ. The latter seemed most likely and, in any case, the choice did not seem to be too material to any estimate or calculation of strength — or so I hoped. I would like to have stopped and looked at the structures in detail but it did seem most unwise. There was a lot of traffic and pedestrians coming and going over the bridges. The latter — the Russians in particular — seemed to have quite a lot of time to stand and stare and to accost anyone suspicious or even interesting or a possible source of cigarettes.

The vertical members were all 9 inch to 12 inch diameter timbers, closely spaced in both directions, and the bracing seemed systematic though not over plentiful to my eye — which again suggested piled construction. The superstructure could not be examined but did not vibrate or bounce too much as we, and heavier traffic, passed over it.

Finally, common sense suggested that the Russians were unlikely to build semi-permanent bridges, over relatively small gaps, for less than their own maximum loads. The only doubt was whether they now needed to bring their top weight tanks into Charlottenburg and Spandau. I felt that the bridges looked like 40 tonners at least, but that 24/30 tons would do for our Army's early needs and I reported them as safe for 24/30 tons.

We were now moving into Tiergarten, the third section of the future British Sector and the equivalent of St James's and the Regents Park areas of London. No further possible obstacles to our troops' entrance presented themselves and, subject to my submitting my report, our mission was accomplished. Not only that, but it dawned on us that — unless some of our colleagues had had the same idea and overtaken us — though that seemed very unlikely — we were the first western troops to enter Berlin other than Montgomery and his entourage and presumably some Americans, who had flown in some weeks before to a conference. We didn't think they counted!

We knew that Hitler's famous bunker must be somewhere near the Unter den Linden and the Brandenburg Gate so we took a cursory look around for it but one pile of rubble looks very much like another. We ventured through the Gate and drove a short distance into the eventual Russian sector but, there too, there seemed to be little else but rubble to look at. If anything, the damage was worse than on the British side of the Gate. At the far end of the Unter den Linden was a huge ruined church but there was little else that was identifiable in any way, so we turned around and drove back. One point of interest was that the eastern side appeared to be far more deserted than the western side, both by the Germans and by Russians.

Returning to Tiergarten one huge feature of interest did present itself and that was a massive concrete anti aircraft fortress built just on the edge of the parkland. We could not resist going in to have a look so, rather rashly leaving our jeep to look after itself, but removing our arms and ammunition, we walked up the steps. They led to what, at first sight, appeared to be a hospital. So it was, because there appeared to be at least two floors of the building, which must have been at least six or seven floors high, devoted to some form of large first aid post. Making our way right to the top we found that the building had four drum towers each of which was crowned with twin 88mm anti-aircraft guns. It was a highly impressive military structure but its effectiveness did not appear to have been very great as the view from the top was one of uniform desolation in every direction. Possibly it attracted more bombs than it fended off.

It now being lunchtime, we decided we had sufficient evidence to give of our penetration to the heart of the enemy capital. So now to reap our reward in terms of the astounded applause of our colleagues. We returned by the way by which we had come in and saw no reason why it should not be a perfectly adequate route of entry according to specification.

The others were well advanced by the time we got to the lunch-room but we were soon surrounded by an excited crowd who rapidly produced maps to check our route and departed as quickly as they could in order to test it out themselves. We did not see any of them again for two hours or so when they began to trickle back triumphant. The Americans had thought to travel well supplied with cartons of cigarettes and had clearly been testing the Reichstag black market. Rumours began to circulate about incredible bargains, including what later became a hardy annual, namely the claim that one bottle of whisky would buy a cow although it was hard to think of any use the Americans would make of a cow. They could produce one in cans any time. Still, one or two fat rolls of bank notes began to appear and we felt we had been outclassed.

Apart from tidying up a map or two there did not appear to be anything much that I needed to prepare in the way of a report, but it did seem necessary to try to organise a pass of some nature in order to get back to the West. Our short stay among them had convinced us that the Russians loved nothing more than a pass with a picture on and I was determined that I had to get one.

Accordingly, I searched out the Russian Liaison Section that we now appeared to have brought with us to Potsdam. There were two or three officers in this Section and, I believe, a sergeant or two who had a smattering of Russian between them. They were united in one thing, they were convinced that Russians did not need to see a pass in order to let a Western officer go back from whence he came. I laboured long at this but there was no way in which they were even going to try to get an official pass from the Russians.

Even less did I believe them when they suggested that, if I had any difficulty, our allies at the frontier post at Magdeburg would telephone and that would make it alright. I was positive that there had been no cables or telephone wires along the autobahn and it seemed to me unlikely in any event that there would be a connection between Magdeburg and Potsdam. Furthermore, the Russian army had shown little few signs so far of being equipped with radio. I went to bed with forbodings of a wasted day ahead of me but I still had a day in hand on my target.

Next morning the jeep was loaded with my gear and White's was left behind with him in Potsdam as I took off on my 60 mile journey to Magdeburg and the West. This was covered quickly enough but the Bridge was even more plastered, if possible, with barbed wire.

A saturnine and barely shaved lieutenant was in charge of the bridge but he quickly summoned up reinforcements from some nearby office. A full colonel, no less, appeared and explained in sign language that I needed a pass with a picture. He seemed highly gratified that I understood him without delay. Nothing else I could produce would satisfy him. Even a photograph of my own was no good unless it was on a pass that had got their rubber stamp on it.

At this stage a rather young interpreter appeared. His other occupation must have been filling the inkwells because he had liberally transferred much of the liquid to himself. Inky Boy filled in the details to the effect that the Colonel was quite certain that if I went back to Potsdam forthwith the Russians there would certainly issue me with the required pass. My protestations that I was equally sure that they would not cut no ice against his bland smiles. So, to maintain the good relations I departed forthwith and drove back the 60 miles to be just in time for lunch at Potsdam.

The sympathy of my colleagues did not extend to the Russian Liaison Section or their Russian counterparts. The best they were prepared to do was to phone Magdeburg themselves and, they said, this was certainly within their powers. Short of promoting an incident there seemed to be no arguing with this. So, inadequately fortified by their assurances, I drove back to the Friendship Bridge again.

The Lieutenant was still on duty and was still unable to let me cross without a pass but kindly invited me to have supper with him. I was feeling hungry by then but viewed the possibility with some trepidation which proved amply justified. It seemed to be a hash of fried potatoes and onions liberally smeared with black motor oil. Game to the last I matched him mouthful for mouthful but was secretly delighted when he too failed the course.

Having earned his trust in this way I was not surprised when he allowed me to go myself and search for the office from which the Colonel had so recently joined us. This was in another small riverside villa and the large sitting room constituted the general office of what I now suspected was a Brigade Headquarters, if not a Divisional Headquarters. It reminded me forcibly of similar temporary headquarters in farmhouses during manoeuvres with 2nd Division a couple of years ago in East Yorkshire, except that no radio was in sight and very little in the way of telephones.

The Colonel was seated at a desk at the back and Inky Boy seemed to be door keeper. There were a couple of other clerks and a young Lieutenant Colonel who introduced himself in very limited English (but infinitely more than my Russian) as the Chief Signal Officer. The senior Colonel did not seem at all surprised to see me or very surprised that I had not got a pass. When I said that Potsdam would be happy to answer a telephone call significant glances were exchanged and I was told that the only person who could make such a call would be the General. Inky Boy was instructed to escort me to his residence.

It had come on to drizzle slightly while we had been inside so as we left the office I let down my gas cape which had been rolled up on my shoulders while I had been driving. Inky Boy was apparently impervious to the thin rain which fortunately stopped as we drove a short distance to a rather more splendid villa which he told me was the General's residence.

We parked outside and dismounted and Inky Boy knocked on the door. No-one answered it but some windows opened and two men appeared on a balcony above the lobby of the house. One was wearing a navy blue uniform with a broad gold stripe down each of his trousers. I recognised his insignia as those of a Major General of the Red Army and that seemed to me to confirm the fact that we were at a Divisional Headquarters.

The other officer looked slightly younger but very much more distinguished, his uniform was tightly tailored and seemed to me to carry infinitely more gold braid than that of the Major General. I could not at that moment see his epaulette insignia but when I did see them later I was no wiser as I could not place his rank at all. However, his air of superiority and the fact that he was smoking a very long cigarette in a very long holder convinced me that he was at least a Colonel-General even though the Major General ignored him. This was no guide at all as he equally ignored the Major General. Both gentlemen were equally and liberally be-medalled.

Only much later did I come to consider that the second officer must have been a member of the OGPU. This is now better known as the KGB and he must have been the General's political left-hand man. The air of superiority was clearly one of class and not of rank. Like the OGPU men I saw later this one was clearly drawn from the intelligentsia while the General was clearly a peasant. Such officers had the duty of advising and dealing with such matters as disloyalty, disaffection and deviation but also he would be the General's guide on etiquette and general social graces.

The General remained in command of the situation and addressed himself to Inky Boy in Russian. "The General wishes to know where is your Officer" he said. Indignantly I nearly answered hotly then realised that my gas cape was obscuring my own insignia so I pushed it back off my shoulders to show the crowns on my battle-dress. "I am a Major of Headquarters British Troops Berlin", I said "and I wish to return to West Germany to report". This seemed to ease the situation and I was instructed to enter below and Inky Boy was told to come with me and continue to interpret.

An orderly who must have been listening behind the door opened it and conducted me to the room upstairs which the two officers had re-entered. The General looked at me grimly but the other smiled and waved at me affably. Still thinking that he was a very superior officer, the fact that the latter had no English did not surprise me at all and I expected nothing more from the General — but who was I to feel superior?

The General had apparently been briefed by the Colonel but explained to me through Inky Boy that he had no instructions and that he would now try and get "them" by telephone. No wonder he looked grim but he departed to a back room and could be heard alternately turning the handle of the machine and bellowing into it. His companion re-charged the cigarette holder, continued to smile at me affably and remained silent although he did once offer me one of his cigarettes which I observed had a three or four inch cardboard tube with about an inch and a half of cigarette on the far end. I could not help him with a match and he acknowledged slightly pityingly that I was a non-smoker. Eventually the General returned and with an air of slight relief told me that I was to return to Potsdam again and they would definitely do something for me. Although I was fed up and half said so his air of authority was such that this time I believed it would work so, having deposited Inky Boy back at his office, I set out again for Berlin to report to the Russian Liaison Section.

Wonder of wonders, next morning something had happened. There was still no pass with a picture on it but a full blown Russian Major instead was to accompany me to the Friendship Bridge. His vehicle itself was impressive enough to be a pass over half a dozen bridges as it was an American jeep completely lined with a leopard skin rug. The Major lolled at his ease in the back seat with his feet over the front seat resting over the dashboard next to his driver.

More than that I was also to be accompanied by a Colonel of the NAAFI (Navy, Army and Air Force Institutes) in his own jeep. My pleasure at his company was largely dispelled by my strong feeling that our escort, in lieu of a pass, had not been secured by my efforts but only by the NAAFI Colonel's superior rank. What a come down for a major of the Royal Engineers! Our little cavalcade set off and soon reached the Bridge. A brief discussion with my friend, the Russian Staff Colonel, soon produced the entire guard from the guard room to pull aside the barbed wire entanglements and we were over the bridge and back in the West in no time at all.

Having reported to Colonel "Bubbly" Brown, he sent me to the headquarters of the brigade which was due to be the first contingent to occupy the British sector of Berlin. A merry party appeared to be in progress. The brigadier who eventually came to the door did not invite me in but accepted my report on the doorstep just as though I were any despatch rider.

He made no demur about the route but then demanded where I had found accommodation for them. This took me right off balance as no mention had been made of it in my briefing. I described the situation in general as we had seen it but admitted that I had spotted nothing that I could say positively would suit a British brigade or its headquarters. I indicated where there appeared to be a few tall buildings still standing but could not be precise. The brigadier seemed to think that I had failed in my mission so I was glad to say goodbye to him. I thought I had done damned well.

CHAPTER 16 Headquarters British Troops Berlin — Occupying Berlin (May, 1945 – April, 1946)

Following my return to the West from Potsdam there was a day or two delay, presumably while some negotiations were completed for the simultaneous transfer of part of Berlin to the western allies and a "compensating" transfer of the province of Magdeburg (within the boundaries of the former state of Brandenburg) to the Russians. It seemed that the Russians thought that, in advancing as far as the Elbe and the site of the Friendship Bridge, the Americans had taken too big a bite of territory that the Russians wished to see as part of the newly established country of East Germany. The transfers were to take place on the same day.

On that day the first convoys (other than the Potsdam convoy in which I had travelled) of British and American troops converged on Magdeburg. On the far side of the bridge there were signs that my friends from earlier in the week were also preparing to move. I had a convoy of my own loaded with Major White's generating and water supply plant which I wished to get up to Potsdam at the same time, although the commander of the main British convoy informed me that he was limited to strictly thirty vehicles for the first day, so I took my extra thirty away and placed them conveniently in one of the back streets leading to the Bridge.

After, by their standards, a very short delay the Russians began to move and I soon saw familiar faces in the vehicles as they came over the Bridge. The Signals Colonel, whom I had met in the Divisional Office, came over riding a bicycle and waving to me cheerfully. The rest of their convoy was similarly made up of nondescript vehicles, including one or two horses and carts. The area they were to take over was quite extensive and moved the boundary post back westwards from the Friendship Bridge to a new situation on the autobahn near Helmstedt, a name eventually to become world-famous.

When the Russians had passed through, and presumably officially taken over, the Americans and then the British passed over the Elbe in the opposite direction, following their respective separate routes to Berlin. As the tail end of our convoy reached me I saw, as I had expected, that the Russians had stopped counting so I quickly ordered up my own convoy of engineer stores to tag onto the back. This they did and I breathed a sigh of relief as they too passed over without interruption, with me at the tail. Quickly I overtook the lot of them and pressed on to get to Spandau comfortably before them. Somehow news that something was happening had already reached the German population, who were thronging the streets with modest crowds, so I eventually joined them and stood on the pavement, waiting to welcome the conquerors, now their rescuers.

The crowds were remarkably cheerful and clearly welcomed the departure of the Russians and the imminent arrival of the British troops in their area of the city. There was even a modest burst of cheering as the first vehicles appeared. The brigadier was in one of the lead vehicles and hailed me in a disgruntled fashion "I didn't think much of your route," he said, "it was all potholes." I refrained from telling him he was lucky to get there at all and wondered how he would get on when he found the accommodation I had vaguely indicated to him had no floors or ceilings, even though the exteriors looked impressive.

The railway line from the West entered Berlin through Spandau and it seemed to me to be a very good idea to use one of the station yards on it as my Engineer Stores Depot. I set off to examine one that I had selected from the map as possibly being suitable and not too likely to invite the envy of others. Staaken Station was fairly near the frontier but seemed ideal from my point of view, as there was plenty of room for stacking material and a fair number of spare spurs, suggesting that space was not at a premium. It seemed just right for the job and there were a few buildings available for offices and troops' accommodation.

I returned to Bielefeld for the last time to fix up one further convoy for White — to go out next day — and further convoys of about the same size to get my depot started at Staaken. I got on to 21st Army Group to let me have a supply of useful house repair equipment and materials — glass, paint, roofing felt and so on — which were obviously going to be very necessary.

Next day, having seen White's second convoy safely over the Friendship Bridge, I departed to seek my own new home in Berlin, which I understood was to be somewhere in Charlottenburg, the Olympic Stadium being mentioned as a good place to start looking.

Sure enough I found that efforts were being made to take over the administrative offices of the Stadium for the purpose. As a task the job compared with the cleansing of the Augean stables, but unfortunately the offices were well above water level. The water available would certainly not have cleaned the rooms as the Olympic training pool, which was nearest, had been used by the Russians as an open latrine.

Those too timorous to squat over the edge of the pool had made free with any corners in any room they could find. Their leavings and their unfinished meals were hidden below a thick carpet of paper as the Russians, presumably searching for military secrets, had emptied every cupboard of the Olympic records and scattered them over every floor in the building. The flies, well aware of the treats being uncovered for them, were there in thousands and the smell was indescribable.

Some twenty or thirty clerks, mess-servants and orderlies were doing their best willingly but tentatively to clear up the ghastly mess. I decided to disappear and look around the city, mentally resolving that nothing would make me sleep in that building unless it had considerably improved by dinner time. Fortunately, by seven o'clock, marvels had been done and the floors were even dry after a very liberal douching with water. Accordingly, I put out my bed roll, washed and went off to dinner.

I had not previously met more than one or two of my own Engineer colleagues, let alone any representatives of other branches of the Headquarters, so I was not surprised when I found I knew practically no one at the meal which, in all the circumstances, was tolerable though totally undistinguished.

During the meal it was announced that a decision had been made to transfer the Headquarters from the stadium to new accommodation, which was being taken over in Charlottenburg itself by the Billeting Officers. We would be given details in the morning and so it was. The Engineer Office and the Junior Officer's Mess that our branch was to use, with others, were in Eichen Allee which was a comparatively undamaged area of the city and district. The offices were in a couple of large flats, comparatively well furnished and the mess was in an elegant and sizeable house a couple of hundred yards further up the road and away from the main traffic.

The Mess President was a Major Longman, a smooth officer of our own branch, and I was his deputy. Accordingly, he and I had quarters in the mess building itself. All signs were that we would be very comfortable both domestically and at work.

At work I reported, nominally, to Lt. Colonel "Freddy" Brown but in practice I ran my own show with occasional reference to Colonel "Bubbly" Brown. With the commencement of fairly rapid releases from the army we were informed that we would have to "manage" with German staff, as all our clerks were being recalled to other duties elsewhere, and that this would be a progressive process. Accordingly, I fairly soon acquired a German stenographer, not much of a thrill to look at but extremely efficient, together with a youth who would help her with the clerical work and an elderly gentleman, Mr Schmidt, who would be my interpreter and outside contact man.

There had been no difficulty in engaging these people as there was massive unemployment in Berlin at the time and — the big attraction — the occupying powers issued their staffs with substantial midday meals of soup. Again, we all settled down very comfortably to try to be ready for all contingencies.

So much of my work consisted of trying to find supplies of engineer stores that I spent a lot of the time out of the office building at the depot or round about Berlin itself looking for sources. Not much was available because the Russians were still hard at work pillaging everything they could carry away. To defeat this, the Germans were hard at work burying everything they could that might be useful to them in getting industry re-started.

Before long, the word got round to Mr Schmidt that, if we could supply some materials, we might get a supply of roofing felt going. Help in getting diamond dies from overseas for the drawing of tungsten filaments might help in re-starting production at the Osram electric lamp works. Both of these came to pass. Strangely, the latter works was in the Russian sector but Mr Schmidt had a contact and for a while we had control of the whole light bulb output of Berlin.

There was, surprisingly, a good deal of coming and going between the Russians, the Americans and ourselves in connection with engineer stores, the other two forces were hopelessly outclassed by our own set-up and our own sources of supply both inside Berlin and outside in the West, where it was organised by 21st Army Group. Glass was in high demand but they had got a supply going and, although it was all on a quota allocation, we were never really short for long. I cannot remember that any other item of stores ever gave us any real difficulty.

In consequence my American and Russian colleagues were actively sponging on us for anything they did not have available themselves and I was writing out requisitions on our depot for hundreds of electric light bulbs, yards and yards of roofing felt, and occasional square feet of glass and the odd pot of paint. My American opposite number always accepted an invitation to lunch or coffee and responded with invitations of hospitality at the weekends. He had used his limitless supply of cigarettes to good effect. He assured me that his flat, his yacht, his butler and his mistress were all funded in this way. We certainly had one or two good trips on his yacht and one or two parties at his flat. The Russians were, on the other hand, very much more coy. Only with the greatest reluctance would they accept mid-morning coffee in the mess and steadfastly refused any other entertainment. I am still convinced that this was because they had no way of returning the hospitality, but good relations were maintained by viewing each others' family photographs.

The Russian pillaging was on a massive scale. They were literally taking apart the great factories with household names. Where a factory had no rail service, they were building spur lines into them and even through the buildings so that they could move to Russia everything the Germans had not hidden away. For a while we existed in a curious state of double occupation. The Russians had certain reserved rights of access to our zone. The site of their striking war memorial near the Brandenburg Gate was one reserved spot and the radio station was another. Then they had an extension of time, rather than reserved rights, over many of the factory sites that I have just mentioned. Not content with the factories alone, they could be seen around the streets of the residential quarters removing the pole-mounted transformers and the distributing wire and cable for the domestic electricity supply.

For the first couple of days, before much in the way of stores had arrived, we ran the depot with a small party of ten sappers under a sergeant and a corporal, but as soon as possible, I visited the Kommandatura — this was still the Russian headquarters in Spandau and it was also the town hall. I spoke to the appropriate German official and asked for a regular working party of not less than thirty. I did not think to specify that they should all be men and, indeed, seeing the hard labour being done by the women in the streets on the rubble I felt that they would probably cope with most of the work they would have to do for us.

The next morning I was standing in the depot waiting for them and saw a party of about the right size approaching, marching smartly in threes, almost entirely made up of headscarved women but at the rear there were half a dozen or so males. Two of these were wounded soldiers, still wearing the remnants of their uniforms, two were quite old men and the last two or three were almost boys.

The party was led and very much commanded by a bearded gentleman wearing a deerstalker hat. He brought the party to a halt, turned it smartly to the front and came up and saluted me even more smartly. He announced, in perfect English, that the party was three short of the requested number but he would see that he got the rest on the morrow. I believed him.

When I had handed the party over to my sergeant they all set to work with a will and with clear interest and intelligence. The sergeant soon handed over to their own "fuhrer" who explained to me that he was from South-West Africa (now Namibia), which accounted for his good command of English. He told me that one or two others in the party also spoke tolerable English.

With this excellent working party everything in the depot was soon going swimmingly until disaster struck. One morning the corporal appeared at my beakfast table to tell me that the Russians had taken over and that the sappers were confined to their quarters. I left immediately after telephoning our Russian Liaison Section — not the Potsdam one, but just about as useful — and asked for prompt help.

On reaching the depot I found a small party of Russian airforce officers waiting for me to arrive. I protested vigorously and produced a map to show that my depot was indeed within the boundaries of Spandau and that therefore I was within my rights to hold it. They said, through their interpreter, a charming female officer, that I was much too near their Staaken airfield. At this point the liaison man arrived and it had all to be explained again to him. He told me that he could not spare me much time as he had much more important business. I told him that he could not possibly have anything more important than a boundary argument but he advised me to let the Russians have the rail yard and find another place for myself. We parted with mutual compliments.

I took over my own negotiations again. I pointed out again to the Russians that, while Staaken airfield was certainly outside Berlin, according to my map, Staaken rail yard was certainly not and it was undoubtedly British territory. We had reached an impasse. They felt they needed further instructions and decided that we should all go down to the Kommandatura. We set off, I securing the lady lieutenant as my passenger and having to take her grim looking male colleague also.

At the Kommandatura the airforce representatives did not invite me to join them but left me outside with my two passengers. We had plenty of time to converse and I remember we spent quite a lot of time looking at the papers, which had reached me from England with my postal vote, for the General Election, which had just been called. They seemed fascinated by this insight into the democratic process but even more in the fact that I was not going to vote for Mr Churchill's man. They seemed far from flattered that I was prepared to support a socialist.

Eventually the senior officers appeared again and bluntly told me that we would hear later the outcome of their talks. I took this to mean that I could now return to the depot and get on with the job. I did not depart before inviting the two lieutenants to come and have dinner with me at the mess and to my surprise they accepted. However, when I turned up to collect them later I was told they had left Berlin and judged that they had run into the same problem as my previous contacts.

I returned victorious to the depot but was certain I had not heard the last of the matter and sure enough, a couple of weeks later, there was an official announcement of a change of boundary which put Staaken rail yard outside Berlin but gave the British forces a face saving concession in putting the whole of Gatow airfield inside the British sector, where it had been half and half before.

When the changeover between Staaken rail yard and Gatow airfield took place we had to find another site for our engineer depot and we picked on an island in the river Spree close to the Havel lake. It was also close to one of the Russian bridges on a main through route in the city. Very little of our material was now coming in by rail so we did not feel the loss of the rail yard too much and the new site was much more convenient for all those wishing to collect material they had requisitioned.

One other change was the loss of our South-West African. Apparently he had been a leading Nazi and the De-nazification Court caught up with him. We were sad to see him go because he had been a very efficient leader of our squad and had fitted well into the administration of the depot. However, we certainly did not disagree with the decision of the Court. One of the wounded army ex-officers took his place and the fact that he only had one leg did not seem to inconvenience him or the work at all.

Personal expenses were few in Berlin and we largely funded ours by abstaining from smoking and selling our spare cigarettes at 1 mark (or 5 shillings) each. Each morning my batman brought a cup of tea and sorted out my room a bit while exchanging the news of the day. He always asked if I needed any money and, if I did, he would take two or three packets of cigarettes from my cupboard and dispose of them for me. The route was that he sold them to the German mess servants who in turn sold them on the black market, where they were bought by the Russians, everyone taking an appropriate cut on the way. The mess servants gave us quite a cachet as they were all highly professional. My only objection to them was that they were so delighted to be handling real sugar again that, given half a chance, they would turn a cup of tea or coffee into treacle.

One morning, my batman hailed me with, "I agree with what the newspapers say about fraternisation, don't you, sir?". "I doubt it," said I, knowing which newspaper he read. "Well sir," he replied, "they're saying it serves the English girls right. Do you know, when we were in England we used to ride around with notices saying 'Don't wave girls we're English,' on the outside of our trucks."

He was referring to the difficulty British troops were having in England in competing with American nylons and chocolates. The issue of fraternisation was indeed uppermost in the minds of all the troops in Germany and in the minds of the British press and the British Government. However, the rules about no fraternisation with German civilians were being openly flouted on all sides and discipline demanded either full enforcement or a change in the rules.

About this time I was personally informed that Field-Marshal Montgomery was coming to Berlin to present medals to those like me who had earned them but who could not be accommodated under normal Buckingham Palace arrangements. The heavy pressure on the

King involved in trying to present all those, that had been gained during the six years of war, would be unacceptable because of his health.

The presentation was to take place in front of the Olympic Stadium where there was a fine parade ground. On the due day a large guard of honour from the 11th Hussars was assembled on the parade ground, together with the twelve officers who would be honoured, mostly, as for myself, with the MBE but with a number to get the MC and even one major to receive the DSO. A large number of other troops had also been gathered from somewhere to make a fair crowd. The great man arrived in a jeep, wearing a well-tailored battledress, his black Tank Corps beret and rows and rows of "fruit salad" (medal ribbons) over a neat gold watch chain. He was accompanied by the Commander of the 11th Armoured Division. After he had inspected the guard of honour, the dozen of us were called forward one at a time.

Monty asked me my present job and then asked whether I had any difficulty getting any items of stores. It was no time to be belly aching about minor difficulties so I assured him that, with small delays, we could usually be satisfied fully enough. He then revealed that he actually knew something about the subject by asking me if my report applied to glass. As I have already said above, glass was available to us from 21st Army Group, but only on a quota basis. Having succeeded in catching me out, he smiled broadly and pinned on the medal above the ribbon I was already wearing. I was gratified and felt as least as honoured as if I had gone to the Palace — though I never did thereafter meet George VI, but then I never did again meet Montgomery.

Incidentally, at that time, we had only just received the medal ribbons for our campaign stars and medals and those films and television shows which show British troops wearing medal ribbons in action during the Second World War are usually incorrect unless the man portrayed was supposed to have served in the First War.

When Monty had finished the line, he summoned up his jeep and mounted in the back of it. He then summoned all the troops present, excluding the guard of honour, to gather round as he wished to address us. He then proceeded to explain the fraternisation situation as he saw it.

In his inimitable style he told us that he had had many discussions with the War Cabinet about the subject. First he had had to explain to them that there was no way in which he could prevent British soldiers from talking to small children. When he had persuaded Winston Churchill to consent to fraternisation with German children he then said that he had tackled the question of age. "At what age", he had asked, "do young ladies stop being children?." There being no answer to that question the War Cabinet had again given ground and we were at present, therefore, authorised to fraternise with Germans of all ages and all sexes in the open air.

"However," he said with a flourish, "I'll have you all inside before Christmas." There were loud cheers and he beamed with satisfaction. It was typical Monty stuff and, I think, it explains why all his ex-soldiers felt that he cared for them and was the greatest commander of all. He certainly exceeded, in their opinions, Eisenhower, Patton and Bradley comfortably and completely overshadowed more junior British commanders like Dempsey. The rest of his address was more pedestrian but still meaningful to the officers present, with talk of the Four Powers' relationships in Berlin and in Western Germany.

During the autumn my contacts with the Americans increased. Finding my way to their headquarters had always been easy, even though it involved crossing large stretches of totally devastated city blocks. The cleared streets between us were marked by a succession of conspicuous signs all saying "to the Coca Cola factory" and it was only necessary to turn off the key route at the right place to reach one's true destination.

With Major Longman or Captain Gimson, a young engineer colleague, and Wes Tennant, an American acquaintance, we went on a number of yachting trips, thanks to American cigarettes, where we met a small crowd of American nurses who were our companions on a number of occasions until their duties took them away from Berlin.

One enjoyable occasion was the grand American football match between the 81st and 101st Airborne Divisions, held in the Olympic Stadium. It was a great show, particularly the half-time parade when squads of American soldiers marched round the arena doing fancy arms drill on the move. Present day exponents of this are the RAF Regiment squad which does the show regularly at the Albert Hall. At that time we had not then seen this form of show before and thought it highly amusing until we saw from the serious faces of our companions, who were all standing "at attention", that we were meant to take it seriously, as a tribute to the United States flag.

Meanwhile, every so often, artillery stationed in the yawning entrance, crashed out round after round of blank while the marching troops smacked their rifle butts. It was all very impressive but not nearly so impressive as the quantity of beer being consumed by the onlookers, each half dozen of whom had entered the stadium rolling a small barrel of beer, of at least firkin (9 gallon) size.

As the season went on I found myself organising rugby in the city — as secretary of the British Troops Berlin Rugby Club. The class of play was highly mixed, in that we had at least three internationals to leaven up the collegiate level of most of the rest of us. We did not aspire to play on the main Olympic Stadium pitch but played mostly on the Champ de Mars behind the stadium. We had a variety of opposing teams — both stationed in Berlin and imported as guests from the West.

Meanwhile, the Potsdam Conference itself took place with Clement Attlee representing Britain in place of Winston Churchill. It was quite clear from just about everyone one spoke to, officer or other rank, that the "soldiers' vote" had gone against the Conservatives and for the Labour Party who had won resoundingly. The initial count of the civilian vote had suggested a Conservative win but the "soldiers' vote" had reversed all that.

The Conference itself passed inconspicuously and Atlee did not visit Berlin officially. The only relevance to me was that, when it was finished, Major White sent up to Berlin the two convoy loads of engineering "goodies" that I had sent him at Potsdam. Apart from the generating and water supply sets which we did not really need there was quite a collection of best British "utility" coffee perculators, electric toasters, toast racks and other breakfast table decorations. These formed an invaluable reserve of largesse which I was able to distribute as the spirit moved me.

Among the beneficiaries was the British Admiral stationed in Berlin. Quite what naval power he actually controlled was far from clear, but he sent along a well-dressed sub-lieutenant armed with a very polite note to see if I would donate some of these "goodies" to the cause of naval peace at the breakfast table. I was moved to sanction this and the sub-lieutenant departed with effusive thanks and great relief. More tangible thanks followed in the form of an invitation to a reception at Admiralty House when the Admiral was to entertain his opposite numbers from the Allied fleets. I duly attended and found the occasion most interesting.

Rather like the Friendship Bridge Major General, most of the Russian admirals looked to be over-promoted peasants but, doubtless, they too were capable and ruthless commanders. It was here that I discovered my mistake about the Major General's elegant companion at Magdeburg whom I had mistaken for a Colonel General. An acquaintance from our Intelligence Department was present and, when I questioned him, he told me that the similar companions of each of the admirals was indeed an OGPU man and had a double duty on this occasion. Firstly it was his task to be a security watchdog and to say occasionally, "Change the subject, Admiral," but he was also an etiquette guardian and would occasionally advise his charge, "Use the fork, Admiral!".

Continuing the discussion I remarked to my associate about the curious way in which the Russians responded to social invitations at my level. He responded that I was probably right in my guess about their inability to return hospitality in an acceptable fashion, from their point of view. Nevertheless, he did advance an alternative theory which was that they were dead scared of being thought to be too friendly with members of the Western forces. They might well imagine that it could earn them a fast trip to the depths of Siberia. He warned me that many of them who came with innocent requests for material might well have another mission which was literally to get to know who was who in the British hierarchy in Berlin. I asked him if he meant that I might well be now on their files and he astonished me by saying that I certainly would be, regardless of whether the emissary had been specially sent for the purpose or not. A fascinating thought!

At about this time a change in our departmental command took place when John Stone, who had been my Chief Engineer during the D Day planning in London and until the Arnhem campaign, but who had then been injured in a car accident and had been convalescing for six months or so, returned to duty and took over from Colonel "Bubbly" Brown as Chief Enginer of British Troops in Berlin. In addition he had the role of being Chief Engineer to the local branch of AMGOT (Allied Military Government Occupied Territories). One or two new officers appeared to swell our staff and presumably give continuity well on into "peacetime". However, these activities did not concern me and it was a delight to be working for John Stone again.

One day he called me to his office and I thought I was in for some minor rocket for sending trucks well into the Russian zone to Dresden to collect supplies of hardboard and plyboard. It was not so but he heard my confession and then said if necessary he would assure the Russians that I had been shot at dawn.

He said that he felt that he wanted to write a testimonial for me and that reminded me that I was well within my last couple of months of service with the forces. I would leave with reluctance and yet with expectation of settling down to civilian life and taking up my career as a mining engineer. Accordingly he scribbled out a few lines, reading them out to me as he did so. It was a flattering picture of my ability and enthusiasm and I thanked him for it in proper style.

"However", I said, "while this is very welcome to me indeed, I feel you should also give me some advice as to my weaknesses and the faults I should look out for if I am to avoid trouble in a new sphere". "Well, Mortimer", he said "you haven't got too many and I meant what I have written but I suppose if there is one thing that may trip you up now and again it is your tendency not to suffer senior fools gladly. I am sure you will meet more, but try to be kind to them."

The days passed rapidly and my only remaining problem turned out to be what to do with the large amount of poker winnings I had accumulated in the mess. Playing with black market Deutchmarks had presented no risk of serious loss and I had a fair aptitude for the game.

We had a pleasant school and it passed quite a few equally pleasant hours but I had accummulated several hundred pounds of winnings and there was no chance of being able to convert them to sterling before departure. In the end I just donated them to the pool, having converted the maximum I was allowed. The only other slight embarrassment on the journey was to be a Brunsvega calculating machine that I had inherited from someone who had undoubtly purloined it from some overrun commercial or military office. It was in fact impounded by the Customs at Dover until the authorities could fix what they considered to be a suitable price for it, and when I had paid the duty I recovered the machine. I took it with me to South Africa and it was the first the mine accountants had ever seen so I sold it eventually, at a time when I was low in funds, to the mining company for which I was working. Otherwise I was 'clean' and could validly pass through with no declaration.

From Dover I went straight to Fulford Barracks at York where I was to be discharged. Here I surrendered my military equipment, including my revolver and its ammunition and a Thompson sub-machine gun which I had inherited somewhere along the line and which I had enjoyed "owning" though I had never fired a shot from it. Next we were passed on to the civilian clothing department which was all "utility" but quite fair quality at that. I chose a check tweed suit which served me well for some years in South Africa. It would have to as my civilian wardrobe was distinctly limited. Then, weighed down by my remaining military baggage and a large brown paper parcel of my new civilian clothes, I walked out of the gate towards the station as a free man on the way to commence my discharge leave with my wife and family of one in County Durham.

POSTLUDE

The "Z" Reserve Recall
(May, 1951)

In 1951 I was due to take long leave from the South African mine on which I was working. At my status as a mine captain this meant that I was entitled to my normal four weeks annual leave plus four extra weeks for each year of service I had given on the mines. This worked out at five and a half months. As the time approached I noticed in the South African newspapers reference to the British Army calling up what they named a "Z" Reserve. This was because of the more and more threatening look of the Korean war which might conceivably degenerate into a full scale world conflict. The "Z" Reserve was presumably seen as the ultimate reserve of trained or semi-trained manpower available to the British forces short of full scale mobilisation and full scale conscription again. It was to be made up of ex-wartime soldiers and those who had completed National Service training as conscripts since the war. As a resident abroad I was one of those who could be exempted. Brigadier Campbell, whom I had worked for on Second Army Headquarters, had, since the war, been promoted and appointed to be Deputy Adjutant General. He had also been knighted and was now Major General Sir Douglas Campbell. Clearly he was a senior man in the right department for me to rely on his good offices and perhaps get the chance, if I so wished, to be recalled to the army with the "Z" Reserve. Accordingly, I wrote to him enquiring what the possibility would be of my doing some service in a suitable "slot" at a mutually convenient time.

It turned out that, though I was fairly elastic as to the available dates that I offered, there was a shortage of really suitable billets to take me. However, he replied that I could be offered a post as a Captain in an Engineer Base Workshops. I snapped at the chance and, so, when I had travelled to England and re-joined my family I was fairly soon, thereafter, on my way to Stratford-upon-Avon with orders to report to the massive engineer depot at Long Marston, about five miles south west of the town. It was a good place to spend a fortnight and the quarters were fairly comfortable, as far as any hutted camp could provide.

If I remember rightly, the unit was about four hundred strong in all and had about twenty officers. It was divided into trade sections but also into two squadrons for discipline and administration. Not being either an electrical and mechanical man or a workshops expert of any nature, it was natural for the colonel to allocate me to be commander of one of the squadrons. This suited me excellently. I did not know any of the officers personally but then, as is not unusual, none of them seemed to know one another either.

I cannot recall any of their names except that one, if not two, of the Costain family were amongst them. The programme was arranged so that each squadron had one week of military training and one week of trade training. It was clearly hoped that, at the end of this time, the men of the unit as a whole would have recollected sufficient of their previous military experience to do a useful job, if we had to be sent to Korea.

At first sight of the unit on parade it seemed a pious hope to reckon that they could be welded so quickly into an effective unit. But it was astonishing how, after a couple of days drill, physical training and general brushing up on weapon training, etc. they all began to look just like soldiers again.

After two or three days someone caught onto the fact that I had managed to re-enter the Army without a medical examination and I was instructed forthwith to report to the Medical Inspection room. The doctor was just another reservist like the rest of us but he put me through a new and rather more searching test than I had faced in 1939. Then it was virtually true that if you were actually breathing you would be certified as A1 grade and passed as fit. Now the test was very much more complex and resembled the one I had had on my South African mine in order to get accepted as a member of the Proto team (the underground fire brigade) which involved wearing the proto type breathing sets which were thought to put a heavy strain on the heart. This involved stepping up and down off a stool and other physical tests and, in particular, I noticed that they now tested for colour blindness. This was done with a series of pages showing a lot of coloured bubbles, some of which presented a contrasting image of a single number. If you were colour blind you could not see it but those with normal sight could detect the numbers fairly readily.

Not only the test was different but the coding of the result had been changed. No longer were we classified as A1, A2, etc. but, reading the form upside down across the doctor's desk, I saw that a whole series of numbers were being placed on the summary page of a fairly full document. I remarked, "I see this is all different these days too; what do these numbers mean?". I pointed to the figures on the sheet and read out "2 2 1 1 1 1 2". Recalling that I had passed fit for the proto training I asked, "Why don't I get all 1's?".

The doctor replied; "If you got "ones" instead of "twos" at the beginning here, you would be fit for commando and paratroop duties anywhere in the world and I'm sure that you don't want that".

Consolingly, he said, "We are all getting a little older, and a little bit more around the waist I see".

"Then, what can I be expected to take on with "twos" at the start," I asked.

"Oh, general duties in any part of the world except commando and paratroop duties" he replied.

"I'll settle for that", I said "but what about this "two" at the end, what's that for?". I was told that that was for "sanity". "Well, don't I get a "one"?", I asked.

He silenced me with a cryptic remark, "No one in the army gets a "one"".

The first week passed quickly. We had one formal dinner in the mess and at work my squadron appeared to be enjoying life and indeed to be regarded with some envy by the other squadron which was doing trade training. An old acquaintance of mine turned up from the War Office to inspect us. He was the Engineer in Chief, Major General Tuck, who I remembered as a brigadier in charge of the airfield construction troops during the Normandy campaign. He did not seem to remember me, even though I had supplied all the material his troops had used. He seemed to feel that my troops were to be pitied because they had only done military training so far but I assured him that he had it wrong. Their view was that they now did their trade work every day of their lives and there was no change in coming into the army to do it again. While, for them, a week of physical training, drill and so on was a real holiday, on the principle that "change is as good as a rest". They tried to explain this to the General but he did not seem to wish to understand them so we all figuratively shrugged our shoulders.

Accordingly, in the second week, most of my squadron went off to the workshops, leaving me with a fair rump who could not be accommodated there or who had no particular trade. We had two jobs to do, the first of which was to remove a First World War armoured trench digger which was occupying a space required for something else. It was, in fact, virtually an old style tank, such as was used at Cambrai in 1917 but it had been ingeniously divided into three which could be taken apart and reduced the individual loads to something we might be able to cope with using jacks and cribbing. We set to work and after a couple of hours we had the first portion high in the air on a rather precarious erection of Rorkee cubes and rolled steel joists. Although the cubes gave a moderately stable footing to the whole erection, there was no certainty that the RSJ's were entirely safely mounted on top of them, so my job consisted largely of keeping the men out of dangerous situations. We maneouvred a low-loader under the RSJ's and lowered the part of the trench digger onto it for removal. I seem to recall that we found an easier method for taking it off the loader than we had had to employ to put it on but, encouraged by our success with the first part, we pressed on with the other two. The last one was the heaviest of all and nearly defeated us but eventually we got it onto the low-loader and safely away. It had been a test of improvisation. We had taken far too many risks for my liking but we had done the job. The second task was much more glamorous and offered us the chance of appearing on television. Near Stratford the River Avon had been canalised in the seventeenth century and one of the lock-gates installed by Charles II had given way under the strain of the years. In order to replace the gate it would be necessary to get a pile driver onto the island in the river. A Bailey bridge had been made available to get this equipment across the lock. As the "Z" Reserve was news, it was decided that we should take a party and erect the bridge so that the contractors could get on with the job while a television crew took pictures for the newsreel.

On the appointed day I arrived on site, with a working party of thirty men, and surveyed the scene. The line for the bridge was obvious and the parts were all spread out on the bank. I had approached the job with confidence but, as I viewed the parts, I realised that I had completely fogotten how to put the bridge together. It was no excuse to say that I had spent most of the war as a staff officer dealing with Bailey bridges by hundreds. In the last resort I would have to get the bridge built by dredging my memory or admit defeat.

Questioning the sergeant and the available corporals and lance corporals did not produce a single man who had any experience of building a Bailey bridge but, displaying all the confidence that I no longer felt, and recalling that the first step was to divide the working party into two, one team for each side of the bridge, I ordered the sergeant to do this and then gave the command to start building.

The sappers walked around the parts with a mystified air and tentatively attempted to join one or two of them together. I walked around looking intelligent and questioning the troops on their work. Although a few seemed to recall a little bit about the work and could name a few parts, none of the NCO's was any help at all. However, the sappers did remind me of the one or two names they knew — an end post, a transom, a stringer and so on — but the bridge showed little sign of making real progress. Fortunately for me, and the BBC, the penny suddenly dropped.

I remembered how to put the bridge together! In a loud voice, I commanded everyone to stop what they were doing and listen while I told them how to build the bridge. "I can see that none of you know", I said, "so I shall have to tell you". I divided the working party into four now and soon we had something that began to look promising. The temporary nose was soon on the rollers and the main bridge began to stretch out behind as we carefully pushed the nose forward towards the other bank. Soon we had the main span over and were putting down the decking when I stopped them and started them taking it to pieces again as the BBC party were due at any minute. It was a tribute to the whole design of the bridge that, with un-trained troops and a rusty officer, we were able to build it finally in convincing fashion. I did not see the BBC version and, as usual, it only lasted about ten seconds, but some of my family saw it — although I did not feature.

So the whole fortnight passed much too quickly. We had been to the Shakespeare Memorial Theatre at least three times and enjoyed those visits thoroughly. We had dined out in Stratford and we had seen a little bit of the beautiful surrounding area. Mostly, however, my recollection is of turning ourselves and our sappers back into soldiers again and feeling at the end of it that Korea would hold no problems which we could not solve. It was almost sad that the opportunity never came but I said goodbye to my colleagues, knowing that I at least was unlikely ever to see them again. If the call came I would doubtless have been required for some staff job or to serve with a Field Company or Field Park Company again. It was the last time I wore uniform but I had enjoyed it all, both the two weeks and the seven years which preceded them.